God's Two Words

God's Two Words

Law and Gospel in the Lutheran and Reformed Traditions

Edited by
Jonathan A. Linebaugh

To Josh,
a fellow hearer of God's
two words.

William B. Eerdmans Publishing Company
Grand Rapids, Michigan

Wm. B. Eerdmans Publishing Co.
Grand Rapids, Michigan
www.eerdmans.com

Published 2018

ISBN 978-0-8028-7475-7

Library of Congress Cataloging-in-Publication Data

Names: Linebaugh, Jonathan A., editor.
Title: God's two words : law and gospel in the Lutheran and Reformed traditions / edited by Jonathan A. Linebaugh.
Description: Grand Rapids : Eerdmans Publishing Co., 2018. | Includes bibliographical references and index.
Identifiers: LCCN 2018002518 | ISBN 9780802874757 (pbk. : alk. paper)
Subjects: LCSH: Law and gospel. | Lutheran Church—Doctrines. | Reformed Church—Doctrines.
Classification: LCC BT79 .G63 2018 | DDC 241/.209—dc23
LC record available at https://lccn.loc.gov/2018002518

To

Dan and Orrey,

Wes and Nate,

& Mike and Zac

Contents

PART III: Law and Gospel in Theology and Ministry

PART IV: Lutheran and Reformed Responses

Acknowledgments

Gathering a group of Lutheran and Reformed theologians to discuss and debate some of the core matters of their shared and respective traditions has been a dream of mine since I learned it was a dream of Thomas Cranmer's. The essays in this book began as part of a colloquium at the Cathedral Church of the Advent (Birmingham, AL) in July 2016. I am grateful to all who met together for those meaningful and fun few days, and especially to those whose contributions make up the contents of this collection.

The loudest thanks—and here I'm sure all the contributors would agree—must go to the Cathedral Church of the Advent. Their hospitality, financial generosity, and encouragement through their commitment to a ministry of preaching and pastoral care informed by the theology of the Reformation made what was an isolated and unlikely wish into a shared and fruitful reality. The entire parish has our gratitude and affection, and special thanks go to Dean Andrew Pearson and Gil Kracke for their support of and participation in the colloquium.

I am grateful to Eerdmans for allowing our conversation to be heard publicly by helping to form a colloquial dialogue into the present book.

This book is dedicated to six friends—Lutherans, Anglicans, Reformed—in conversation.

JONATHAN LINEBAUGH
Jesus College, Cambridge

Abbreviations

AC	Augsburg Confession, in *The Book of Concord: The Confessions of the Evangelical Lutheran Church*. Edited by Robert Kolb and Timothy J. Wengert. Minneapolis: Fortress, 2000
Ap	Apology for the Augsburg Confession, in *The Book of Concord: The Confessions of the Evangelical Lutheran Church*. Edited by Robert Kolb and Timothy J. Wengert. Minneapolis: Fortress, 2000
BC	*The Book of Concord: The Confessions of the Evangelical Lutheran Church*. Edited by Robert Kolb and Timothy J. Wengert. Minneapolis: Fortress, 2000
CCCM	Corpus Christianorum: Continuatio Mediaevalis. Turnhout: Brepols, 1969–
CR	*Philippi Melanthonis opera quae supersunt Omnia*. Edited by Karl Bretschneider and Heinrich Bindseil. Vols. 1–28 of *Corpus Reformatorum*. Halle: A. Schwetschke and Sons, 1834–1860
CSEL	Corpus Scriptorum Ecclesiasticorum Latinorum. Vienna, 1866–
FC	Formula of Concord, in *The Book of Concord: The Confessions of the Evangelical Lutheran Church*. Edited by Robert Kolb and Timothy J. Wengert. Minneapolis: Fortress, 2000
FC SD	Formula of Concord, Solid Declaration, in *The Book of Concord: The Confessions of the Evangelical Lutheran Church*. Edited by Robert Kolb and Timothy J. Wengert. Minneapolis: Fortress, 2000
HC	Heidelberg Catechism, in *Reformed Confessions in the Sixteenth Century*. Edited by Arthur Cochrane. Louisville: Westminster John Knox, 2003

LW	*Luther's Works.* American Edition. 55 vols. Saint Louis: Concordia; Philadelphia: Fortress, 1955–1986, 2010–
MBW	*Melanchthons Briefwechsel: Kritische und kommentierte Gesamtausgabe.* Edited by Heinz Scheible. Stuttgart–Bad Cannstatt: Frommann-Holzboog, 1977
MW	*Melanchthons Werke in Auswahl.* Edited by Hans Engelland and Robert Stupperich. Gütersloh: C. Bertelsmann, 1951
OE	*Ioannis Calvini Opera Omnina.* Series II: *Opera Exegetica.* Edited by Helmut Feld. Geneva: Librairie Droz, 1992–
PG	Patrologia Graeca. Edited by J.-P. Migne. 162 vols. Paris, 1857–1886
PL	Patrologia Latina. Edited by J.-P. Migne. 221 vols. Paris, 1844–1864
SPT	*Synopsis Purioris Theologiae: Synopsis of a Purer Theology.* Latin Text and English Translation. Vol. 1, *Disputations 1–23.* Edited by Dolf te Velde. Studies in Medieval and Reformation Traditions 187. Leiden: Brill, 2014
ST	Thomas Aquinas. *Summa Theologiae.* Latin Text and English translation, introduction notes, appendices, and glossaries. 60 vols. London: Blackfriars; Eyre and Spottiswoode, 1962–1980
WA	*D. Martin Luthers Werke. Kritische Gesamtausgabe. Schriften.* 73 vols. Weimar: H. Böhlau, 1883–2009
WABr	*D. Martin Luthers Werke. Kritische Gesamtausgabe. Briefwechsel.* 18 vols. Weimar: H. Böhlau, 1930–1985
WADB	*D. Martin Luthers Werke. Kritische Gesamtausgabe. Die deutsche Bibel.* 15 vols. Weimar: H. Böhlau, 1906–1961
WATr	*D. Martin Luthers Werke. Kritische Gesamtausgabe. Tischreden.* 6 vols. Weimar: H. Böhlau, 1912–1921
WCF	Westminster Confession of Faith, in *Westminster Confession of Faith.* Glasgow: Free Presbyterian Publications, 1995
WLC	Westminster Larger Catechism, in *Westminster Confession of Faith.* Glasgow: Free Presbyterian Publications, 1995
WSC	Westminster Shorter Catechism, in *Westminster Confession of Faith.* Glasgow: Free Presbyterian Publications, 1995

Introduction

JONATHAN A. LINEBAUGH

On October 4, 1529, Martin Luther wrote a letter to his wife. He was in Marburg at the urging of Landgrave Philip of Hesse, who had brought together several leading Lutheran and Reformed theologians in an attempt to secure the theological agreement necessary to establish a united evangelical front against the Hapsburgs. The participants in this Marburg Colloquy were able to produce a joint doctrinal statement, the "Marburg Articles," and the list of signatories reads like a who's who of the early Reformation: Martin Luther, Philip Melanchthon, Justus Jonas, Andreas Osiander, Johannes Brenz, Johannes Oecolampadius, Huldrych Zwingli, Martin Bucer, and Caspar Hedio.

Despite far-reaching agreement on such essentials of the evangelical faith as the doctrine of the Trinity, Christology, original sin, and justification *sola fide*, the Marburg Colloquy is mainly remembered for what it did not accomplish: full theological concord between the Lutheran and Reformed traditions. According to the final article, "we have not been able to agree at this time whether the true body and blood of Christ are corporeally present in the bread and wine."[1] This admission reflects the record of the exchange between the loudest Lutheran and Reformed theologians at Marburg—Luther and Zwingli. Luther continually cited the "clear words" of Scripture—"This is my body"—and invited Zwingli to "submit." Zwingli marshaled texts like John 6:63, "the flesh profits nothing," insisting "this passage breaks your neck." "Don't be too proud," Luther replied. "German necks don't break so easily."[2]

1. WA 30:3.160–71.

2. See C. Hedio's report in *Das Marburger Religionsgespräch* (1529), ed. G. May (Gütersloh, 1970), 23, cited in H. A. Oberman, *Luther: Man between God and the Devil* (New Haven: Yale University Press, 1989), 237n22.

Luther's letter to his wife, Katharina, captures this dynamic of broad and basic agreement together with particular but pointed disagreement: "[We are] of one opinion in almost everything," but "at the Lord's Supper they will allow bread to be only physically present and Christ to be only spiritually present."[3] This "but" proved to be a line in the sand. As Heiko Oberman points out, the following year, at the Diet of Augsburg, the evangelicals were unable to offer a unified confessional document, submitting instead the Augsburg Confession, a statement from Zwingli, and the Tetrapolitian Confession.[4]

This event is more than an episode on the way to distinct Lutheran and Reformed identities, however. It is an instance of concrete conversation between Lutheran and Reformed theologians. Considered in these terms, Luther's characterization of the discussion and debate in his letter to Katharina reads, with five centuries of retrospect, like a prophecy: when Lutherans and the Reformed talk, "we are of one opinion in almost everything, but . . ."

In 1529 at Marburg, the definitions of and distinction between law and gospel seem to fall under the "almost everything" of which the Lutherans and Reformed were of "one opinion." Article 7 explicitly affirms "justification before God . . . for the sake of his Son, in whom we believe" apart from the law, and articles 4 through 7 all implicitly employ the distinction between law and gospel as a criterion by which Christ *alone* is identified as the subject of God's saving grace: "no deed, social status, or religious order can free us" (article 5); "all of humanity would be damned had not Jesus Christ come to help with his life and death" (article 4).[5]

The distinction between law and gospel began germinating in Luther's theology at least as early as his 1513–1515 lectures on the Psalms, as he modulated the traditional distinction between the letter and the spirit from the fourfold method of interpretation into the key of God's killing and resurrecting words.[6] By 1518 and 1520, however, this distinction had fully broken the surface, first as a soteriological and epistemological criterion in the Heidelberg Disputation—"the law says 'do this,' and it is never done. Grace says, 'believe in this,' and everything is already done"[7]—and then as a hermeneutic in *The Freedom of the Christian*—"the entire scripture of God is divided into two parts: commandments and promises."[8]

3. WABr 5:154.16; October 4, 1529.

4. Oberman, *Luther*, 237.

5. WA 30:3.160–71.

6. See G. Ebeling, "The New Hermeneutics and the Early Luther," *Theology Today* 21 (1964): 34–46.

7. *LW* 31:56.

8. *LW* 31:348.

For Luther, this was the theological crux: "Anyone who can properly distinguish the gospel from the law may thank God and know that he is a theologian."[9] Translating this distinction from hermeneutics to homiletics, Luther writes: "This is the sermon which we should daily study. . . . In it both imprisonment and redemption, sin and forgiveness, wrath and grace, death and life are shown to us. . . . The first thing about sin and death is taught us by the law, the second about redemption, righteousness and life by the gospel of Christ. One must preach both. One must preach the law so that people come to a knowledge of their sins. . . . One should preach the gospel so that one comes to know Christ and his benefits."[10] This begins to express the meaning of and difference between law and gospel as Luther understood them. The law is God's word by which he diagnoses sinners: condemned and dead. The gospel is God's word by which he delivers sinners: forgiven and made alive. God's law reveals sin and seals the coffin of the old Adam. God's gospel is preached at the graveside of the old, and it is a word that redeems and resurrects. The law sounds like Nathan's words to David: "You are the man" (2 Sam. 12:7). The gospel sounds like Jesus's words to the dead: "Lazarus, come out" (John 11:43). The distinction between law and gospel is not first a hermeneutical and homiletical strategy that provides categories by which to index, interpret, and announce God's word. Law and gospel name the actions of the "living and active" word (Heb. 4:12) by which God interprets hearers, imprisoning in disobedience in order to have mercy (Rom. 11:32), killing and making alive (1 Sam. 2:6). For Luther, therefore, this was never just theological or pastoral theory; it was personal experience. In one of his reminiscences about the "Reformation breakthrough," he recalls, "I regarded both [God's law and his gospel] as the same thing. . . . When I realized the law was one thing, and the gospel another, I broke through and was free."[11]

As Luther's letter indicates, this is not just his own unique theology or experience. The distinction between law and gospel is shared by Lutheran and Reformed theology; it is part of the "almost everything" on which the traditions are of "one opinion." Zacharias Ursinus, commenting on the structure of the Heidelberg Catechism, says, "the catechism in its primary and most general sense, may be divided as the doctrine of the church, into the law and gospel. . . . The first treats of the misery of man, the second of his deliverance

9. *LW* 26:115.

10. WA 45:3.19, quoted in H. J. Iwand, *The Righteousness of Faith according to Luther*, trans. R. H. Lundell (Eugene, OR: Wipf and Stock, 2008), 90n77.

11. *LW* 54:442.

from this misery."[12] John Calvin spoke repeatedly of "the antithesis between legal and gospel righteousness"—the way "the gospel differs from the law"—and insisted that an awareness of this distinction "can extricate us from many difficulties," as it reveals "that the righteousness which is given us through the gospel has been freed of all conditions of the law."[13] Theodore Beza, in his *Confessio*, both distinguished law and gospel—"We divide this word into two principal parts or kinds: the one is called 'law,' the other the 'gospel'"—and echoed Luther's sense of the significance of this distinction: "Ignorance of this distinction between law and gospel is one of the principal sources of the abuse which corrupted and still corrupt Christianity."[14] William Perkins, again like Luther, made the move from hermeneutics to homiletics: "The basic principle in application is to know whether the passage is a statement of law or of gospel." This is crucial because, "when the word is preached, the law and the gospel operate differently. . . . The law exposes the disease of sin . . . but provides no remedy for it. . . . By contrast, a statement of the gospel," which differs from the law in that "it has the power of the Holy Spirit joined to it," does not call for "works" and pronounce a "curse" but "speaks of Christ and his benefits."[15] Quotations like these, which could be multiplied many times over, confirm Louis Berkhof's assertion that "The churches of the Reformation"—not the Lutheran or Reformed tradition but "churches of the Reformation"—"from the very beginning distinguished between the law and the gospel as the two parts of the word of God. . . . The law comprises everything in scripture which is a revelation of God's will in the form of a command or prohibition, while the gospel embraces everything, whether it be in the Old Testament or the New, that pertains to the work of reconciliation and that proclaims the seeking and redeeming love of God in Christ Jesus."[16]

This kind of basic agreement on the distinction between law and gospel is significant. For the reformers, this was something they shared, something that

12. Z. Ursinus, *The Commentary on the Heidelberg Catechism*, trans. G. W. Williard (Phillipsburg, NJ: Presbyterian and Reformed, 1852), 13.

13. J. Calvin, *Institutes of the Christian Religion*, ed. J. T. McNeill, trans. F. L. Battles (Philadelphia: Westminster, 1960), 3.11.14, 17, 18.

14. *The Christian Faith, by Theodore Beza*, trans. J. Clark (Lewes, UK: Focus Christian Ministry Trust, 1992), 41.

15. W. Perkins, *The Art of Prophesying* (Edinburgh: Banner of Truth, 1996), 54. For these and more references on the distinction between law and gospel in the Reformed tradition, see M. S. Horton, "Post-Reformation Reformed Anthropology," in *Personal Identity in Theological Perspective*, ed. R. Lints, M. S. Horton, and M. Talbot (Grand Rapids: Eerdmans, 2006), 45–69.

16. L. Berkhof, *Systematic Theology* (Grand Rapids: Eerdmans, 1941), 612.

picked them out as evangelicals and differentiated them from their theological opponents. In Luther's words, "You will find nothing about this distinction between law and gospel in the books of the monks, the canonists, and the recent and ancient theologians."[17] But you do find it in the books of both Lutheran and Reformed theologians. While "for centuries there has been a remarkable silence about [the distinction between law and gospel] in all the schools and churches," the Reformation schools—Lutheran and Reformed alike—speak: "The word of God is both law and gospel."[18]

Agreement, however, is only half the story. As Luther discovered through long experience with the distinction between law and gospel, it is a difficult art. At "the level of words," the difference between law and gospel is obvious: "There is no one so stupid that he does not recognize how definite this distinction between law and grace is."[19] One particularly memorable rendition of this "definite distinction" comes from a preface to a piece of Elizabethan Protestant propaganda, John Foxe's *Acts and Monuments of the English Martyrs*:

> There is nothing more comfortable for troubled consciences than to be instructed in the difference between the law and the gospel. The law shows us our sin; the gospel shows us the remedy for it. The law shows our condemnation; the gospel shows our redemption. The law is a word of ire; the gospel is a word of grace. The law is a word of despair; the gospel is a word of comfort. The law is a word of unrest; the gospel is a word of peace. The law says pay your debt; the gospel says Christ has paid it. The law says you are a sinner, despair you shall be damned. The gospel says your sins are forgiven, be comforted you shall be saved. The law says where is your righteousness? The gospel says Christ is your righteousness.[20]

Here, as Luther suggests, the distinction is concrete and clear. But it is also said to be "comfortable." This gestures toward a more fundamental level at which the distinction between law and gospel operates, what Luther termed "the level of reality and experience." If at the "level of words" the distinction is so obvious that "no one is so stupid that he does not recognize" it, at this

17. *LW* 26:313.

18. *LW* 26:313; 33:105. Cf. Herman Bavinck, *Reformed Dogmatics*, vol. 4, *Holy Spirit, Church, and New Creation*, ed. John Bolt, trans. John Vriend (Grand Rapids: Baker Academic, 2008), 448: "the word of God, both as law and gospel, is the revelation of the will of God."

19. *LW* 26:143–44.

20. Adapted from "Patrick's Places," trans. John Frith, in J. Foxe, *Acts and Monuments of the English Martyrs*, vol. 4, ed. S. R. Cattley (London: Seely and Burnside, 1837), 566.

lived level—"the level of reality and experience"—the distinction between law and gospel "is the most difficult thing there is."[21] For Luther, the reason this simple linguistic distinction is a near existential impossibility is that when a person is suffering and aware of his or her sin, it "is the most difficult thing" to ignore the condemning voice of the law that speaks against the person and listen instead to the forgiving voice of the gospel that speaks for the person. What this means—theologically, pastorally, and personally—is that "There is no one living on earth who knows how to distinguish rightly between the law and the gospel. . . . Only the Holy Spirit knows this art."[22]

If "no one living on earth . . . knows how to distinguish rightly between the law and the gospel," then perhaps it is unsurprising that this is not simply a theme on which Lutheran and Reformed theologians have agreed but has also been a source of debate and self-differentiation. It does not, in other words, only live under Luther's "almost everything" on which the traditions are of "one opinion." Rather, when Lutheran and Reformed theologians talk about the distinction between law and gospel, the conversation on this shared theme tends to run along the lines of Luther's letter to Katharina: "we are of one opinion in almost everything, but . . ."

Herman Bavinck articulates this dynamic of agreement-and-disagreement in his *Reformed Dogmatics*. Both the Lutheran and Reformed traditions agree, "the word of God, both as law and gospel, is the revelation of God's will."[23] Despite this shared affirmation, Bavinck argues that Reformed theology and Lutheran theology have "a very different view."[24] One symptom of this difference, as Bavinck diagnoses it, is that while "Lutherans almost exclusively have an eye for the accusing and condemning function of the law," for the Reformed this "pedagogical use of the law" is only "accidentally necessary because of sin," and as such, "among the Reformed the law occupies a much larger place in the doctrine of gratitude than in that of misery."[25] This exposes a potential fault line: Is the law fundamentally or even exclusively for the world as fallen and

21. *LW* 26:445.

22. *LW* 54:127.

23. Bavinck, *Reformed Dogmatics*, 4:448. Note, however, that whereas Bavinck says that "law and gospel . . . differ especially in content" because the former demands "human works" and the latter invites the acceptance of "the righteousness of Christ" (4:454), Iwand insists, "both the law and the gospel have the same content," quoting Luther, who writes, "The law requires that we must have love and have Jesus Christ, but the gospel offers both and brings both" (*The Righteousness of Faith*, 42; cf. *LW* 25:326).

24. Bavinck, *Reformed Dogmatics*, 4:455.

25. Bavinck, *Reformed Dogmatics*, 4:454–55.

thus the person as sinner, or is the law originally and principally for the world as created and thus the person as redeemed?

One way to approach this question is via the threefold use of the law. The Lutheran and Reformed confessions both affirm a political use of the law (i.e., restraining sin), a theological use of the law (i.e., revealing sin), and a third use (i.e., a use of the law for Christians). This formal agreement, however, can mask deep discontinuity. As Bavinck notes, for Lutherans, the third use of the law "is solely necessary since and insofar as believers continue to be sinners."[26] This captures a recurring theme in Luther's *Antinomian Disputations*: "the law needs to remain . . . insofar as we live and act here in the flesh"; "the law is still given to the holy and righteous . . . not insofar as he is righteous and holy, but insofar as he is flesh"; "because we are not perfect and sin in the present life, the law is to be taught."[27] For Luther, texts like Galatians 3:19 and 1 Timothy 1:9 indicate that the law, while "holy, righteous, and good" (Rom. 7:12; cf. 1 Tim. 1:8), is given "because of transgressions" and is "not for the righteous but for . . . sinners." *The Book of Concord*, the collection of Lutheran confessional documents, takes the same line. The law, like the gospel, should be preached to Christians, not because they are righteous *extra nos*, but because they are sinners *in se*—because "the old Adam hangs on" like an "obstinate donkey."[28]

It is just here that Bavinck insists, "The Reformed held a very different view."[29] Whereas Luther takes his bearings from the law given at Sinai in the context of sin, Bavinck starts in Eden, "before the fall."[30] Because "the law" was given "before the fall," its political and theological functions—that is, God's uses of the law in relation to sin—can only be "accidentally necessary."[31] This reflects Calvin's view that while "the law, which among sinners can engender nothing but death, ought among the saints to have a better and more excellent

26. Bavinck, *Reformed Dogmatics*, 4:455.

27. M. Luther, *Solus Decalogus est Aeternus: Martin Luther's Complete Antinomian Theses and Disputations*, ed. and trans. H. Sonntag (Minneapolis: Lutheran Press, 2008), 267, 269, 283.

28. FC SD 6.7, 24, in *BC*, 588, 591. There are internal Lutheran debates, related to the third use of the law, about the implications of insisting that the law is for the old age and thus for the Christian *qua peccator*: Does the third use mean the political and theological uses are still operative for the Christian, does third use name an additional, distinctive, and didactic use for the Christian, or is the notion of a third use of the law problematic?

29. Bavinck, *Reformed Dogmatics*, 4:455.

30. Bavinck, *Reformed Dogmatics*, 4:455.

31. Bavinck, *Reformed Dogmatics*, 4:455. Luther, in his lectures on Genesis, addresses the question of the relationship between the law Paul refers to in texts like 1 Tim. 1:9 and the command and prohibition of Gen. 2:16–17 and concludes that it is necessary to make a "distinction between the law given before sin and that given after sin" (*LW* 1:109).

use."[32] This means that, in contrast to Luther, who called the theological use of the law the "primary purpose" and "chief and proper use,"[33] for Calvin the third use is the "principal use," the use of the law that "pertains more closely to the proper purpose of the law."[34] On Bavinck's reading, "proper" and "principal" seem to mean something like "original" and "created." His rendering of the distinction between law and gospel is thus oriented to creation "before the fall" and its restoration: "the gospel is temporary; the law is eternal and precisely that which is restored by the gospel."[35]

It is exactly this complex of themes that Werner Elert, a Lutheran theologian who taught at Erlangen, picks up in his short book *Law and Gospel*.[36] Elert's publication was provoked by Karl Barth's 1935 reversal of the traditional order of law and gospel, "Gospel and Law."[37] As the title of chapter 9 of Elert's book suggests, however, his polemic is as much "a critique of Calvin" as it is a response to Barth. Taking up the question of the third use of the law, Elert agrees with Bavinck that for the Lutheran confession the Christian requires the sin-restraining and the sin-revealing law because the Christian is a "pardoned sinner," because in his or her "earthly existence" the "old Adam still infects [the person's] nature."[38] Elert critiques Calvin for thinking that there is a "nomological existence in which the law does not turn against the man who lives with it" (*lex semper accusat*) and thereby rejects Calvin's notion of a "better and more excellent use" of the law among the saints.[39] Following Luther, the theological use is not accidental for Elert; rather, "the proper and absolute use of the law is to terrify with lightning (as on Mt. Sinai) . . . with a thunderbolt to burn and crush that brute which is called the presumption of righteousness."[40] This leads to Elert's most basic critique. Where Bavinck declared "the gospel is temporary; the law is eternal and precisely that which is restored by the gospel," Elert voices the apparently opposite pole: "[Calvin] sees in the law the ultimate criterion for measuring man's relation to God. This means that the gospel did not provide a new way of salvation, but served only to clarify

32. Calvin, *Institutes* 2.7.13.

33. *LW* 26:309.

34. Calvin, *Institutes* 2.7.12.

35. Bavinck, *Reformed Dogmatics*, 4:455.

36. W. Elert, *Law and Gospel*, trans. E. H. Schroeder (Philadelphia: Fortress, 1967).

37. K. Barth, "Gospel and Law," in *Community, State, and Church* (New York: Doubleday, 1960), 71–100.

38. Elert, *Law and Gospel*, 41–42.

39. Elert, *Law and Gospel*, 43, 45.

40. *LW* 26:310.

the law. It stepped in as an auxiliary aid since the law alone did not achieve its goal. For Calvin, the gospel stands in service of the law. . . . [But] it is not the gospel that serves the law, but the law that serves the gospel. . . . Either the law or the gospel is the end of God's ways with men, but not both."[41]

Listening in on these moments of this centuries-old and ongoing conversation puts some of the recurring topics on the table. Does the law operate in Eden or only east of it? What is the "proper" function of the law, and is the third use for the Christian *qua peccator* or *qua iustus*? Is the divine-human relation fundamentally legal or evangelical? Other voices in the conversation between the Lutheran and Reformed tradition would add other questions. For Hermann Sasse, the real "difference" is that "the Reformed believe that both law and gospel are parts of Christ's real work" whereas "the Lutheran Church . . . teaches that the preaching of the law is the 'strange,' and the preaching of the gospel is the 'real,' work of Christ."[42] Berkhof identifies a "difference between the Lutherans and the Reformed" in that the Lutheran emphasis on the theological use of the law considers the function of the law in justification while the Reformed stress on the third use pays "more attention to the law in connection with the doctrine of sanctification."[43] The Reformed, at times, seem to define the law more in terms of its nature as a "revelation of the will of God" and "an expression of God's being,"[44] whereas Lutherans regularly define the law by its function: "Whatever shows sin, wrath, and death exercises the office of the law"; "The law and the showing of sin, or the revelation of wrath are synonymous terms."[45]

If these themes indicate some of the specific points of debate, there are also more fundamental ways of framing the conversation. In the wake of the Westminster Standards, Reformed theology has tended to understand law and gospel within the frame of covenant theology. On the one hand, this preserves a distinction, as the difference between the covenant of works and the covenant of grace names distinct modes of God's relation to creatures. At the same time, covenant provides a category more basic than law and gospel, a theological space capacious enough to hold God's two words *together*, even if

41. Elert, *Law and Gospel*, 47–48.

42. H. Sasse, *Here We Stand: Nature and Character of the Lutheran Faith*, trans. T. G. Tappert (Adelaide, Australia: Lutheran Publishing House, 1979), 129.

43. Berkhof, *Systematic Theology*, 615.

44. Bavinck, *Reformed Dogmatics*, 4:448, 455.

45. Luther, *Solus Decalogus est Aeternus*, 137. See, however, Ursinus, who in the *Commentary on the Heidelberg Catechism* defines the law and differentiates it from the gospel in terms of its "effects" as well as its "mode of revelation" and "conditions" (497).

they are only together in distinction.[46] For at least some Lutherans, any theology that holds law and gospel together within a more basic category (e.g., covenant, word of God, revelation) differs so fundamentally from the Lutheran conviction that such "unity can only be asserted in the face of agonizing spiritual struggle (*Anfechtung*)" that the two approaches represent "fundamentally different ways of studying theology."[47] Another root of these divergences may lie in differing understandings of the scope and subject matter of theology. For Calvin, theology is concerned, quite expansively and comprehensively, with "the knowledge of God and of ourselves."[48] Within this frame questions about the prelapsarian law and its relation to and reflection of God's eternal being are entirely apropos. For Luther, however, theology's purview is narrower: "the real subject of theology is the human being, accused of sin and lost, and God, the one who justifies and rescues the sinful human being."[49] Here, where the focus is not God and the human being in general but only the sinning human and the justifying God, theology's task is not the consideration of all truth from before creation to the consummation; it is the distinction between and delivery of the word that kills (law) and the word that makes alive (gospel).[50]

And so the conversation goes. The Marburg Colloquy was one episode in this discussion, but Luther's description of it in his letter to Katharina captures the long course of the conversation: "we are of one opinion in almost everything, but . . ." The extent of this "almost everything" encouraged other reformers that the "but" was temporary, that further dialogue could end in full confessional unity. On February 10, 1549, Thomas Cranmer wrote to Philip Melanchthon: "I am aware that you have often desired that wise and godly men should take counsel together, and, having compared their opinions, send

46. See especially Michael Allen's essay in this book. Covenant theology is therefore part of the way Reformed theology would answer Elert's charge that in the Reformed tradition the creator-creature relationship is regulated by the law rather than the gospel. Because the relationship is covenantal, it includes nomistic aspects, but the relationship itself is anchored in grace, in an act of "voluntary condescension on God's part" (WCF 7.1).

47. G. Ebeling, *Word and Faith*, trans. J. W. Leitch (Philadelphia: Fortress, 1963), 270. For Oswald Bayer, any attempt to posit a unity (*Einheit*) of law and gospel forgets that "the theology we do en route as pilgrims (*theologia viatorum*) is stamped by the . . . irreducibly different ways which God encounters us," namely, law and gospel, though Bayer would also include divine hiddenness (*Theology the Lutheran Way*, trans. J. G. Silcock and M. C. Mattes [Grand Rapids: Eerdmans, 2007], 105).

48. Calvin, *Institutes* 1.1.1.

49. *LW* 12:311.

50. Katherine Sonderegger and Erik Herrmann, in their essays in this book, consider this issue of the scope of theology, in terms of both the range of what God does through his word (Sonderegger) and the characteristic theological modes of the Lutheran and Reformed traditions (Herrmann).

forth under the sanction of their authority some work, that should embrace the chief subjects of ecclesiastical doctrine. . . . This object we are anxiously endeavoring to accomplish with our utmost power. We therefore request you to communicate your counsels and opinions to us in person."[51] John Calvin received a similar letter, and as his reply from Geneva in April 1552 indicates, he supported such a gathering: "Most illustrious Lord, you truly and wisely judge that in the present disturbed state of the church no more suitable remedy can be adopted than the assembling together of godly and discreet men, well disciplined in the school of Christ, who shall openly profess their agreement in the doctrines of religion."[52] Calvin, however, like Melanchthon, never sailed for England: "if I can be of any service, I shall not shrink from crossing ten seas," he wrote. Nevertheless, he added, "I hope my want of ability will occasion me to be excused."[53]

The meeting never happened. There never was "an agreement of learned men . . . well framed according to the standard of scripture" that would allow "the churches . . . far separated from each other . . . to unite."[54] This book is far from the product Melanchthon, Cranmer, and Calvin dreamed of. It does not take up all the "chief subjects of ecclesiastical doctrine"; it carries no more authority than all honest and open conversation; and whether its contributors are "wise and godly" is for the one who said "judgment is mine" to decide. But this book does join in a conversation and invites its readers to listen in and keep it going.

51. Cranmer to Melanchthon (1549), in J. E. Cox, *Miscellaneous Writings and Letters of Thomas Cranmer* (Cambridge: Parker Society, 1846; reproduced by Regent College Publishing), 426.

52. Calvin to Cranmer (1552), in *Original Letters Relative to the English Reformation*, ed. H. Robinson for the Parker Society (Cambridge: Cambridge University Press, 1847), 711.

53. Calvin to Cranmer, 713.

54. Calvin to Cranmer, 713.

PART I
The Law Is Not the Gospel

Chapter 1

The Law in the Lutheran Tradition

Piotr J. Małysz

The distinction between the law and the gospel was a hallmark of Luther's theology, its formal principle. Its purpose was to keep in view theology's proper subject, that is, "man guilty of sin and condemned, and God the Justifier and Savior of man the sinner."[1] As early as the Heidelberg Disputation (1518), Martin Luther insisted, "The law says, 'do this,' and it is never done. Grace [or divine promise, or precisely the gospel] says, 'believe in this,' and everything is already done."[2] The law-gospel distinction has ever since been a watchword of the Lutheran theological repertoire and one of Lutheran theology's treasures.

Our objective is to investigate the first element of the distinction—the understanding of the law in Lutheran theology. The task is deceptively simple. To be sure, it can only be undertaken in light of the distinction itself. It will be necessary, therefore, to attend to questions of both theological anthropology (the human person under the law) and the doctrine of God (the one thanks to whom everything is already done). But beyond that, things are less obvious. Even on an issue so fundamental, the tradition has certainly not spoken with a single voice, let alone in a monotone manner. In the following, we shall grant a privileged voice to Luther himself as a *doctor ecclesiae*, officially recognized as such in the last of the Lutheran confessional writings, the Formula of Concord (1577).[3] We shall also give some attention to Luther's medieval context and the Formula of Concord itself, which claims Luther's mantle. Yet there are many other voices, including that of Luther's friend and colleague on the Wittenberg faculty, Philip Melanchthon, and a long line of their often-warring

1. Martin Luther, *Psalm 51* (1532), in *LW* 12:311; WA 40.II:328.

2. *LW* 31:56; WA 1:364.

3. FC SD 9, in *BC*, 528–29.

disciples. The tradition's polyphonic voice not infrequently turns into the dissonance of controversy, stretching well into the present, and we cannot avoid stepping into that world. We cannot avoid taking sides, if only implicitly, as the law-gospel distinction refracts into a multitude of thorny and hotly contested issues. The law and the gospel are to be distinguished, but what is their underlying connection that enables their distinction in the first place? How old is the law; is it eternal? What kinds of law are there? How many uses of the law are there? Does the law have a place in the church and in the Christian life? There are challenges from outsiders, too, including Karl Barth's charge, first, that the distinction rests on shaky biblical and dogmatic foundations that attribute to God "not one intrinsically true and clear Word of God, but . . . two Words in which he speaks alternately and in different ways to man," and his further charge that the law in the distinction seems to contradict "the self-understanding of the Old Testament," and finally his incomprehension in regard to how the law can lead to the gospel.[4] We shall touch on some of these in-house and external issues in the course of our exposition.

Our approach is expository rather than polemical. The line of argument pursued here will amount to the claim that the law cannot be properly understood outside of a robust relational anthropology, and this means, in particular, outside of God's communicative being as both Creator and Redeemer. It was as a result of an impoverishment of this anthropological framework that the distinction of law and gospel lost its broader clarity.

Edenic Anthropology and the Law

To understand the law and its work, we must begin by considering humanity as God's creation, created in God's image. For Luther, the law was present already in the garden of Eden. The question of what it was and is, therefore, is inseparable from broader anthropological considerations. This will allow us to inquire into humanity after the Fall and investigate Luther's theology of the law against the broader picture of what the reformer understands as the human predicament.

In his *Lectures on Genesis,* delivered in the last decade or so of his life, Luther challenges the received tradition that views the *imago Dei* in terms of

4. Barth admits that "there is perhaps more than one Luther" in addition to the Luther he encountered in the German Lutheran theology of the first half of the twentieth century. *Church Dogmatics* IV/3.1 (Edinburgh: T. & T. Clark, 1961), 370–71.

natural human endowments, such as memory, will, and mind.[5] Though Luther does not discount those, the image of God, for him, is constituted rather in the use of those faculties as that use is enabled by and oriented to God's actual, public work. It is thus not so much an internally ordered human being, keeping fleshly inclinations under control by means of a grace-fortified will and so able to attend to higher things, that expresses the image and similitude of God. It is humans' openness to God at work, which in turn enables them to live "just as God lives."[6] What Luther emphasizes as an essential part of the image is the intimate knowledge of God by the first humans and, as its corollary, their openness to each other and an intimate knowledge of other creatures. All this enters into Luther's definition of original righteousness.[7] Adam and Eve find themselves "completely engulfed by the goodness and justice of God." And just as God is toward them, they, being in God's image, are able to be toward each other in "a singular union of hearts and wills."[8] God has, as it were, preached himself—spoken his own character—into Adam and Eve's being.

The first couple's knowledge of God has the more specific character of faith: "in man there was the most admirable confidence [*fiducia*] in God, and man could not have been afraid even if he had seen the heavens collapse."[9] Adam "knew God and believed [*credidit*] that He was good."[10] It is this overwhelming sense of divine goodness—Adam's being "content with God's favor"—that enables Adam not only to trust another human being but also to exercise dominion over creation without fear, that is, to make "use of the creatures only for the admiration of God and for a holy joy which is unknown to us in this corrupt state of nature."[11] In this manner, Adam's life was "wholly godly; that is, he was without the fear of death or of any other danger." In faith, Adam and Eve received their very selves from God and were able to risk themselves not only for each other but also for creation itself. For this they had been created.

Their ecstatic being determined Adam and Eve's attitude to God's command. Luther is of the opinion that there was law in Eden. For one thing, God as part of his blessing had issued a command to be fruitful, etc. (Gen. 1:28). Even more obviously, he forbade the eating of the fruit from the tree of

5. *LW* 1:61. Luther delivered his lectures on Gen. 1–3 in 1535 and early 1536.
6. *LW* 1:63; WA 42:47.
7. *LW* 1:113; WA 42:86.
8. *LW* 1:67; WA 42:50.
9. *LW* 1:171; WA 42:128.
10. *LW* 1:62–63; WA 42:47.
11. *LW* 1:71; WA 42:54.

the knowledge of good and evil, and to this particular command attached the threat of death (Gen. 3:16–17).[12] But this was not law as we come to experience it in our being. In the context of Adam's faith, obedience to the command became Adam's "outward physical way of indicating his worship of God and of demonstrating his obedience by an outward work."[13] With the tree, "God gave Adam Word, worship, and religion," so that humans might obey and praise him, so much so that the tree itself actually was "Adam's church, altar, and pulpit. Here he was to yield to God the obedience he owed, give recognition to the Word and will of God, give thanks to God, and call upon God for aid against temptation."[14] The command, it seems, was a vehicle of Adam's *recognition* of his creaturely limitation, and the tree the place where the wise God, whom Adam knew so intimately, could be taken at his word, not just in Adam's whole ecstatic existence as its innermost determinant, but also in a willed external act by the creature itself. Luther, therefore, denies that the command was anything weaker than that, that is, exhortation rather than law, albeit prelapsarian law.[15] The command with its explicit threat enabled Adam's *self*-expression as a creature basking in the overwhelming goodness of God. It was, according to Luther, "Gospel and Law."[16] In that order!

It should come as little surprise that the serpent's temptation in Genesis 3 is not really into disobedience to the command as such. The violation of the command—just as obedience to it—could only come as a symptom of something far deeper: the subversion of one's whole being in the loss of faith. The focal point of the chapter is, therefore, God. Luther depicts Satan, speaking through the serpent, as one who apes God. Satan is in effect a preacher of another word, or to put it more precisely: "Satan attacks the Word and works of God" in such a way that "a new god is invented by Satan for men without their even being aware of it."[17] As a result, behind the good will of God there now looms another will, not good but uncertain and untrustworthy. "The serpent directs its attack at God's good will,"[18] with the result that one no longer feels "safe in God's goodness," as Adam and Eve used to.[19] For Luther, "the chief temptation is to listen to [this] other word and to depart from the one

12. *LW* 1:110; WA 42:83.
13. *LW* 1:94; WA 42:71–72.
14. *LW* 1:106, 95; WA 42:80, 72.
15. *LW* 1:108–9; WA 42:82
16. *LW* 1:146; WA 42:110.
17. *LW* 1:147–48; WA 42:111–12.
18. *LW* 1:146; WA 42:110.
19. *LW* 1:143; WA 42:107.

which God had previously spoken."[20] When one succumbs, the first thing that has—already!—happened is the loss of the knowledge of God, and with it a complete collapse of the person's being.[21]

Luther speaks of a "prodigious fear which followed sin."[22] He explains: "By nature we have become so thoroughly frightened that we fear even the things that are safe." This postlapsarian fear is crystallized chiefly in humans' fear of God, which now takes the place of humans' natural faith: "Adam and Eve lose their confidence [*fiducia*] in God and are so filled with fear and terror that . . . they immediately think God is approaching to punish them." God now appears to Adam and Eve as an oppressive taskmaster whose command—now an arbitrary command because the giver is not to be trusted—they have transgressed, a powerful deceiver whose sole goal is to keep the man and the woman ignorant and submissive. Therefore, God's question "Where are you?" is heard by them as nothing but words of the law.[23] God's whole being—in its inscrutability and unreliability—is now a threat. Unmoored, uncontained, and sheer law. It is, of course, "our will [that] makes a devil out of God and shudders at the mention of His name, especially when it is troubled by God's judgment."[24] But Adam and Eve do not know that—for "sin itself is the real withdrawal from God," and, in light of the false image that stands at its center, it can only be followed by flight.[25]

Luther identifies unbelief "in the inmost heart" as "the root and source of all sin"; in fact, "unbelief alone commits sin," and actually is "the only sin."[26] Acts done in unbelief produce further acts of unbelief, in that the sinner does not believe—because he or she does not know—that unfaithfulness can be brought before God. "This is the nature of sin—that the farther man withdraws from God, the farther he still desires to withdraw."[27] The postlapsarian "fear is

20. *LW* 1:147; WA 42:111.

21. "In the case of the soul the outstanding fact is this: that the knowledge of God has been lost; that we do not everywhere and always give thanks to Him; that we do not delight in His works and deeds; that we do not trust Him; that when He inflicts deserved punishments, we begin to hate God and to blaspheme Him; that when we must deal with our neighbor, we yield to our desires and are robbers, thieves, adulterers, murderers, cruel, inhuman, merciless, etc." (*LW* 1:114; WA 42:86).

22. *LW* 1:170; WA 42:127.

23. *LW* 1:173; WA 42:129.

24. *LW* 1:142; WA 42:106.

25. *LW* 1:172–73; WA 42:129.

26. *Preface to the Epistle of St. Paul to the Romans* (1522/1546), *LW* 35:369; WADB 7:9.

27. *LW* 1:173; WA 42:129. Kierkegaard may have captured this the most pointedly: "every unrepented sin is a new sin and every moment that it remains unrepented is also new sin" (Søren Kierkegaard, *The Sickness unto Death*, ed. H. V. Hong and E. H. Hong [Princeton: Princeton University Press, 1980], 105).

really an avoidance and hatred of God,"[28] as "man not only does not love God any longer but flees from Him, hates Him, and desires to be and live without Him."[29]

The Law of Unbelief

That Adam and Eve hear God's question "Where are you?" as law, rather than loving concern, for example, is one aspect of the collapse of their being. But the ripple effects of the loss of the knowledge of God are far more pervasive. Luther implies that something like God's question, a bare and unmitigated threat, now continues to echo in the sinner's conscience and wreaks havoc there. "Where am I? Who am I?" For the loss of the knowledge of divine goodness brings with it a loss of the knowledge of self, which was founded upon the former. The man and the woman "do not know their Creator, [and so also] their origin, and their end; they do not know out of what and why they were created."[30] Furthermore, when one no longer knows what one is, not to mention what one was, the transgression itself, one's very guilt, also becomes unknowable. The knowledge of sin is thus lost as well.[31] Coming back to one's true self becomes impossible. The sinner neither has the means nor knows the path. Reality itself must take the form of a cipher and a trap. If God exists, he appears unjust, and even satanic; or perhaps there is no God, and everything is at the mercy of fate's own iron law.[32] This sweeping uncertainty takes its toll on the conscience: "our conscience is no longer quiet but, when it thinks of God's judgment," or perhaps what it only takes for God's judgment, it "despairs and adopts illicit defenses and remedies."[33]

Chief among such defenses and remedies is for the unbeliever to attempt to make sense of his or her being, to make something of himself or

28. *LW* 1:171; WA 42:128.

29. *LW* 1:165; WA 42:124.

30. *LW* 1:67; WA 42:50. Or, as Luther puts it in *Disputation concerning Man* (1536), humans have lost the knowledge of their efficient and final cause. *LW* 34:138, 140; WA 39.I:175, 177.

31. *LW* 1:141; WA 42:106. Cf. "we are so corrupted by original sin that we cannot see the magnitude of sin" (WA 39.I:449; Luther, *Solus Decalogus est Aeternus: Martin Luther's Complete Antinomian Theses and Disputations*, ed. and trans. H. Sonntag [Minneapolis: Lutheran Press, 2008], 333).

32. "God so orders this corporal world in its external affairs that if you respect and follow the judgment of human reason, you are bound to say either that there is no God or that God is unjust" (*The Bondage of the Will* [1525], in *LW* 33:291; WA 18:784). Cf. *LW* 33:41; WA 18:617–18.

33. *LW* 1:114; WA 42:86.

herself, to justify the self[34]—regardless of whether the thought of God even enters the mind. For all the relative security one might enjoy, postlapsarian life turns into an existence under sin, the curse of the law, death, and the devil.[35] (It is all that without faith in Christ, of course.) Importantly, sin, law, death, and the devil are not so much punitive impositions, or even privations; they are rather positively manifested from within individual and collective life. At their mercy, the unbeliever cannot but become a "restless worker" (to borrow Luther's phrase from a somewhat different context),[36] bound to their logic and law. First of all, one finds oneself doomed to a life of self-creation—a self-contradictory posture in which, as Luther notes, one attempts to be simultaneously the material and the worker.[37] One is thus constantly delivered up to oneself, inexorably faced with being less than one desires to be, or feels one ought to be. To make matters even worse, self-justification can take place only within some coordinates beyond the person—according to some law, as it were. This is a surprising vestige of humanity's original openness to God's goodness. One must thus make for oneself a god—if only in the form of one's own thoughts—whom one will trust just enough to provide both the coordinates and the stamp of approval on one's self-making.[38] Hence unbelief ineluctably turns into idolatry. True idols, says Luther, are "in the heart" in the form of "false righteousness, glory in works, unbelief, and everything else that takes the place of Christ in the heart in the form of unbelief."[39] Even as it "denies the truth of God," unbelief "invents a new god."[40] This demonstrates further its ultimate presumption: one not only makes oneself, as if one were nothing, but one also makes for oneself a god to aid one in the process. "All hypocrites and idolaters try to do the works that properly pertain to the Deity and belong completely and solely to Christ."[41] The unbeliever is thus—to sum all this up with Luther's famous adage—a *homo incurvatus*

34. Those who "deny faith" have to "bless themselves by their own work, that is, to justify themselves" (*Lectures on Galatians* [1531/1535], *LW* 26:257; WA 40.I:404).

35. *LW* 26:281ff.; WA 40.I:440ff.

36. Luther used this phrase to draw attention to the damage that Erasmus's concept of a neutral human will did by turning Christians away from God's grace to their vastly overblown capacities. *LW* 33:34–35; WA 18:613.

37. *LW* 26:259; WA 40.I:407b.

38. *LW* 1:149; WA 42:112. Cf. Large Catechism (1528), Part I: The First Commandment, 2–3; *BC*, 386.

39. *Against the Heavenly Prophets* (1525); *LW* 40:94–95; WA 18:78.

40. *LW* 1:149; WA 42:112.

41. *LW* 26:258; WA 40.I:440.

in se ipsum, a human curved in upon his or her vacuous self, desperately yet with abandon.[42]

Any further consideration of natural law in Luther's theology must take into account the fact that the unbeliever already enacts the formal law of his or her collapsed self, the law that now drives the unbeliever to the contradictory self-expression as both a would-be god and an unfinished creature. This law is at the same time externalized subjectively in the form of a material or conceptual idol to which the unbeliever cannot but submit. Yet there is also a truly objective dimension to this law. Whatever idolatrous principle may drive one, it manifests the threat of God's law ("you will surely die"). Unbelievers are in the end delivered up to God's own law, now a pervasive and sheer law, in that, precisely in the face of denying God's goodness, they are now driven to manifest their creatureliness as bare, unsustainable, and moribund finitude, but never more than that. The notorious pseudo-Augustinian image of a human as a beast of burden ridden by Satan is a mythological way of expressing this compulsion and captivity to sin, death, and the devil—to the law of another who is hidden behind it.[43] The very denial of God's goodness compels one to confess that one is not (a) God or even like (a) God. God alone is God. This thought is positively terrifying in its tautological implications.

Luther captures the logic that fallen human nature follows in his disputations against the antinomians of the late 1530s. To be sure, the disputations have as their topic the need for preaching the law to Christians (more on this below). In making the argument that the law has its place even in what the church says to the faithful, Luther does not argue from incidents of moral failure or incontinence on the part of believers. He points instead to the *inescapable undertow of law that permeates human existence* in the fallen world. He opens the fifth disputation with a brief thesis: "The law rules in man as long as he lives."[44] The sixty-nine theses that follow form a commentary on this initial statement. Certainly, insofar as believers are "crucified and dead in Christ by faith . . . the law is fulfilled [in them], sin is deleted, death is destroyed" (theses 11, 10). "Yet *if we are alive*," Luther hastens to add, "then we are not yet in Christ, but dwell outside of Christ under law, sin, and death" (thesis 12). Such simply is the nature of embodied historical existence in the world. To disentangle the righteous from the law would require that one "prove first that the righteous

42. *Lectures on Romans* (1515–1516), *LW* 25:291, 313, 345; WA 56:304, 325, 356.

43. *LW* 33:66; WA 18:635.

44. ". . . quanto tempore vivit" (*Fifth Set of Theses against the Antinomians*, thesis 1; WA 39.I:355; Luther, *Solus Decalogus est Aeternus*, 240–49).

are completely without any sin and death" (thesis 21). What these statements make clear is that Luther's criticism of the antinomians and his affirmation of the law are *ontologically* grounded. Faith makes it possible for believers to be in Christ; this is their unquestionable, true, and real identity (we elaborate on this below); but faith does not, strictly speaking, abolish human nature as it has become manifest as part of the world and as we know it, insofar as physically, biologically, and historically believers have not yet undergone death, and "the sin which clings to nature is destroyed by death alone."[45] "For," Luther explains, "*relatively*, not formally or substantially, is sin eliminated, law abolished, death destroyed" (thesis 48). To think differently "is nothing else than assuming that all [the antinomians'] hearers have been taken out of this life" (thesis 31). Luther famously compares antinomian preaching to a play enacted before "an empty theater," without any actual audience; the antinomians put on a show "for and by themselves" (thesis 32).[46]

The Law, Politically

It is small wonder humans' profoundly law-saturated existence leads them to think that one comes to be, one becomes something and acquires inherent worth, by means of being what one is and doing what one does. It makes all the sense in the world, as we have come to know it, that doing makes a doer, perhaps with the added qualification that "a good will and right reason to do well" should motivate one's actions for them to be genuinely praiseworthy![47] That humans should have this attitude even to God's law makes sense, too: "*by nature* all men think that the Law justifies."[48] Thus when God gives his law, he runs the risk that human beings will smugly use it for self-justification. The law may actually fuel humans' sense of security. For the deeper question—whether we, and not just our affections, actually are as we ought to be, especially before God—is only rarely asked.

But God does give the law. He gives it for two reasons and in two ways. First, to prevent humans' self-justifying pursuits from destroying humankind

45. WA 39.I:491; Luther, *Solus Decalogus est Aeternus*, 255.

46. "Hoc [i.e., omnes auditores eorum ex hoc vita sublatos esse] autem putare est sibi ipsi in vacuo theatro ludos fingere et spectare" (WA 39.I:355; Luther, *Solus Decalogus est Aeternus*, 244–45).

47. À la Kant. *LW* 26:262; WA 40.I:410. "A [moral] philosopher or a lawyer does not ascend any higher," Luther adds. For Luther's theological critique of Aristotelian ethics on this issue, see also *LW* 26:255–56; WA 40.I:401–2.

48. *LW* 26:307; WA 40.I:477–78 (emphasis added).

altogether. This is the so-called *civil use* of the law. Further, God gives the law principally to prevent the sinner's self-justification, to wrest open the sinner's self-referential being, caught up in the vicious Creator-creature dynamic. This is the law's spiritual or *theological use*. Beyond these, God, first and foremost, interprets his own being. In the face of the human perversion of the image of God, God discloses his goodness by taking upon himself the consequences of sin and in doing so simultaneously reiterates his own image in the humanity of Jesus Christ. The law, as Luther sees it, is given by God ultimately for the sake of this *good news*. Luther speaks repeatedly of a *duplex usus legis* (twofold use of the law),[49] though he distinguishes also between laws and types of law.

The purpose of the political use of the law (*usus civilis, politicus*), as it is embodied in worldly government, is to restrain transgression. In this political form and role, the law, just like civil authority whose prerogative it is, is divinely sanctioned. The temporal authority is entrusted by God with the coercive power of the sword, "so that those who do not want to be good and righteous to eternal life may be forced to become good and righteous in the eyes of the world."[50] Importantly, its task is accomplished when it "bring[s] about external peace and prevent[s] evil deeds."[51] Materially, civic law systems are of course numerous. Yet their grounding in divine providence is disclosed by their single formal and teleological thrust, namely, that "every law was given to hinder sins."[52] Even bad civic laws, in that their deficiency is recognized, confirm this aspect of the law.

For Luther, all law can ideally be reduced to the Golden Rule. Seen from this angle, the law aims at togetherness and reciprocity. But Luther also invokes another maxim that he considers to be a pithy summary of the law: no one ought to be the judge in his or her own case (*nemo iudex in causa sua; Niemand soll sein eigen Richter sein*). He regards the maxim to be a summary not only of natural law but also of the justice that the law crucially presupposes and that nonetheless transcends the law.[53] It is this aspect of the law, I believe, that links Luther's *usus politicus* with the deeper ontological foundation of the law.[54] Consider that, at creation, it was God in his own

49. E.g., *Lectures on 1 Timothy* (1527–1528), *LW* 28:233; WA 26:15; and *LW* 26:274, 308; WA 40.I:429, 479; and WA 39.I:441; Luther, *Solus Decalogus est Aeternus*, 171.

50. *Whether Soldiers, Too, Can Be Saved* (1526), *LW* 46:99; WA 19:629.

51. *Temporal Authority: To What Extent It Should Be Obeyed* (1523), *LW* 45:92; WA 11:252.

52. *LW* 26:308; WA 40.I:479.

53. *LW* 46:108; WA 19:636.

54. On Luther's use of the maxim, as well its relation to the Golden Rule, see Piotr J. Malysz, "*Nemo Iudex in Causa Sua* as the Basis of Law, Justice and Justification in Luther's Thought," *Harvard Theological Review* 100, no. 3 (July 2007): 363–86.

good work who guaranteed the justice of human beings. God justified humans in the context of his creation: God was the generous giver of human character, and he made sure humanity received pride of place within God's world in accordance with its dignity. Correspondingly, when they obeyed God's command, humans affirmed their existence in such a way that all the focus was on God as the one who justifies this existence and makes sense of it.[55] Fallen humanity, by contrast, acts as judges in their own cases (cf. Gen. 3:12–13). Humans' failed self-making and even their inveterate idolatry emphasize an inability to trust another with rendering a righteous judgment in regard to themselves. The purpose of the law in its first use is, in this light, to take away from humans their self-serving misuse of justice, to emphasize that what cannot succeed ontologically (self-justification as self-creation) simply must not be done. Period. It ought not to be attempted. The law's purpose, in other words, is to mitigate the consequences of the single sin that is the motor of fallen human nature and in this way to reduce those among sin's manifestations—taking justice in one's own hands—that threaten the peace of the community or polity.

The noteworthy thing about this use of the law, which affords a significant insight into the law's very nature, is that the law cannot ultimately accomplish this purpose of peaceful wholeness. The problem lies not even in hypocrisy, in humans' ability to hide their true selves behind the facade of their actions; neither does it lie in the possible misuse of the law. It lies in the law as such. The law, Luther notes, cannot by itself guarantee justice. It cannot do it without a just judge who sees not so much the law as the person whom the law concerns. "If we do not make exceptions and strictly follow the law we do the greatest injustice of all."[56] We ought to note this carefully. Even in its political use, the law points beyond itself. Following the Aristotelian notion of equity (*epieikeia*),[57] Luther speaks of justice (*Billigkeit*) as that which must be brought *personally* to the law. Justice entails the law's proper application in accordance with the law's very essence—a just application of that which aims at justice. To try to avoid this and attempt, instead, to insulate the law as law against failure is to destroy the law and to pervert it into casuistry. Yet even in this ersatz form,

55. What helps to clarify this is Bernard of Clairvaux's distinction between grades of loving God. Bernard considers the highest form of love to be, not that one loves God for God's sake, but that one loves oneself for God's sake. That is, one is able to accept one's entire self—before the self even reciprocates divine love—as a gift of this very love. See Bernard of Clairvaux, *On Loving God* 10.27–11.30, in *Selected Works*, trans. G. R. Evans (New York: Paulist, 1987), 195–97.

56. *LW* 46:100; WA 19:630.

57. See, for example, *Nicomachean Ethics* 5.10.

the law will not be able to account for every eventuality and to assure justice, while its inherent simplicity and hence usefulness will be compromised. Consequently, "all laws that regulate men's actions must be subject to justice, their mistress, because of the innumerable and varied circumstances which no one can anticipate or set down."[58] Justice transcends the law. In calling for it, the law calls for that which can only precede the law and which the law cannot generate or sustain: *personal regard*. Without it the law is not what it is meant to be. The essential role of Christians in the structures of civil government finds its rationale in this paradox.

The Law, Theologically

The second use of the law, its theological use (*usus theologicus*), is, for Luther, the law's chief and right use. Its principal objective is to accuse and terrify the conscience.[59] To accomplish this purpose the law must "reveal [transgressions] theologically" and even increase them.[60] Luther explains at length: "the proper use and aim of the Law is to make guilty those who are smug and at peace, so that they may see that they are in danger of sin, wrath, and death, so that they may be terrified and despairing, blanching and quaking at the rustling of a leaf. To the extent that they are such, they are under the Law. For the Law requires perfect obedience toward God, and it damns those who do not yield such obedience."[61]

We shall take up the question of the material content of the law in this use presently, and this will allow us to specify what it means to be before God. For the moment, we must consider the second use from a formal angle, as a use. The second use of the law, Luther appears to be saying, has two aims. One is to place one under the law. The other, related aim is to place one before God.

Whereas the political use of the law brings one's *actions* into the orbit of the law to enforce their integrity and thus prevents one from acting as judge in one's own case, the theological use places the *entire person* under the law. Now, human existence is, as we have noted, inescapably law-saturated. What the *usus theologicus* does is make this existence visible and, in doing so, pose the question of the doer's personal integrity. The theological use distances one from oneself and

58. *LW* 46:103; WA 19:632.
59. *LW* 26:310; WA 40.I:482.
60. *LW* 26:316–17; WA 40.I:491–92.
61. *LW* 26:148; WA 40.I:257.

shows with painful clarity that one is not what one desires to be, let alone what one ought to be. It shows with equal clarity that one is not what one thinks one is: a free god on the brink of breaking through to sovereign self-determination. One is rather chained to the Sisyphean hill of self-justification, bearing uphill the ever-increasing burden of one's failure. Failure does not let itself be waved away by a wish for a clean slate and a resurrection. Unrepented actions give rise not to repentance but to further evasion. To put it less colorfully, the law's theological use undercuts the possibility of ethical redemption. To put it radically, it shows the impossibility of ethics, that is, the impossibility of fulfilling the law, any law, with a view to achieving personal integrity. The ethical agent, wishing to make something of himself or herself through the law, must be above reproach; he or she must already have personal integrity as demanded by the law, rather than being saddled with the guilt of exploiting the law by means of that which the law seeks to prevent, being a judge in one's own case.[62]

Luther remains skeptical whether the law can accomplish all this by itself rather than falling prey to "the most destructive beasts, security and presumption."[63] Upon hearing the law, one is more likely to seek to secure divine favor for oneself through doing the works demanded, without giving as much as a thought to how much the law demands, namely, "a free, willing and happy heart."[64] When it comes to the law in a Christian context, it will more likely than not transform one into a "holy hypocrite [*sanctus hypocrita*]."[65] This leads Luther to insist that the theological use of the law is, in the end, *God's* use. "God has to make use of that hammer of His, namely, the Law, to break, bruise, crush, and annihilate this beast with its false confidence, wisdom, righteousness, and power, so that it learns that it has been destroyed and damned by its evil."[66] All this takes place through the agency of the Holy Spirit, who alone can use the law.[67]

62. Kierkegaard addresses the issue with a clarity uncommon among Lutheran theologians of a more conservative stripe: "An ethics that ignores sin is an altogether futile discipline, but if it asserts sin, then it is for that very reason beyond itself. . . . As soon as sin is introduced, ethics runs aground precisely upon repentance, for repentance is the highest ethical expression but precisely as such the deepest ethical self-contradiction." What makes repentance such, it seems, is that it is a confession of one's lack of integrity, one's consequent inability, and the burden of both. This confession the theological use of the law seeks to elicit. See Søren Kierkegaard, *Fear and Trembling*, ed. C. S. Evans and S. Walsh (Cambridge: Cambridge University Press, 2006), 86.

63. WA 39.I:426; Luther, *Solus Decalogus est Aeternus*, 151.

64. *LW* 35:377; WADB 7:23.

65. *LW* 26:125; WA 40.I:221.

66. *LW* 26:314; WA 40.I:488.

67. WA 39.I:370–77; Luther, *Solus Decalogus est Aeternus*, 55, 57.

The opposite extreme is despair that is not met with any hope. Now, the law certainly aims at despair, but despair is not its final end. Accordingly, "the law urges to do what is impossible," but it does not do this in an unqualified or absolute sense. Although "sin and Satan made the possible and enjoyable law impossible and terrifying," there already is one who both bore the curse of the law for us and fulfilled the law the way it was meant to be.[68] For Luther, as is to be expected, the word of the law is not self-standing (since God never at any point intended it to be so): "the Law only shows sin, terrifies, and humbles; thus it prepares us for justification and drives us to Christ."[69] The law is thus to be "a minister and a preparation for grace,"[70] and the despair worked by it ultimately is useful and salutary.[71] Importantly, however, this qualification can be made only from the perspective of grace. "For the teaching of the law is such that, if it truly touches the heart, the entire world becomes too small for that person. Then there is no help left besides Christ."[72] Luther's observation here is a factual one: only Christ can help. But it is not that Christ, or even the idea of Christ, is somehow given from within the law. As such, the law leads to despair and offers no relief. The despair must not be watered down, as if the law inherently presupposed the gospel, or as if divine grace corresponded in a direct fashion to the predicament the law puts one in. Still, despair is not the ultimately desired goal.

Despite the law's being properly ordered to the gospel, there is essential discontinuity between the law in its theological use and the gospel itself. They must be distinguished! The second use of the law cannot determine what the gospel is, or subjectively will be, simply because it does *not restore the proper knowledge of God*. Instead, the law places the one it accuses before God as he "works life and death and all in all,"[73] an inscrutable judge who refuses to let one forget that one is a failed creature, a mere finite being, a plaything.[74] Even if God should actually be known as the giver of a positive law, without trust God's good will remains questionable. Luther is obsessively adamant: "the law is not a gift, but the word of the eternal and almighty God, who is fire

68. WA 39.I:364–65; Luther, *Solus Decalogus est Aeternus*, 47.

69. *LW* 26:126; WA 40.I:224.

70. *LW* 26:314; WA 40.I:488.

71. "Utilis desperatio" (WA 39.I:445; Luther, *Solus Decalogus est Aeternus*, 177); "salutaris desperatio" (*LW* 33:190; WA 18:719).

72. WA 39.I:456; Luther, *Solus Decalogus est Aeternus*, 191.

73. *LW* 33:140; WA 18:685.

74. "True repentance begins with the fear and with the judgment of God. He sees that he is such a great sinner that he cannot find any means to be delivered from his sin by his own strength, effort, or works" (*LW* 26:131; WA 40.I:231).

for consciences."[75] All this entails a vital qualification of the law's accusatory character. Because of what it does—or rather, does not—disclose about God, the law reveals *sin only as individual transgressions* and as their cumulative effect. It focuses the sinner's attention on its own letter and character and actually distracts the sinner from God's actual character. Consequently, while it is true that "the first step in Christianity is the preaching of repentance and the knowledge of oneself," that is, "that man first acknowledge, through the Law, that he is a sinner, for whom it is impossible to perform any good work"[76]—this first step is *not yet* Christianity, and neither does it intimate what it could be. To be sure, one may, in the midst of despair, even be led to the thought of a mediator between God and humans.[77] But even this pious idea is not Christianity; nor does it grasp conceptually God's own mediatorial work. However convicted by the insufficiency of his or her works, the sinner does not know what will provide healing because the sinner does not know God in the actuality of God's work. The gospel, to put it from its perspective, is not some general message determined by the sinner's need; the gospel is specific. It announces God's actual works.

Sin thus remains beyond "legal restraint . . . [and] our range of choice." Luther explains this further, writing early on against one of his Roman opponents: Commandments have to do with *sins*; "they have to do with our own actions." But sin cannot be addressed in the same way as sins. Even if one were to propose specific imperatives aimed at sin, they would be pointless as an attempt to regulate being's essential orientation. So Luther: "What sort of law would this be: Do not obey ulcers, do not obey fever, do not obey hunger and thirst, do not obey nakedness and bondage; and do not obey the passions of any one of these?" Where sin is concerned, only God's action will do. "Who can slay death . . . except God alone, [acting] without [dependence on] us?" the reformer asks rhetorically.[78]

The Law, Materially

So far we have discussed God's self-disclosure in the law as the latter *functions* theologically. The theological use of the law already presupposes the law as the

75. WA 39.I:370–71; Luther, *Solus Decalogus est Aeternus*, 57.

76. *LW* 26:126; WA 40.I:223.

77. *LW* 26:131; WA 40.I:232.

78. *Against Latomus* (1521), *LW* 32:214; WA 8:97.

more fundamental dynamic of the sinner's historical existence in the world. We have shown this dynamic to be not only a subjective logic of the sinner's nature or an outcome of its externalization but also essentially a vestige of God's paradisiacal law. Whereas Adam expressed and affirmed his self with gratitude, seeing his self as the gift of being *God's* creature in God's own image, fallen humans are now doomed to recognize themselves time and again as nothing more than godless and moribund creatures, doomed to a debilitating dissonance within their very selves. Luther repeatedly emphasizes the primacy of this formal natural law over positive articulations of law.

Positive laws, however, are also necessary. The deep subjective structure, as we have noted, rarely comes to light in *all* its desperate contradiction. To be sure, it takes the Holy Spirit to lead one into the depth of one's being and to undercut one's presumption of integrity as a doer of the law.[79] But the Spirit does not work without means. There must be an encounter with the law in which the law's demand discloses the hearer's desperate condition. In principle, any positive law may function as the Spirit's vehicle to lead one to despair—even godly despair—over oneself. In reality, since positive law is by and large civic law and requires only outward conformity, chances are rather slim. That is why biblical law is important, for it explicitly raises the question of the heart (paradigmatically Isa. 29:13 and Matt. 15:8). "The little word 'law' you must not . . . take in human fashion," Luther warns. "It makes its demands on the inmost heart."[80]

Luther favors and privileges biblical law also because he is very much aware that one can make up laws, even in the name of God, and by means of them oppress both hearts and minds. Monastic vows, as they were used in early modern Europe, are one such handy and oft-mentioned example as far as Luther is concerned.[81] A rule of thumb for determining whether something may function as law is the grammatical mood of the utterance: "the Law de-

79. Or, to echo Kierkegaard, to breathe enough self into the person for despair to be able to set in.

80. *LW* 35:366; WADB 7:3–5.

81. "I reject and condemn also as sheer deceptions and errors of the devil all monastic orders, rules, cloisters, religious foundations, and all such things devised and instituted by men beyond and apart from Scripture, bound by vows and obligations, although many great saints have lived in them, and as the elect of God are misled by them even at this time. Because these monastic orders, foundations, and sects have been maintained and perpetuated with the idea that by these ways and works men may seek and win salvation, and escape from sin and death, they are all a notorious, abominable blasphemy and denial of the unique aid and grace of our only Savior and Mediator, Jesus Christ" (*Confession concerning Christ's Supper* [1528], *LW* 37:363–64; WA 26:503–4).

mands: 'Do this!' The promise grants: 'Accept this!'"[82] In keeping with this basic rule, Luther then addresses the further, long-standing distinction between ceremonial, judicial, and moral laws in the Bible. He is quick to point out that the distinction, though heuristically of some value, is limited in its application. It may not even be as clear-cut as it promises. Even the Ten Commandments commingle ceremonial and judicial law.[83] More importantly, the distinction must not be used to isolate some aspect of the law, such as its spiritual, charity-oriented intention, in order to prop up the gospel with it, or make it conditional upon it. Hence Luther's insistence: "Whatever is not grace is Law, whether it be the Civil Law, the Ceremonial Law, or the Decalog. . . . One should not make a distinction between the Decalog and ceremonial laws."[84] The distinction is "old and common, but it is not an intelligent one."[85] A different approach to the law in its entirety is needed, rather than a partial salvage job. This leads Luther to draw attention, instead, to the actuality of God's dealing with Israel as that law-giving foreshadows Christ. On his reading, the biblical law—the covenant at Sinai in particular—in its entirety constitutes a renewal of the "law in general" for a particular people. Scripturally, as testimony to God's dealing with Israel—and this is the first thing that must be said—it carries no explicit universalizing mandate. And so Luther can make the claim: "even the Ten Commandments do not pertain to us."[86] Rather, all of the Mosaic law, including the Decalogue, anticipates Christ.[87] For he was to fulfill it, not through a further reiteration of the law for yet another era, but through his gospel.[88]

What all this means is that, although the Bible has the advantage that it contains laws given by God, biblical laws cannot be resourced and applied directly or indiscriminately. Luther's encounters, beginning in the early 1520s, with more radical reforming programs that claimed the Scriptures' sanction led him to realize how easily and profoundly the gospel could be compromised also by unreflective biblicism, leading souls to either despair or presumption. This realization resulted in Luther's insistence that proper discernment between biblical laws, with a view to their application, must be based on two

82. *LW* 26:303; WA 40.I:472.

83. *LW* 40:93; WA 18:77.

84. *LW* 26:122; WA 40.I:218.

85. *LW* 40:93; WA 18:76.

86. *How Christians Should Regard Moses*, *LW* 35:165, 166; WA 16:373, 376.

87. *LW* 35:168–73; WA 16:381–90.

88. Hence Luther's frequent warnings not to make Moses out of Christ. See, for example, *LW* 26:132; WA 40.I:232; "Preface to the New Testament," *LW* 35:360; WADB 6:9.

criteria: one has to do, as we have already suggested, with natural law considerations, and the other with the law's fulfillment in Christ.

Recall that the theological use of the law aims at "the old man"—those who live under the all-pervading bare law, and inexorably yet keenly enact this law with their entire being (this includes also Christians, who are still tempted to succumb to the pull of this inner law). It is this "natural" law that the person must confront and do so as a person, with heart and mind. Biblical laws that speak to this law are therefore applicable and may function as a mirror of the sinner's soul. In his exposition of biblical law, Luther therefore repeatedly invokes and emphasizes the critical importance of "the law in general" laid down for the entire human race and inscribed on people's hearts.

This law finds its expression in the Decalogue, though not to the exclusion of "many laws that are useful for this life," presumably the Golden Rule and the maxim *nemo iudex in causa sua*, and possibly also others.[89] All positive biblical law must be seen and evaluated in its light. In the end, Luther does, therefore, affirm the abiding value of the Decalogue as a particular statement of natural law: "the natural laws were never so orderly and well written as by Moses."[90] One need look no further for proof than Luther's use of the Decalogue in his catechisms. In Luther's usage the Decalogue may thus come to stand for that which it expresses: "from the foundation of the whole world the Decalogue was inscribed in the minds of all men."[91] As such, "the Decalogue does not belong to the law of Moses, and he was not the first one to give it, but the Decalogue pertains to the entire world, it is written and etched in the minds of all people from the beginning of the world."[92]

Still, it must be remembered, even this law—as it exposes the law of creaturely self-justification—is fulfilled in Christ. The christological criterion is particularly important to Luther. The law—all law—has, in the end, become void insofar as it is law of and for a nature that no longer has reason to be. The completed work of redemption makes possible this deeper grasp of the law and all its positive articulations. We may characterize Christ's work, in relation to what we have already said about the law, as follows. In Christ's work, the law meets its objective end (Rom. 10:4). There is no more rationale for unmoored, uncontained, bare law. In Christ's work, the law finds its fulfillment as that which it was meant to be in the first place: the creature's self-affirmation as a creature

89. WA 39.I:539; Luther, *Solus Decalogus est Aeternus*, 321.

90. *LW* 40:98; WA 18:81.

91. WA 39.I:454; Luther, *Solus Decalogus est Aeternus*, 187.

92. WA 39.I:478; Luther, *Solus Decalogus est Aeternus*, 217.

already affirmed by God. Christ fulfills the law by allowing God the Father to be the justifier of his human Son, and that justifying act is nothing short of a new creation, the rising to life of a new man. "Christ fulfilled the whole law. For he is the end of the law, not only of the ceremonial laws or the judicial laws, but also of the Decalogue itself."[93] Christ himself is now the "reality [*res*]" of the Decalogue, which now exists eternally no longer as the law's letter (*lex*), but as the creature's—this creature's!—worshipful rest in God's self-donation.[94] We shall speak to what this means for Christian conduct momentarily.

One more qualification needs to be added. The fundamental feature of biblical law, as noted, is that it is concerned with the whole person, with the self. In the end, any aspect of the biblical message that a person may find to pose a *threat* to his or her seeming integrity may function theologically as law. Imperatives will accomplish this the most naturally. But the self-satisfied Pharisee may also be shattered by the message of God's goodness, in which case the message functions theologically as law. "I do not know," Luther comments, "whether any law can strike the mind and press the heart harder than this contemplation of God's goodness."[95] What comes into play here is precisely the problem of ethics, which we discussed earlier. One may feel perversely, demonically condemned by divine goodness in that one now finds oneself unworthy of such great condescension. It is plausible that in the face of overwhelming forgiveness one may not be able to forgive oneself, to let go of the self, to abandon being a judge in one's case, especially in this case! One may be crushed by the judgment that God's generosity implicitly passes on one, the light that it puts one in and the self-revelation that it brings, and yet one may still not allow God to be the final judge in the matter, despite the verdict of acquittal. All this is the work of the law; all this is despair.

For Luther the law, insofar as it functions theologically, must in the end also be defined theologically. "'Law' ought not to be taken in a technical or material or grammatical sense . . . but *as it is and sounds forth in your heart, urging and battling your heart and conscience*, so that you do not know where to turn" and "the entire world becomes too small . . . and there is no help left but Christ."[96] Theologically speaking, "law" belongs to the new vocabulary where meanings of ordinary terms are defined by and in light of the work of God.

93. WA 39.I:453; Luther, *Solus Decalogus est Aeternus*, 187.

94. WA 39.I:413. To the christological eternity of the Decalogue, in the context of Luther's antinomian disputations, see Nicholas Hopman, "Luther's *Antinomian Disputations* and *Lex Aeterna*," *Lutheran Quarterly* 30, no. 2 (Summer 2016): esp. 164–67.

95. WA 39.I:536; Luther, *Solus Decalogus est Aeternus*, 317.

96. WA 39.I:455; Luther, *Solus Decalogus est Aeternus*, 189–91.

The Christian and the Law

The work of God, in the end, determines what it means to fulfill the law—in very much the same way that it did in Paradise. Human attempts to keep the law must run aground. Theologically, the law demands personal integrity from the doer. One who has already violated a single command, who is already at odds within his or her self, does not have the requisite integrity (James 2:10). The law cannot be fulfilled by keeping it as such. To insist, despite this, that one can use the law to achieve personal integrity is to want to create oneself, from nothing, as it were, in the face of one's past. It is not only to be deceived, but it is to offend against God, whose law it is that permeates human existence. One's creatureliness will not be wished away. At any rate, the very idea of keeping the law for the sake of personal integrity violates the law, for it suggests exactly what the law seeks to prevent: using the law for one's own sake and thus being a judge in one's own case. The upshot of all this is that there is a distinction between doing the works of the law and fulfilling the law; those actually are "two very different things."[97] (This distinction also belongs to the new vocabulary of the Spirit.) The law itself suggests it, for it says that one shall love God and one's neighbor (Matt. 22:37–40). To love is to stake one's whole being on another and to risk it for the sake of another.

The law can only be fulfilled by *faith*. Faith alone is that which grants integrity and bestows new being, outside of the works of the law. Faith alone justifies.[98] Faith does this because it grasps God's work in Christ and takes God at his word, recognizing in Christ's work an expression of God's abiding good will. "Faith is nothing else but . . . the right knowledge of the heart about God."[99] As such, it allows one to receive one's entire self anew from this work and self-attestation of God. To be justified is to be whole, a truly human creature, Luther insists.[100] The reformer articulates the meaning of faith in terms of both union with Christ and an exchange of being. To be a human creature is to be a bearer of God's image, without a trace of an internal contradiction. "The chief article and foundation of the gospel is that . . . you accept and recognize [Christ] as a gift, as a present that God has given you and that is your own. This means that when you see or hear of Christ doing or suffering something, you do not doubt that Christ himself, with his deeds

97. *LW* 35:367; WADB 7:7.

98. "Faith alone makes a person righteous and fulfills the law" (*LW* 35:368; WADB 7:7).

99. *LW* 26:238; WA 40.I:376.

100. *LW* 34:133ff.; WA 39.I:175 (thesis 32).

and suffering, belongs to you. On this you may depend as surely as if you had done it yourself; indeed as if you were Christ himself."[101] Luther compares faith to a marital union, in which the spouses exchange their property and, indeed, their very being in that they will now be known as the husband or wife of the other.[102] "[Christ] gave to all who believe, as their possession, everything that he had. This included: his life, in which he swallowed up death; his righteousness, by which he blotted out sin; and his salvation, with which he overcame everlasting damnation."[103]

In faith, one finds oneself—and finds one's self—beyond the law. One already has the integrity that the law both required and seemingly promised. One is thus free from the bare law that drove and defined one's very being, which forced one to acknowledge and enact one's creatureliness and to seek to justify oneself by means of it. The law, in its deceptive promise and reproach, is now empty or quiescent (*lex vacua seu quiescens*).[104] Luther can therefore conclude that faith is "something omnipotent" in that it shares in the majesty of God.[105] "[A] Christian, properly defined, is free of all laws and is subject to nothing, internally or externally. . . . For the Christian . . . the entire law has been abrogated—whether it be the Ceremonial Law or the Decalog—because he has died to it." The one for whom the world was formerly too small to offer any help "is now greater than the entire world. . . . [Christians] are lords over all the laws of the entire world."[106]

Yet the Christian remains involved with the law (the word "involved" is apropos here), as faith now issues in love, or rather love finds its possibility and fulfillment in faith. To take God at his word is to be *able* to love him—and to *love* him—for who he is. Christians believe and trust God and, in the intimate knowledge that faith brings, love God. As those who trust God enough not to be judges in their own case, Christians are able to commit their dealings in the world to God. They are able, specifically, to love the neighbor and to take responsibility for the neighbor, without the debilitating need to live up to some benchmark. It is in their love for God and so also the neighbor that Christians

101. *A Brief Instruction on What to Look for and Expect in the Gospels* (1521), *LW* 35:119; WA 10.I:11.

102. "By the wedding ring of faith he shares in the sins, death, and pains of hell which are his bride's. As a matter of fact, he makes them his own and acts as if they were his own and as if he himself had sinned; he suffered, died, and descended into hell that he might overcome them all" (*LW* 31:352; WA 7:25, 55).

103. *LW* 35:359; WADB 6:4.

104. WA 39.I:433; Luther, *Solus Decalogus est Aeternus*, 161.

105. *LW* 26:227; WA 40.I:360. Cf. *The Freedom of a Christian* (1520), *LW* 31:355; WA 7:57.

106. *LW* 26:134, 156–57; WA 40.I:236.

exhibit the freedom from the self—and so from sin, death, the devil, and the sheer law—that faith grants.

Luther comments on the Christian's existence: "I do indeed live in the flesh, but I do not live on the basis of my own self"; rather, "this life . . . is the life of Christ, the Son of God, whom the Christian possesses by faith."[107] My life becomes "a mask of life [*larva vitae*]" hiding Christ, who lives in me.[108] Because the gospel is for the Christian God's final word, the sheer miracle of a new life, Christian existence embodies not the question, "How can I now be myself?" or, even worse, "How must I now be myself?"—as if the gospel were cheap, easy, deficient, and one's by right. Instead of the question, "How can and must I now be myself?" the question that the Christian life embodies is rather "For whose sake—for the sake of what *persons!*—am I this new person-in-Christ?" That this is, indeed, the question that defines the Christian's active life is a corollary of the safe haven (heaven!) from the law's accusation that the gospel provides, a consequence of being rescued from preoccupation with the self.

Concern with the neighbor is actually embodied in the Christian's personal being, in the very act of his or her person. The Christian life, like the eternal Son's life, is a life of descent into the neighbor. Though the Son was (is) in the "form of God" and enjoyed the fullness of God (Luther interprets this in terms of the Son's intimate relation to the Father rather than Christ's two natures), he became a man and took the form of a servant—to serve *us* as opposed to some abstract act of self-abnegation—precisely because he knew the Father.[109] Likewise, the Christian life is one of putting on the neighbor with his or her anxieties, enslavements, and sins. It is a life of first justifying the neighbor as a person before applying the law to judge the neighbor's works. In this, Christians "do of their own accord much more than all the laws and teachings can demand."[110] They love. In other words, even though the will of those who are in Christ is, to use Philip Melanchthon's apt phrase, "the Spirit, the living law," the Christian life is hardly a life without form, or laws—hardly a life of self-serving freedom.[111] It is rather a Christlike life of more than equitable service to the neighbor, of being a righteous judge in the neighbor's case because one does not have to be one in one's own. Christians serve the political

107. *LW* 26:171–72; WA 40.I:289–90.

108. *LW* 26:170; WA 40.I:288.

109. *LW* 31:366; WA 7:65.

110. *LW* 45:88; WA 11:250.

111. Philip Melanchthon, *Loci Communes Theologici* (1521), in *Melanchthon and Bucer*, ed. Wilhelm Pauck (Louisville: Westminster John Knox, 2006), 124.

community in the awareness that even the best of laws do not sustain justice. Christians' Christ-formed freedom from the law is, therefore, also freedom to engage in *moral reasoning*, the freedom to become responsible.

Here it is important to qualify what we have said about the love of God. The Christian life is, above all, a life of loving God. But it is love of a particular sort. One does not so much love God for God's sake. One rather loves oneself for God's sake. In doing so, one affirms not that one has any love of one's own to give to God. What one affirms, instead, is oneself as the workmanship of a righteous God. This makes the love of God indirect. It is in living the life to which one has been freed—a life of loving the neighbor—that one loves God. To love God is to be in God's own image. In this way, one truly glorifies God as the giver of all good gifts.[112] Service to the neighbor as an outworking of this faith is the Christian's worship.[113]

And yet the Christian is not only entirely righteous, even though the Christian's "conscience and soul" already are on the other side of "death and the grave and in heaven with Christ."[114] The Christian remains also entirely a sinner (*simul iustus et peccator*).[115] Throughout his disputations against the antinomians, Luther insists that the law in its second use must continue to be applied to Christians. The Christian is alive, as a being in Christ, but the Christian is also dead as a being of the world caught up in the iron law of self-justification, of making something of oneself. The Christian's conscience is "lord and king," because as a Christian "I do not live on the basis of my own self." As an embodied historical being, however, "I do indeed live in the flesh."[116] The Christian finds oneself in two loves: the love of self for God's sake, and the quiescent love of God for one's own sake. A Christian inhabits the sacramental economy of divine love, which shapes the Christian, and one remains in the order of the world where self-justification, at whatever cost, is the only way to be. For this reason the Christian requires the law's accusation to realize that

112. "God has none of His majesty or divinity where faith is absent. Nor does God require anything greater of man than that he attribute to Him His glory and His divinity; that is, that he regard Him, not as an idol but as God, who has regard for him, listens to him, shows mercy to him, helps him, etc." (*LW* 26:227; WA 40.I:360).

113. "A Christian lives not in himself, but in Christ and in his neighbor. Otherwise he is not a Christian. He lives in Christ through faith, in his neighbor through love. By faith he is caught up beyond himself into God. By love he descends beneath himself into his neighbor. Yet he always remains in God and in His love" (*LW* 31:371; WA 7:69).

114. *Commentary on 1 Corinthians 15* (1534), *LW* 28:110; WA 36:548.

115. *LW* 26:232; WA 40.I:368.

116. *LW* 26:158, 170–71; WA 40.I:271, 288.

what one still needs is not divine aid on the path to personal integrity but an altogether new being. The law accuses, insofar as one's very being tempts one to use grace to do what one does naturally, loving God for one's own sake instead of loving oneself for the sake of God.

Only beyond death will one be free from the law altogether. So, it seems, would have been Adam had he not sinned.[117]

In summary, Luther's theological anthropology posits three modes of human being in relation to the law. For Adam, the law furnished a mode of worshiping God by affirming his own self as a God-given self. Adam was in what Luther terms "a middle position/condition."[118] Christians, who are in union with Christ, affirm their selves in freedom from the law by doing spontaneously and doing more than what the command would have prescribed. In doing so, they attend to the person before they consider the person's works according to the law. In their very being, they thus do what Christ has done for them before the Father. They stand before God the justifier and, in being free for the neighbor, declare God righteous as the only one who indeed can justify one's whole being into Christlike love.[119] The Edenic ontology of their being is not only renewed but becomes cemented, as it were, as it is subtended upon Christ's own act of being. As they become translated into God's direct presence, believers will be free from the self-justifying flesh and the temptation to justify themselves through their love. They will only love themselves for God's sake. And the triune God will be all in all (1 Cor. 15:28).

Looking Back and Looking Forward: Theological Anthropology and the Law's Third Use

In articulating his theology of the law, Luther departs from the predominant medieval understanding of the law, held by theologians from Augustine, through Thomas, all the way to Erasmus. The law, according to this construal, constitutes God's fundamental relation to human beings. For Thomas, there comes, first, the eternal law, which orders all things in accordance with divine reason. It, in turn, establishes creaturely natures in their natural acts. The natural law of human being, for example, is to act in accordance with reason. Further comes the divine

117. *LW* 1:110–11; WA 42:84.

118. *LW* 1:110; WA 42:84–85.

119. "Faith . . . consummates the Deity. . . . It is the creator of the Deity, not in the substance of God but in us" (*LW* 26:227, cf. 233; WA 40.I:360, cf. 369).

law. It directs humans in the performance of their natural acts beyond those acts' natural goals and toward eternal blessedness, which lies beyond the grasp of human nature as such.[120] Fallen humanity now finds itself in the grip of disordered affections. Those have weakened the governance of reason and allowed sensuality to run rampant. Humans now fall short of the full potential of their nature, let alone the divine law.[121] This can be remedied only by healing inward grace, which forms the centerpiece of Christ's new law of charity and which is given only to those who believe in him.[122] Grace enables one to perform true works of charity, whose essential feature is not the observance of ceremonies, or even outward conformity, but a morally ordered, upright, and God-loving heart. This is what the new law requires: not literal adherence but a spiritual fulfillment through love. In short, to use Erasmus's phrase, the law of faith actually demands "more arduous things";[123] yet it comes with the grace to fulfill it. Grace, on this understanding, is essentially connected to the law, in that the gospel both enables and calls upon one to fulfill the spirit of the law, to keep the nonceremonial law in a loving fashion now that one can.[124] And to do so with a view to meriting eternal blessedness. The law is thus the primary determinant of human being, while the gospel provides a solution to the problem the law engenders. The person confirms one's being a Christian in exhibiting the spirit of the law.

Luther, it seems, stands in the tradition of Bernard of Clairvaux,[125] for whom divine love and grace are the primary determinants of human being. Bernard affirms the eternal law, but he identifies it not so much with divine reason, and its determination of a hierarchy of natures in the cosmos, as with God's triune being. Bernard's ontology has thus a fundamentally relational thrust. The law, he writes, by which even God himself lives, "is nothing else but love. For what preserves the supreme and ineffable unity in the blessed Trinity

120. *ST* I-II, q. 91.

121. *ST* I-II, q. 109, a. 2.

122. *ST* I-II, q. 107, a. 1.

123. Erasmus, *On the Freedom of the Will*, in *Luther and Erasmus: Free Will and Salvation*, ed. E. Gordon Rupp and Philip S. Watson, Library of Christian Classics (Philadelphia: Westminster, 1969), 49–50.

124. *ST* I-II, q. 108, a. 2. Cf. Augustine: "The law, then, was given in order that we would seek after grace; grace was given so that we might fulfill the law. . . . Through faith we obtain grace to struggle against sin; through grace the soul is healed from the wound of sin; through the good health of the soul we have freedom of choice; through free choice we have the love of righteousness; through the love of righteousness we fulfill the law. The law is not done away with, but strengthened by faith, because faith obtains the grace by which we fulfill the law" (*The Spirit and the Letter* 19.34 and 27.47, in *The Works of Saint Augustine* I/23, ed. J. E. Rotelle [Hyde Park, NY: New City, 1997], 171, 185).

125. The following draws on Bernard's *On Loving God* 12.34–14.38, in *Selected Works*, 200–203.

but love? . . . It is that divine substance which is in no way other than itself. . . . This is the eternal law, creating and governing the universe." Because God is love, God communicates and imparts his character as a gift. "Where [love] signifies the giver, it is the name of substance. Where it signifies the gift, it is a quality." To be human is to exist as God does, by first of all honoring God the way a son honors his father.

For Bernard, those who do not recognize divine love but only divine power, or recognize divine goodness without, we might say, acknowledging his good will, suffer in their very being. Their being as such suffers damage. They become turned in on themselves in the manner of a slave or a mercenary. A slave lives a life of fear on his own account. A mercenary uses even God for his own profit. "One does not love God, the other loves something more than God. They have a law which is not of the Lord." Sinners believe they are like God when they abandon God's order and give themselves a new law, "wickedly wishing to imitate [their] creator." Yet it is precisely in this that they become not only unlike God but also an unbearable burden to themselves. Even though the law of their being is set in opposition to the law of God, they are nevertheless caught up in "the changeless order of the eternal law," in that their lawlessness and unbelief retain the character of law. Both the slave and the mercenary are painfully ruled by themselves and delivered over to their selves.

Bernard's placement of emphases in his conception of the eternal law anticipates Luther's relational anthropology. It anticipates the reformer's insistence that the law's fulfillment lies not in works of love but in faith, in the ability, first and foremost, to receive one's entire being anew from God. Bernard's identification of the highest degree of love with loving oneself for the sake of God, as opposed to loving God for one's own sake, or even loving God for God's sake, may serve as a lens that distinguishes the two medieval anthropologies. It also helps us understand the way Luther stands over against the dominant medieval conception of the human being. A person who loves God for God's sake is still one who stands over against God as a person whose existence is characterized first of all by an obligation, even if this obligation can be fulfilled only by divine grace. A person who loves himself or herself for God's sake is a being characterized fundamentally by relation because what such a person is, is entirely a gift. The person acknowledges that he or she has no love to give and would have no love to give were it not for God's gift of the very lover! He or she can only love out of divine donation.

If we now look forward to Luther's successors, we observe a loss of the relational foundation of human being. For Luther, the person is constituted in and by an act of being. Faith is the reception of one's entire self from God, where the recipient comes into being in the act of reception.[126] The believer's trust in God, therefore, does not really orient some previously neutral capacity toward God but, in the first place, grants his or her entire self. To believe is to trust God with one's very self, to receive oneself from his goodness. One is what one is in God's giving. Unbelief, by contrast, is a refusal to receive oneself from God. The unbeliever exists entirely in the contradictory logic of self-justification, according to which one attempts to receive oneself from oneself over against what one already is. To lack faith is to be viciously turned in on oneself. On this side of the grave, believers exist in both of these acts. They therefore require that the law be applied to them theologically, to reveal the quiescent but present dynamic of self-justification into which the sinner will not hesitate to draw even God himself.

The Formula of Concord loses sight of this dynamic character of the Christian's existence as *simul iustus et peccator*, each totally. It does so, first of all, in its understanding of sin.[127] It interprets human being not in terms of existential acts but in terms of natural endowments. On this interpretation, it cannot but view sin as an inexplicable corruption, a debilitating flaw inherent in the material out of which God created the human and which has now "contaminated and corrupted all of human nature like a spiritual poison and leprosy . . . so that in our corrupted nature no one can show or prove what is unmistakably human nature and what is original sin."[128] The Formula thus juxtaposes not belief with unbelief, faith with sin, but rather creaturely makeup with sin, seeing the first as essential and the second as mysteriously privative.

Further, this substance-centered anthropology is also evident in the Formula's understanding of justification as a forensic verdict.[129] Recall that Luther views the believer as *simul* to insist on a genuinely *Christ-formed self* in the face of the very real possibility that one can be a *self over against God*, or even without God. In other words, what Luther's adage expresses is the asymmetrical reality of union with Christ and, more broadly, *essential* though *extrinsic* rest in divine self-donation. This union is always threatened, on our part as historical beings, with dissolution into an ontology of self-contained essences, monads striving to be simultaneously makers and material. Now, when this relational

126. "Faith . . . is a divine work in us which changes us and makes us to be born anew of God. . . . It kills the old Adam and makes us altogether different men, in heart and spirit and mind and powers; and it brings with it the Holy Spirit" (*LW* 35:370; WADB 7:11).

127. I discuss this in considerably more detail in "Sin, between Law and Gospel," *Lutheran Quarterly* 28, no. 2 (Summer 2014): esp. 159–72.

128. FC 1.33, in *BC*, 537.

129. FC 3.17, in *BC*, 564.

framework within which to construe being human is replaced by a seemingly neutral ontology of self-contained substances, defined by their natural endowments, it is grace that falls victim. The only choice one is left with is either to view grace as an infused quality (but that would undermine the Lutheran insistence on the finality of God's justifying act and the assurance to be derived from the fact), or to see grace purely in terms of external divine favor but no longer as effecting the rise of an entirely new subject, performing an entirely new act of being in a vital relation to God and the neighbor.

Thrusting Luther's *simul* into a substance-based view of the person in the end either leaves the believer to his or her own devices, demanding that he or she perform the existential feat of living from from remote grace that is solely in the eyes of God, and do so in the face of what is really only a depraved and recalcitrant nature; or it makes the believer, as nothing but a *peccator* in himself or herself, complacent, for all the believer's works, despite appearances and the believer's own self-perception, must be dismissed as still and necessarily falling short of the divine law. It is hard to understand why, within this kind of personal ontology, one would not rather embrace the more compellingly realist Augustinian, that is, transformational, view that the believer is partially a saint and partially a sinner, a *viator* doing his or her best to keep sinful affections in check and to put to work the grace received, thus awaiting in hopeful expectation God's justifying verdict.

The third use of the law, affirmed by the Formula of Concord, is in fact such an accommodation, though stripped of the notion of a second, final justification.[130] The use finds its rationale in the substance-based theological anthropology adopted by the confession and is only reinforced by the intersection of its theology of sin and justification.[131] The use is applicable to believers alone, and it incorporates some aspects of the theological use of the law. The goal of the third use is, principally, "to instruct [the believer] to live and walk in the law" (§1), and to do so, in part, by admonishing, warning, and threatening (§9). This work is necessary because believers are still dragged down by the "old Adam," who remains part of their nature (§§7, 18,

130. To the duality of justification in medieval theology, see Heiko A. Oberman, "'*Iustitia Christi*' and '*Iustitia Dei*': Luther and the Scholastic Doctrines of Justification," in *The Dawn of the Reformation* (Edinburgh: T. & T. Clark, 1992), 104–25. The concept of the *tertius usus legis* harks back to Philip Melanchthon, and arises initially out of the question of whether the law, as such, should be preached to believers. See, for example, Melanchthon's *The Chief Theological Topics* (1559), trans. J. A. O. Preus, 2nd ed. (Saint Louis: Concordia, 2011), 123–24.

131. The following will quote article 6 of the FC SD, in *BC*, 587–91. References will be given parenthetically in the text.

19, 24). To be sure, believers now possess the Holy Spirit. But there is no sense in which the believer is somehow also Christ-formed in the believer's very being. There is thus always a danger that believers will "fall back on their own holiness and piety and under the appearance of God's Spirit establish their own service to God on the basis of their own choice, without God's Word or command" (§20). Hence believers require that what constitutes proper works be disclosed to them by the law. The law, however, "does not give the power and ability to begin or to carry out the command" (§11). This is the Holy Spirit's role. The Spirit both admonishes and empowers. Now, whether one can call that work "killing and making alive," as the Formula wishes to see it, is debatable. One would much rather want to see this claim made in regard to the theological use of the law and the gospel. (Recall that even the Edenic commandment was not exhortation.) What all this amounts to is the Formula's reinterpretation of Luther's dynamic and dialectical conception of the *simul*, now seen in terms of elements overlapping *partim-partim* within the same substance. Instead of two acts of being—one extrinsic and one self-referential—we have sin viewed as a mysterious force in the lower parts of the human nature, and justification understood as bearing no ontological but only judicial consequences. Instruction in the law and empowerment by the Spirit must now help one move forward.

> If the faithful and elect children of God were perfectly renewed through the indwelling Spirit in this life, so that in their nature and all their powers they were completely free from sin, they would need no law and therefore no prodding. Instead, they would do in and of themselves, completely voluntarily, without any teaching, admonition, exhortation, or prodding of the law, what they are obligated to do according to God's will, just as in and of themselves the sun, the moon, and all the stars follow unimpeded the regular course God gave them once and for all, apart from any admonition, exhortation, impulse, coercion, or compulsion. (§6)

Where Luther believes that the law's accusation and the proclamation of the gospel and its sacramental economy suffice, the Formula resorts to another use of the law to repair human nature. In all, one gets a sense that there is a tremendous missed opportunity here in terms of articulating human agency as participation in the life of the triune God, who grants (the Father), shapes (the Son), and animates (the Spirit) human being and agency. One finds important and more pronounced contours of that in the theology of Luther—but not in that of his followers.

The Law Is for the Gospel

Much more could be said about the law in Luther's theology and that of his predecessors and successors. Its hallmark, formally speaking, is the distinction between the law and the gospel. It aims, as we have shown, at maintaining a strict focus on God's self-revelation in Jesus Christ as the giver of *all* that is good, including the gift of one's very self. The law has a rationale only as part of this goal. It has no independent role to play, and it attests to this itself. Whether we see it as a vehicle of Edenic worship, or consider its incapacity to render true justice in its first use, or recoil from its accusation, the law points beyond itself to the genuinely interpersonal. But the interpersonal is ultimately nothing short of participation in the life of the triune God—of being his very image—till we behold him face-to-face. Here the law finds its end for good.

Chapter 2

The Law in the Reformed Tradition

MICHAEL ALLEN

Reformed churches care to proceed decently and in order. While everything from systematic theology to Robert's Rules of Order may be invoked with such a statement, the claim does accurately mark a characteristic of the tradition. It should not be surprising then that Reformed churches have had much to say about the law. Confessions, commentaries, theological treatises, dogmatic systems, and even homilies have insistently and in great detail addressed the place of the law in life with God. But such is not distinctive, for we know that Lutheran churches have done the same. As we seek to consider commonalities and differences regarding law in Lutheran and Reformed thought, we will need to tend to connections between this topic and related matters, most especially the doctrine of the covenants.

In this essay we will proceed not by pointing to the dogmatic elaboration or moral theology of any single Reformed theologian. They are numerous, of course, and well worth one's attention. Yet the Reformed tradition has always been an ecclesiastical tradition with a high view of the creedal, confessional, and catechetical role played by those vested with ministerial offices in the body of Christ. While the Reformed tradition differs from the Lutheran tradition in that it has not consolidated around a single confession or set of confessional resources (as found in the *Book of Concord*), it shares the confessional rhythm in common with Lutheranism.[1] In seeking to elaborate upon the law in the

1. One can gain an instructive, though somewhat homogenizing, account of Reformed teaching on the law in Jan Rohls, *Reformed Confessions: Theology from Zurich to Barmen*, trans. John Hoffmeyer, Columbia Series in Reformed Theology (Louisville: Westminster John Knox, 1998), 193–205. Interestingly, there is rather little discussion of the law beyond its immediate context in the covenant of works in the handbook of Heinrich Heppe, *Reformed Dogmatics*, ed. Ernst Bizer, trans. G. T. Thomson (San Francisco: HarperCollins, 1950; reprint, London: Wakeman, n.d.), 399–403, 567, and

Reformed tradition, then, we will tend to two texts that have marked its development. First, we will attend to the discussion of the law in the Leiden Synopsis (the *Synopsis Purioris Theologiae*), wherein the various meanings of the word "law" are framed, so that we can see how discussion of the law in the divine economy or covenant relates to wider discussions of law in Christian theology (for example, eternal law). Second, we will consider the chapter on the law of God in the Westminster Confession of Faith, noting parallels in the Larger and Shorter Catechisms as well. In so doing we will intentionally deal with texts that played a role in communal theologizing, albeit differently in the university setting and in the ecclesiastical realm of confession. We will also engage with texts from both the European continent and the British Isles. Finally, we will seek to reflect on commonalities and trends that mark the wider Reformed tradition.

Terminological Help from the Leiden Synopsis

The *Synopsis Purioris Theologiae* was composed by four professors of theology at the University of Leiden—Johannes Polyander, Andreas Rivetus, Antonius Walaeus, and Anthonius Thysius—and published in 1625; owing to the institutional location of its authors, it has been referred to more commonly as the Leiden Synopsis. Disputation 18 concerns the law of God. In its opening pages it orients the reader to some matters fundamental to locating the doctrine of the law within Reformed thought.

The synopsis identified six uses of the term "law" in Sacred Writ. "In Holy Scripture 'law' is used with different meanings, and firstly for anything that has been instituted by God (Psalm 1:2 and 19:8)," specifically both the Old and New Testaments. Second, "the word is used with particular meaning for moral law (as in Luke 10:26), ceremonial law (as in Luke 2:22), or forensic law (as in John 19:7)." Third, "it is used for the books of Moses that contain the teaching of the law, as in Luke 24:44." Fourth, it may refer to "all the books of the Old Testament, as in John 10:34." Fifth, "as a metonym of the adjunct," it may refer to facets of the law such as the Levitical priesthood (e.g., Heb. 7:12) or the curse of the law (e.g., Rom. 6:14). Sixth, it can be "used figuratively for the natural directive of human reason (Romans 2:14)."[2]

569–70. Precisely because the material is parceled out into piecemeal discussions of the law vis-à-vis the covenant of grace and sanctification, there is no summative statement regarding the law beyond its role in the covenant of works.

2. *SPT*, 433–35 (from Disputation 18: On the Law of God).

These six uses, which not only vary but at times overlap, are then located amidst a deeper theological backdrop. "From these usages, it appears that 'law' in the sacred writings is not used for the eternal law, or for the essential conceptual content that exists in the divine understanding as in an archetype, but for a legal rule that is drawn down by God . . . for the human race within time, and communicated and declared to it in various ways."[3] While other verbiage communicates the notion of eternal law (e.g., tracing righteous standards to a righteous law and, ultimately, to the very righteousness of God in Ps. 11:7), and though *summae* would typically begin with eternal law, the synopsis turns directly to laws given for and communicated to creatures.[4] The synopsis has also touched on the "approving will" (*voluntas Approbans*) in its sixth disputation on the nature of God and his divine attributes. Here the authors attested that God wills and approves of things "as they accord with his nature and the structure of his mind, and whereby he necessarily disapproves of the things that are opposite to them."[5] And his will is not coerced or manipulated by anyone else, but is free and, because free, is truly expressive of his being and character: "what He wills He wills from Himself and on account of Himself."[6]

Discussion of the divine will (as was common in some medievals such as Hugh and dominant in the later Reformed tradition) or the eternal law (to use the terminology of Thomas) is similarly intended to attest to the fact that human laws (laws given to legislate human interactions, whether by God supernaturally or by other humans naturally) are rooted ultimately in God's own eternal character. Of course, laws from God bear his character perfectly, whereas other laws are faint echoes of his being yet marred by sin. But the very shape of law giving flows from the identity of the one who is himself the rule or standard. Honoring the freedom of God's election, creation, legislating, covenanting, and redeeming creatures, alongside the concern to also note that God's works (*ad extra*) express God's own being (*ad intra*), continued to shape

3. *SPT*, 435.

4. For eternal law, see, for example, Thomas Aquinas, *ST*, I-II, q. 91, a. 1 and q. 93, a. 1–6. Others address many of the same notions under the rubric of the divine will (without using the language of eternal law): see, for example, Hugh of St. Victor, *On the Sacraments of the Christian Faith*, trans. Roy Deferrari (Eugene, OR: Wipf and Stock, 2007), compare part 4 (on the will of God) with parts 11–12 (on the natural and written law, no mention of eternal law); and Francis Turretin, *Institutes of Elenctic Theology*, ed. James T. Dennison Jr., trans. George Musgrave Giger (Phillipsburg, NJ: Presbyterian and Reformed, 1994), with the justice of the divine will occurring in the third topic, question 18 (1:232–33), and law (minus discussion of eternal law) in the eleventh topic (2:1–168).

5. *SPT*, 173.

6. *SPT*, 175.

these writings.[7] Far more could and should be said on these relations of what is internal and external to God, and yet that is neither where the tradition nor our key texts have focused.

As we investigate the Westminster Standards, then, it is worth noting that the discussion of law occurs within the context of the divine economy of God's grace and communication for, to, and with his human creatures. Thus, we see shades of these varied semantic fields outlined by the Leiden Synopsis appear throughout, and, like the Synopsis, their roots in eternal law are assumed at this point (having been attested already in WCF 2.2, where God is "most holy in all his . . . commands"). God's law does not come arbitrarily but bears his own character. Just as election mysteriously flows from his persona, so his law carries with it *his* constitution.

The Westminster Standards

In the 1640s Parliament convened an assembly to revise and then to replace the Articles of Religion in the Church of England. Now known as the Westminster Assembly, this august gathering of divines produced a number of resources, none of which was officially adopted by the Church of England, yet each of which has had remarkable influence in the wider Christian world (first in Scotland, later on multiple continents). The assembly produced a directory for public worship, a confession of faith, and a larger and shorter catechism. In seeking to address the law in the Westminster tradition, we do well to begin with the nineteenth chapter of the Westminster Confession of Faith: "On the Law of God." Exposition of that passage may then be supplemented by comment upon relevant portions of the catechisms.[8]

> 1. *God gave to Adam a law, as a covenant of works, by which he bound him and all his posterity to personal, entire, exact, and perpetual obedience, promised*

7. In making sense of realities *ad intra* and *ad extra*, those seeking to appreciate the commonalities as well as tensions within the Reformed tradition will be significantly aided by Willem J. van Asselt, "The Fundamental Meaning of Theology: Archetypal and Ectypal Theology in Seventeenth-Century Reformed Thought," *Westminster Theological Journal* 64 (2002): 319–35.

8. Interpreting this chapter of the confession, unlike some others, is not notably shaped by a reading of the minutes and papers of the assembly. One can find the relevant discussions in *The Minutes and Papers of the Westminster Assembly, 1643–1652*, ed. Chad Van Dixhoorn (Oxford: Oxford University Press, 2012), 3:735, 737–38, and 4:252–60, 426–39. Interestingly, while there was discussion as to whether or not to include an affirmation of law and nature, there was no discussion regarding the idea of eternal law.

> *life upon the fulfilling, and threatened death upon the breach of it, and endued him with power and ability to keep it.*

The law is gift. The first thing that must be said about the law is that it is of God; the second thing that must immediately follow is that this divine law is a gift unto humans. Law is not constituted by humans, nor is law laden oppressively upon them. Rather, God lavishes his favor upon his children by instructing them in his ways. We can catch the nature of this gift more fully if we also take in the limits upon law defined in the following chapter 20 on Christian liberty, wherein we learn of the sufficiency of divine instruction and, thus, of the fact that others cannot bind the conscience regarding religious duties for faith or practice beyond what has been so bound by God's own Word (20.1).

The primal law came "as a covenant of works."[9] Here the confession hearkens back to chapter 7, wherein "God's covenant with man" is described in twofold fashion (hence the language of bicovenantalism is used to describe the covenant theology found in Westminster and elsewhere). The covenant of works bound Adam and his descendants "to personal, entire, exact, and perpetual obedience."[10] In this occasion law was the canon or rule for remaining in possession of life and the presence of God. Note, of course, that Genesis 2:17 threatens death upon disobedience ("in that day that you eat of it, dying you shall die," with the infinitive absolute), though the actual shift that is tangibly observed upon this transgression is dismissal from God's presence (Gen. 3:23–24, where, interestingly, there is a repetition to match the infinitive absolute of Gen. 2:17).

Law in this covenant leads to life or death. This merism marks all possibilities; there is no neutral position before God. All—"both Adam and his posterity"—walk in the way by which the die has been cast. Reformed theologians have debated what precisely was involved in the offer of life—whether

9. A number of Reformed theologians refrain from terming this administration between God and Adam a "covenant"; this question is engaged at greater length in the excursus at the end of this chapter.

10. The precise demands, which must be exposited beyond the overt words of either Gen. 1:28–30 or 2:17, are elaborated at greater length in WLC 20: "What was the providence of God toward man in the estate in which he was created? A. The providence of God toward man in the estate in which he was created, was the placing him in paradise, appointing him to dress it, giving him liberty to eat of the fruit of the earth; putting the creatures under his dominion, and ordaining marriage for his help; affording him communion with himself; instituting the Sabbath; entering into a covenant of life with him, upon condition of personal, perfect, and perpetual obedience, of which the tree of life was a pledge; and forbidding to eat of the tree of the knowledge of good and evil, upon the pain of death."

heavenly or earthly.[11] That death involves both spiritual and physical ills has proven sadly obvious.

> 2. *This law, after his fall, continued to be a perfect rule of righteousness; and, as such, was delivered by God upon Mount Sinai, in ten commandments, and written in two tables: the first four commandments containing our duty towards God; and the other six, our duty to man.*

Law must be thought *post lapsum* ("after his fall"), for law "continued to be a perfect rule of righteousness." Notice that the language here describes its nature and position in this moment of the economy. Whereas section 1 marked law as gift, this second section depicts law as possessing a stable substance (continuing to be). It is a "perfect rule of righteousness" wherein the language of perfection speaks to fullness or wholeness. We see this wholeness in that the confession quickly speaks of commandments "written in two tables . . . containing our duty towards God; and . . . our duty to man."[12] The law instructs every facet of our existence, both in our upward glance by which we behold God and in our sideways facing of our neighbor or our enemy.

The confession speaks of continuity; the law continued to rule in this way. The confession also speaks of interjection, however, with words that point to the Exodus account and Sinai in particular. The law "was delivered by God upon Mount Sinai." Interesting, of course, that a law that had been given so long ago must again be delivered. The language of rule here serves to differentiate the law's function in this covenant of grace from its role in the covenant of works. This distinction has been a hallmark of Reformed ethical thought, displayed powerfully in a contemporaneous text of ongoing significance, Edward Fisher's *Marrow of Modern Divinity*.[13] It has been matched by the distinction between "legal obedience" and "evangelical obedience"; John Owen offered the most astute reflections on how the justification received wholly in Christ—for his work imputed to us—reorients our call to and gift of lived holiness such that it is no longer legal holiness, in the sense of fulfilling

11. See Mark Herzer, "Adam's Reward: Heaven or Earth?" in *Drawn into Controversie: Reformed Theological Diversity and Debates within Seventeenth-Century British Puritanism*, ed. Michael Haykin and Mark Jones (Göttingen: Vandenhoeck & Ruprecht, 2011), 162–82; J. V. Fesko, *The Theology of the Westminster Standards: Historical Context and Theological Insights* (Wheaton, IL: Crossway, 2014), 142n67.

12. The language of duty here parallels the principal description of Scripture's revelation in WSC 3.

13. Edward Fisher, *The Marrow of Modern Divinity* (Fearn, UK: Christian Focus, 2009), 125.

the law for justification, but "evangelical holiness" that fulfills the law out of a position of adoption and justification already granted fully in the singular work of the Son.[14] The role of the law as rule for believers—and not as a covenant of works—reappears in related fashion in WCF 20.1, wherein the first element of Christian liberty is freedom from sin, death, and the devil and freedom for God's presence and service, because of justification wholly in Christ.[15]

Debates have swirled regarding the way in which the law of God functioned in this covenantal framework. Chapter 7 identifies the Mosaic economy as an instance of the covenant of grace, one of its "diverse administrations." Yet the covenant of grace has not been mentioned yet in this chapter, and the Mosaic deliverance of the Decalogue precedes its entrance into this discussion. Does this bespeak a divergence in emphasis, if not in substance, between chapter 7 and chapter 19? Before we seek to address the question of republication, we do well to observe two more facets of this deliverance upon Sinai. Then we can return in section 5 to ask hermeneutically how the confession suggests that we hear this legislation delivered to the liberated.

> 3. *Beside this law, commonly called moral, God was pleased to give to the people of Israel, as a church under age, ceremonial laws, containing several typical ordinances, partly of worship, prefiguring Christ, his graces, actions, sufferings, and benefits; and partly, holding forth divers instructions of moral duties. All which ceremonial laws are now abrogated, under the new testament.*

Apparently section 2 addressed moral law, or at least that is the starting point for section 3's comparison. That other laws will be noted in addition to this moral law does not suggest, as has been taken by many recent readers, that other laws are not moral; no, other laws are moral (indeed, the first sentence ends here by identifying part of this ceremonial law to regard "moral duties") but not simply, exclusively, or even primarily moral. For we read here that "God was pleased to give . . . ceremonial laws," which "are now abrogated, under

14. On "evangelical holiness," see John Owen, *Pneumatologia*, in *The Works of John Owen*, vol. 3 (Edinburgh: Banner of Truth Trust, 1955), 279, 323, 371, 380, 413–14, 446–47, 467, 472, and 514. See the helpful analysis by Kelly Kapic, "Evangelical Holiness: Assumptions in John Owen's Theology of Christian Spirituality," in *Life in the Spirit: Spiritual Formation in Theological Perspective*, ed. Jeffrey P. Greenman and George Kalantzis (Downers Grove: IVP Academic, 2010), 97–114. "Legal obedience" has been identified with the false path of "works" in classic Reformed exegesis of texts such as Rom. 3:19–20 because of the pairing of law and sin as identified in Rom. 7:11, 13.

15. Helpful commentary is provided on this point by Fesko, *Theology of the Westminster Standards*, 269.

the new testament." Cultic laws—found not only in the book of the covenant (Exod. 25–40) but especially throughout the book of Leviticus—are also a gift of God, in this case "to the people of Israel, as a church under age."[16] They are specific to Israel, not the nations; yet their particular delivery to Israel is under one aspect of her being, as a church in her immature phase ("under age").

These ceremonial laws contain "several typical ordinances" and are "partly of worship" and "partly . . . moral duties." Notice that the emphasis here is on typological (read "typical" in this manner, as opposed to a synonym for "common") and figural (read "prefiguring Christ") functionality. These laws for liturgy and obedience more broadly are meant to prepare a church by pointing ahead. We are finally reminded that the goal of these typological prefigurations has been reached "under the new testament," such that all these "laws are now abrogated."

Categories of laws are not discerned within the Old Testament itself, but these distinctions are drawn based on later canonical judgments regarding what is or is not binding as such. The Jerusalem Council in Acts 15 clearly discerns that the so-called ceremonial laws are no longer binding as such, choosing not to place the whole yoke of Moses in that way upon Gentile converts (see esp. Acts 15:19–21, 28–29). The apostle Paul would later reiterate these protocols in various settings (perhaps most famously in Gal. 2 and 5:6). Similarly, we see a shift with regard to the civil legislation from the book of Deuteronomy, which is no longer enforced given the new political epoch. Rather than calling for or instituting theocracy again, God commissions obedience unto pagan powers (Mark 12:14; Rom. 13:1–7; 1 Pet. 2:13–17). And yet the law—specifically, the Decalogue—continues to be upheld and, in fact, is "fulfilled" by Christians (Rom. 8:4; 13:8–10). The tripartite distinction was not needed in the Old Testament era, where the law addressed the people as a whole. The distinction is useful to make sense of what is "abrogated" (by which the confession means fulfilled for one reason or another, whether by its climaxing in Christ's work, in the case of cultic law, or by its contextual obsolescence, owing to providential changes in the political situation) in the New Testament writings.

4. *To them also, as a body politic, he gave sundry judicial laws, which expired together with the State of that people; not obliging any other now, further than the general equity thereof may require.*

16. The distinction between moral and ceremonial laws goes all the way back to Augustine, *Answer to Faustus the Manichaean*, in *Works of St. Augustine* I/20, ed. Boniface Ramsey, trans. Roland Teske (Hyde Park, NY: New City, 2007), 93–94 (book 6, section 2).

A third category of law appears here: "judicial laws." These laws are also a gift of God; they are a grace, not a mere human achievement. God gives unto Israel by legislating for her "as a body politic." God was not the mere inspiration for human legislation. God was not merely the animating principle of constitutional invention or revision. God himself gave or legislated a constitution ("sundry judicial laws") unto a particular "State of that people."[17]

As this civil law was given to a particular "State of that people," however, the expiration of that political entity mandated the expiration of that civil law. Judicial laws no longer "[oblige] any other now," not "as such," though they may inform others insofar as the "general equity . . . may require." The divines do not wish to deny that there are principles worthy of emulation even in later centuries, but they do distinguish between legislation that directly binds as such and that which only requires general and equitable gleanings by others indirectly.[18] So, for example, Deuteronomy's specific statutes and ordinances regarding judicial proceedings (19:15–21) are not binding directly upon any country today—for the political entity to which they were given does not exist anymore—though they may guide wise legislation by way of principle or "general equity."

> 5. *The moral law doth forever bind all, as well justified persons as others, to the obedience thereof; and that, not only in regard of the matter contained in it, but also in respect of the authority of God the Creator, who gave it. Neither doth Christ, in the gospel, any way dissolve, but much strengthen this obligation.*

That law, which was "commonly called moral" in section 3, "doth forever bind all . . . to the obedience thereof." It is not merely that those who are in Adam, through the covenant of works, are to keep this law of old, but "as well justified persons as others." Indeed, the Mosaic writings end with a foreshadowing of a future work wherein God would circumcise the heart of Israel so that "you shall again obey the voice of the LORD and keep all his commandments that I command you today" (Deut. 30:8). The prophets pick up on this emphasis. Jer-

17. This third category of laws—and hence the notion of a tripartite distinction of the law as a whole—can be traced back to Thomas Aquinas, *ST*, I–II, q. 99, a. 4. It has been picked up by a number of Reformed divines: famously, by John Calvin, *Institutes of the Christian Religion*, ed. John T. McNeill, trans. F. L. Battles, Library of Christian Classics (Louisville: Westminster John Knox, 1960), 364–65 (2.7.16) and 1504–5 (4.20.16); notably, the Second Helvetic Confession, 12.1.

18. For a classic exposition of the distinction between ongoing application in a direct and binding form and application indirectly according to general equity, see Martin Bucer, "De Regno Christi," in *Melanchthon and Bucer*, ed. Wilhelm Pauck (Louisville: Westminster John Knox, 2006), 174–394.

emiah's famous "new covenant" promise ranges more widely but does clearly speak of God putting the law within Israel and writing the law upon their heart (31:33). Ezekiel points to a "covenant of peace" (34:25), and this future intervention involves another work upon Israel's heart: "I will give you a new heart, and a new spirit I will put within you . . . and cause you to walk in my statutes and be careful to obey my rules" (36:26–27). In each case the work upon the heart leads to obeying the law, employing language drawn from Deuteronomy.

The fifth section goes a step further and provides a link between Jesus and the law of old in its moral form. "Neither doth Christ, in the gospel, any way dissolve, but much strengthen this obligation." That Christ does not dissolve or abrogate the law's demand can be drawn from his famed Sermon on the Mount (Matt. 5:17–19). He not only programmatically speaks of fulfilling the law therein (5:17) but also illustrates the need to honor the full moral demand of the law in the six contrasts found later in Matthew 5. Reformed interpreters have consistently pointed to Jesus's work in interpreting the Decalogue faithfully and holistically, rather than opposing it, such that the "You have heard . . . but I say to you" corrects truncated or foreshortened misperceptions of Sinai's moral law, not the law itself. And Jesus strengthens the binding character of this law in the justified also. Notice that the first sentence in section 5 speaks of how God's authority as creator adds to the intrinsic authority of this moral legislation; now Jesus the justifier of the ungodly affirms this legislation and, thus, adds still further to its authority. The moral law not only is true in and of itself, but is also good as the design of our almighty Creator and beautiful as the intent of our incarnate Redeemer.

As noted earlier with regard to section 2, some have argued that the law of Eden was promulgated again upon Sinai, so that we can speak of the republication of the covenant of works. It is worth distinguishing between two affirmations here, one held virtually universally within the tradition and the other held by a significant minority. First, virtually all held that the moral law had been given to Adam and Eve and then written by the very hand of God upon the tablets delivered to Moses on Sinai. Hence, the lasting nature of the moral law is rooted in its creational reality (notice that section 5 here states that it is not only authoritative "in regard of the matter contained in it, but also in respect of the authority of God the Creator, who gave it," wherein most have read the giving of it to be creational and not simply a later act of one who had previously created). Second, some significant theologians in the tradition believe that while the Mosaic economy was an "administration" of the "covenant of grace," it also served symbolically and typologically to republish the covenant of works (in the principle of obedience, as in Lev. 18:5, read through

Paul's lenses in Rom. 10:5–8 and possibly also Gal. 3:10–14) and point to God's people's need for one who would fulfill that original covenant on their behalf. In other words, republicationists argue that while the Mosaic economy does provide grace and forgiveness, it also republishes the deeper need for genuine justice that it does not itself satisfy and, in so doing, points to a later provision by God (logic, it is argued, rooted in reading Rom. 3:21–26).[19]

> 6. *Although true believers be not under the law, as a covenant of works, to be thereby justified, or condemned; yet is it of great use to them, as well as to others; in that, as a rule of life informing them of the will of God, and their duty, it directs and binds them to walk accordingly; discovering also the sinful pollutions of their nature, hearts, and lives; so as, examining themselves thereby, they may come to further conviction of, humiliation for, and hatred against sin, together with a clearer sight of the need they have of Christ, and the perfection of his obedience. It is likewise of use to the regenerate, to restrain their corruptions, in that it forbids sin: and the threatenings of it serve to show what even their sins deserve; and what afflictions, in this life, they may expect for them, although freed from the curse thereof threatened in the law. The promises of it, in like manner, show them God's approbation of obedience, and what blessings they may expect upon the performance thereof: although not as due to them by the law as a covenant of works. So as, a man's doing good, and refraining from evil, because the law encourageth to the one, and deterreth from the other, is no evidence of his being under the law; and, not under grace.*

That the moral law binds even the justified does not mean that the Christian relates to these commands in the same fashion as the unredeemed. The justified "be not under the law, as a covenant of works," and thus do not obey it for the sake of fulfilling their duty for righteousness. Nevertheless, it is a "rule of life informing them of the will of God, and their duty." The language of its rule is nonreductive, for the confession quickly identifies a number of ways whereby the moral law aids the reception of life from God. First, "it directs and binds them to walk accordingly." Second, it aids them in "discovering . . . the sinful pollutions of their nature, hearts, and lives," which enables them to see the insidious ignominy of sin as well as the breadth and sufficiency

19. For a helpful survey and analysis, see Mark Jones, "The Old Covenant," in Haykin and Jones, *Drawn into Controversie*, 183–203; see also Mark Beach, *Christ and the Covenant: Francis Turretin's Federal Theology as a Defense of the Doctrine of Grace*, Reformed Historical Theology (Göttingen: Vandenhoeck & Ruprecht, 2007), ch. 4.

of Christ's redemption. Third, it helps them "restrain their corruptions" by showing the just deserts of sin and the judgments looming for its exercise. Fourth, the promises found within the law—that is, statements of divine blessing premised upon fulfillment of its ways—are heard as well. The law guides, convicts, warns, and elicits.

A final sentence is added to this section: "So as, a man's doing good, and refraining from evil, because the law encourageth to the one, and deterreth from the other, is no evidence of his being under the law; and, not under grace." Clearly a pastoral or polemical concern generates this finale. Action impelled by the law's carrot or its stick does not suggest that one is thereby "under the law" and "not under grace." Indeed, the preceding sentence qualified the final function: when the law elicits obedience through its promises, these are not heard as blessings "due to them by the law as a covenant of works."

> 7. *Neither are the forementioned uses of the law contrary to the grace of the gospel, but do sweetly comply with it; the Spirit of Christ subduing and enabling the will of man to do that freely, and cheerfully, which the will of God, revealed in the law, requireth to be done.*

Whereas we regularly hear of the Reformed teaching about the harmony of word and Spirit, here we see a more specific unity between the law and the Spirit. The preceding functions of the law are here defined, for the first time, as "uses of the law." They "sweetly comply with" the gospel rather than being "contrary to the grace of" it. The preceding section specified that they function outside a covenant of works, for the justified believer relates to God now through a covenant of grace (which itself fulfills the covenant of works by means of a mediator and surety; on which see ch. 8). Another element is added here by way of explanation: the Spirit "subduing and enabling the will of man" for free and cheerful obedience unto the "will of God, revealed in the law." In the gospel of Jesus, then, we see the promise of healing and transformation by the Spirit, such that the human will freely chooses to obey God according to his lawful instructions. So far from undermining the integrity of human volition by affirming divine sovereignty, we see here that this gracious and lordly intervention leads to "cheerful" obedience.

Sweet compliance between law and gospel occurs here not in that the gospel abolishes or negates the law, but that the gospel provides for the fulfillment of the law. Such language can speak, of course, to the way in which the gospel involves the promise of Christ's law-keeping work on behalf of or in the place of those united to him by faith. His substitutionary work under the law's demands holds a central and leading place in the promise of the gospel.[20] Yet sweet compliance here focuses upon the fact that the gospel also involves the promise of healing and transformation, such that the one united to Christ fulfills the law. Romans 8:3–4 speaks to such fulfillment occurring with regard to the "law of the spirit of life," and Romans 13:8–13 identifies love—Christian love as teased out in chapters 12–15 and expressed according to the second table of the law (see 13:9)—as the "fulfilling of the law."

John Calvin famously spoke of the double grace (*duplex gratia*) of the gospel.[21] "With good reason, the sum of the gospel is held to consist in repentance and forgiveness of sins [Luke 24:47; Acts 5:31]. Any discussion of faith, therefore, that omitted these two topics would be barren and mutilated and well-nigh useless. Now, both repentance and forgiveness of sins—that is, newness of life and free reconciliation—are conferred on us by Christ, and both are attained by us through faith."[22] He repeatedly returns to this structuring principle: "The whole of the gospel is contained under these two headings, repentance and forgiveness of sins";[23] and "By partaking of him, we . . . receive a double grace: namely, that being reconciled to God through Christ's blamelessness, we may have in heaven instead of a judge a gracious Father; and secondly, that sanctified by Christ's spirit we may cultivate blamelessness and purity of life."[24] Whereas later doctrinal discussions typically front the language of justification and sanctification—over Calvin's preference for forgiveness of sins and repentance—the double grace becomes a key rubric for understanding Reformed soteriology.[25] God reconciles us to himself through

20. The WCF addresses this work not only in 19.6 but also in 8.3–5. I have reflected at length upon the relation of these two facets of the gospel in Michael Allen, *Justification and the Gospel: Understanding the Contexts and the Controversies* (Grand Rapids: Baker Academic, 2013), chs. 1–2.

21. Calvin and the Reformed tradition do not invent this way of speaking of a twofold grace. Cyril of Alexandria, the great fifth-century theologian, notes how this mediator is "both the altar of incense since he is the pleasing aroma of sanctification and the altar of burnt offering since he is the sacrifice for the life of the world" (Cyril of Alexandria, *Commentary on John*, vol. 1, 256 [on 6:68]). Similar comments noting a twofold rubric for the work of Christ can be found in Athanasius's *On the Incarnation* (ch. 2, §10) as well as Augustine's *On Faith and Works* (9.14).

22. Calvin, *Institutes* 3.3.1.

23. Calvin, *Institutes* 3.3.19.

24. Calvin, *Institutes* 3.11.1.

25. Illustrated notably in HC 1, which speaks of the double grace twice (first, "He has fully paid for all my sins with his precious blood, and has set me free from the tyranny of the devil"; and second, "Because I belong to him, Christ, by his Holy Spirit, assures me of eternal life and makes me wholeheartedly willing and ready from now on to live for him"), and Augustus Toplady's "Rock of Ages," which includes the lines "Be of sin the double cure, save me from its guilt and power."

the work of Christ outside us (his sin bearing as well as, in most iterations, his perfect obedience to the law), and God also restores us to the image of God in Christ through the renovating work of the Holy Spirit within us. With this rubric of double grace, then, the Reformed have been able to keep their eyes on both the converting work of God in accepting sinners through the substitutionary role of Christ and the transformative and progressive work by God over the long haul of the Christian life.[26]

Here we see the final affirmation of this chapter, returning to locate this discussion of the law within the orbit or matrix of the gospel. Speaking of a "rule of life" governing the justified believer and instructing the believer's way does not denigrate grace and will not oppose the gospel precisely because we can attest that not only is the law a gift but the Spirit is also given to transform our hearts to delight in that law. Sanctification, then, is only secondarily something that we participate in or play any active role within. First and foremost, sanctification is an action of God and, specifically, of Jesus Christ, wherein he restores the image of God within us, conforms us to his own example, and by his Spirit reshapes our heart that we might fulfill his law.[27]

26. There are historiographic debates on the way Calvin's theology of union with Christ is or is not similar to that of the Lutheran tradition and whether it is or is not consistently developed by later Reformed theologians, such as those federal divines who prepared the Westminster Standards in the seventeenth century. Mark Garcia and others (in the so-called Gaffin School) have argued that Calvin offers a very different approach to union with Christ than does the Lutheran tradition, and that Calvin in no way identifies justification as a cause for sanctification. James Torrance, Thomas Torrance, and Charles Partee, among others, argue that Calvin was not faithfully followed by the later Calvinists, who failed to maintain his focus on union with Christ. Yet leading scholars of Reformation and post-Reformation theology on just these doctrines—in particular, J. Todd Billings, J. V. Fesko, and Richard A. Muller—have argued at length from primary sources that both dichotomies are false: Calvin stood alongside Lutherans (like Melanchthon, in particular) in affirming the priority of justification as well as the necessity of sanctification; and Calvin's insistence on union with Christ as the context for the double grace was developed in a faithful or continuous way by later federal theologians (and in the Westminster Standards). See especially Billings, "The Contemporary Reception of Luther and Calvin's Doctrine of Union with Christ: Mapping a Biblical, Catholic, and Reformational Motif," in *Calvin and Luther: The Continuing Relationship*, ed. R. Ward Holder (Göttingen: Vandenhoeck & Ruprecht, 2013), 158–75; as well as his larger study, *Calvin, Participation, and the Gift: The Activity of Believers in Union with Christ*, Changing Paradigms in Historical and Systematic Theology (New York: Oxford University Press, 2007).

27. On active and passive sanctification, see, for example, Herman Bavinck, *Reformed Dogmatics*, vol. 4, *Holy Spirit, Church, and New Creation*, ed. John Bolt, trans. John Vriend (Grand Rapids: Baker Academic, 2008), 252–56. On locating sanctification christologically, see Michael Allen, "Sanctification and the Gospel," in *Sanctification*, New Studies in Dogmatics (Grand Rapids: Zondervan Academic, 2017), ch. 1.

Law and Gospel within the Covenant Theology

What, then, shall we say of the law? Nothing, without attending to the way in which it has been heard and confessed by the saints. In listening to two great witnesses from the Reformed tradition, we might be in a better position to hear certain things in the law and to testify more fully and convincingly of it. As we consider ways to reflect thoughtfully upon the voice of the law and its various tones in Holy Scripture, much less the way we are called to attest of it in our praise and proclamation, we do well to follow the instruction of those who have gone before us. We do well to remember the fifth commandment even as we think about the very nature and function of those commandments, that we might not only set apart God's law as holy but do so by honoring our fathers and mothers in the faith.

Perhaps the most significant thing to catch in listening to those ancestors is the way in which the law and gospel have not tended to be discussed in Reformed circles, at least not this side of Westminster, apart from the thick development of covenant theology. The covenant of works and the covenant of grace have provided rubrics for talk of ways in which one relates to God and, perhaps, for the way in which one receives various scriptural words appropriately, depending upon one's own spiritual standing before God (whether in the covenant of grace through Christ or simply in the covenant of works through Adam).[28] The law—the very same instructions—can be and should be heard by various persons as a merely legal or as a delightfully evangelical word based upon whether it is heard within the one or the other covenantal context. In short, the Reformed approach to law and gospel through the prism of covenant theology—either the covenant of works or the covenant of grace—reorients the individual within a canonical, communal, but especially also an eschatological frame.[29] One must not only ask of a verse or portion of a sermon, *what do I hear?* But to do so, one must locate that question within a nest of others: *Where am I? Whose am I? In what time am I?*

Without offering a deconstruction of other approaches, be they Lutheran or Reformed, I can conclude only by suggesting that covenant theology—and

28. For further elaboration of the connection between law and gospel and the covenant of works/covenant of grace distinction, see Beach, *Christ and the Covenant*, ch. 4, section D.

29. For more on the eschatological shape of such discussions, see the work of Brian J. Lee, "Johannes Cocceius as Federal Polemicist: The Usefulness of the Distinction between the Testaments," in *Church and School in Early Modern Protestantism: Studies in Honor of Richard A. Muller on the Maturation of a Theological Tradition*, ed. Jordan J. Ballor et al., Studies in the History of Christian Traditions 170 (Leiden: Brill, 2013), 567–82.

viewing the law and gospel within that frame—helps avoid some of the ambiguity and vagueness that so often affect discussions of law and gospel as well as some of the far worse problems wherein law and gospel might be confused, separated, or misidentified.[30] To appreciate them and to rightly distinguish them, perhaps Westminster and the tradition of federal theology show that one needs some more basic categories helpfully attested in the realm of God's covenant with humanity.

Excursus: On the Covenant with Adam

A number of Reformed theologians refrain from terming this administration between God and Adam a "covenant," since the Bible does not explicitly do so. Some have argued, and many still do, that Hosea 6:7 compares Israel's covenantal responsibility and failure in that day to that of Adam before them. But this is a debated text, for "Adam" may refer to a specific human, a generic human, or even a particular city in that day. It is notable that this text was not employed as a scriptural proof text for the confession and catechisms (likely owing to its exegetical difficulties).

Some object to the very existence of a covenant that is distinct from the "covenant of grace" (e.g., Karl Barth, James B. Torrance, T. F. Torrance). They argue that the development of a bicovenantal approach to covenant theology is theologically ruinous, in particular that it brings disaster to the doctrine of God by suggesting that God is akin to a schizophrenic (gracious sometimes, demanding at others). These theologians (and others) have tried to argue that federal theology (this bicovenantal approach as exemplified in the Westminster Standards) is a marked divergence from the theology of Calvin and that it is owing to the "legal" or even "legalistic" tendencies of these later Reformed theologians who failed to honor Calvin's biblical principles. And they call for a return to Calvin's more "evangelical Calvinism." Further, they argue that anything shy of a covenant theology that delivers a universal atonement fails to be "good news" for anyone.

Response to this line of criticism takes many forms. First, their control or baseline is arbitrary, for neither is Calvin the first to articulate the doctrine of the covenant (following Tyndale, Zwingli, and Bullinger, among others) nor is he the definitive figure in the Reformed development of the covenant concept.

30. For further elaboration of such a project, see "Grace and Discipline," in Michael Allen, *Sanctification*, ch. 10.

Second, while Calvin does not use the language of a "covenant of works" or "covenant of life" of Eden before the Fall, he does at times and in various places suggest the idea itself as being biblical.[31] Third, as the covenant of works/covenant of life concept was developed (and with it the very hermeneutic of bicovenantal distinctions, broadly conceived) throughout the latter sixteenth century and early seventeenth century (especially in the work of Wolfgang Musculus, Zacharias Ursinus, and Caspar Olevianus), it was not a legal mind-set foreign to the Scriptures but the very language and breadth of canonical teaching that drove this development (e.g., the teaching of Hebrews, the Adam/Christ parallels in Rom. 5 and 1 Cor. 15, the distinction between the universal extent of Adam's sin and the particular redemption accomplished by Christ for his elect, and the tradition of expositing Gen. 1–3). Historical theologians of the sixteenth and seventeenth centuries have shown for over three decades that the purported dichotomy between "Calvin and the Calvinists" here is a fiction in the minds of these mid-twentieth-century theologians. While there are still advocates of this opposition to the covenant of works along the lines posed by Karl Barth and the Torrance brothers, they do so in the face of the detailed and extensive arguments of the finest historical theologians.[32]

Others object simply to the terminology of covenant being applied where the Bible does not apply it. John Murray, a strong advocate of the bicovenantal approach to Scripture, believed that "Scripture always uses the term covenant, when applied to God's administration to men, in reference to a provision that is redemptive or closely related to redemptive design."[33] Murray's main dispute is terminological, though he also disagrees with some elements within the tradition of federal theology (namely, with the argument that there was no grace before the Fall, on the grounds that grace is always and only redemptive; and also with the argument that the covenant of works was republished in the Mosaic

31. See Peter Lillback, *The Binding of God: Calvin's Role in the Development of Covenant Theology*, Texts & Studies in Reformation & Post-Reformation Thought (Grand Rapids: Baker, 2001); see also Fesko, *Theology of the Westminster Standards*, 127–37.

32. See, for example, Richard A. Muller, "The Covenant of Works and the Stability of Divine Law in Seventeenth-Century Reformed Orthodoxy: A Study in the Theology of Herman Witsius and Wilhelmus à Brakel," in *After Calvin: Studies in the Development of a Theological Tradition*, Oxford Studies in Historical Theology (New York: Oxford University Press, 2003), 175–90. For a more recent, measured argument along the lines of Barth, albeit with an eye historically to the rejoinders of Muller and others to the Torrance approach to Reformed history, see Paul Nimmo, "The Law of God and Christian Ethics," in *Christian Dogmatics: Reformed Theology for the Church Catholic*, ed. Michael Allen and Scott R. Swain (Grand Rapids: Baker Academic, 2016), 291–310.

33. John Murray, "Adamic Administration," in *Collected Works of John Murray*, vol. 2, *Systematic Theology* (Edinburgh: Banner of Truth Trust, 1977), 49.

covenant as a typological precursor of the coming Messiah). But both of these are disagreements he holds with positions that, while they do occur amongst federal theologians, in no way mark the confession or even mark the majority tradition. In broad strokes, Murray remains at one with the tradition of covenant theology in the Westminster vein (though, admittedly, some contemporary advocates of republication and those influenced by Meredith Kline, a former professor at Gordon-Conwell and Westminster Seminary California, consider him to be a foe of the whole tradition).

To Murray's question, though, we should offer a response. Can there be a covenant here if the Bible does not explicitly call it a covenant? Chad Van Dixhoorn is especially helpful here:

> We do not always need to see a term employed to know that the thing really exists. If you spot four English ladies sipping tea, eating scones and savoring the local gossip at four o'clock in the afternoon, you do not need a label to know what is going on: there is a tea party. Yes, it is possible you have stumbled on an international spy ring or the caucus of a drug cartel; but if you are familiar with tea parties you should be able to spot the difference. We could call this the "tea party principle" and it easily applies to covenants. Any time one spots a sovereignly determined and administered arrangement between God and man, with penalties and promises, you have a covenant.[34]

In conclusion, then, we can note that the key elements of a biblical covenant are found here. Even if Hosea 6:7 and Isaiah 24:5 (which references the "eternal covenant" broken and likely refers either to the Noachian covenant or to a prelapsarian Edenic covenant) do not refer to the covenant of works, the idea itself is biblical, and use of the terminology of covenant only makes explicit what is otherwise conveyed in implicit fashion.

---

34. Chad Van Dixhoorn, *Confessing the Faith: A Reader's Guide to the Westminster Confession of Faith* (Edinburgh: Banner of Truth Trust, 2014), 97.

PART II
The Gospel Is Not the Law

Chapter 3

The Gospel in the Lutheran Tradition

Charles P. Arand

Where does one turn for what Lutherans teach about the gospel? One's first instinct is to turn to Martin Luther—and for good reason. Lutherans bear his name. He launched the Reformation movement of the sixteenth century that spread across the entire continent of Europe. And for that matter, he represents something of an ecumenical figure to which all can look, much as we do with a Saint Augustine or a Gregory of Nyssa. But where has Luther's teaching been set down most definitively—the teaching that has been most accepted and transmitted across the generations? In other words, where does one turn for an authoritative account of what Luther taught, and with him, his Lutheran followers?

For Lutherans, that would be a series of confessional statements at the head of which list stands the Augsburg Confession presented to Emperor Charles V on June 25, 1530, and its Apology published a year later. Although these texts were written by Philip Melanchthon and not by Luther (as he was forced to remain at Coburg Castle during the Diet of Augsburg), they have always been regarded as definitive statements about what Luther taught on justification. One cannot overstate the importance of these statements in setting the direction for Lutheran theology in the decades to follow.[1] So for this essay, I am going to turn to Melanchthon's exposition of the gospel as set forth in the Apology of the Augsburg Confession.

1. Citations are from Robert Kolb and Timothy J. Wengert, eds., *The Book of Concord: The Confessions of the Evangelical Lutheran Church* (Minneapolis: Fortress, 2000).

The Distinction of Law and Gospel for Luther and Melanchthon

Martin Luther's arrival at a biblical understanding of the gospel can be illustrated by the way in which he wrestled with Paul's statement in Romans 1:17 that "the righteousness of God" has been revealed in the gospel.

As he describes it later in life, he had understood the phrase to mean the righteousness that God demands from us. It appeared as if Christ was a greater lawgiver than was Moses in that he demanded far more from us. After all, Moses demanded primarily external works from us as set forth in the Ten Commandments. Christ, by contrast, now demanded in the Sermon on the Mount even more difficult works by speaking to our thoughts, attitudes, and emotions. For example, where Moses said "thou shall not kill," Jesus stated, "But I say to you that everyone who is angry with his brother will be liable to judgment; whoever insults his brother will be liable to the council; and whoever says, 'You fool!' will be liable to the hell of fire" (Matt. 5:22).

Luther's recovery of the scriptural gospel occurred when he came to a different understanding of that phrase. Rather than seeing the righteousness of God as a righteousness that God demands from us, he realized that the righteousness of God was a righteousness that God bestows upon us on account of Christ! The gospel reveals and bestows upon us the righteousness of another, an "alien righteousness," namely, the righteousness that Christ acquired for us by means of his life, death, and resurrection. And with that discovery the distinction of law and gospel was born. Luther describes the discovery: "It seemed as if the very heavens had been opened."[2]

The distinction of law and gospel became key for Philip Melanchthon's argument in article 4 of his Apology of the Augsburg Confession. This article provides one of the longest and most sustained treatments of justification in Lutheran literature. And by its inclusion in the *Book of Concord*, it should be regarded as the first and most authoritative exposition of the Lutheran position on justification in general. To understand his argument, one must see how he constructed the article by utilizing the categories of rhetoric (on which he wrote several times).[3]

Melanchthon chooses the *genus iudicale* (judicial type of speech) for composing the Apology. One might thus think of a courtroom as the setting, in which the Lutherans are the defendants, the papal legate, Cardinal Compeggio, is the prosecutor, the emperor is the judge, and the German audience is the

2. *LW* 34:336–37.

3. See Charles P. Arand, "Melanchthon's Rhetorical Argument for *Sola Fide* in the Apology," *Lutheran Quarterly* 3 (Autumn 2000): 281–308.

gallery (whom Melanchthon often addresses as "dear readers"). The speech follows the pattern of an introduction (*exordium*) by which the speaker engages the listeners and prepares them for what will soon follow. Then follow what one might call the opening statements (*narratio*), by which a lawyer rehearses the events that brought the discussion to this point and in the process sets forth the position or thesis of his opponent (*minor proposition*) and then his own thesis (*major proposition*). After both positions have been laid out, the arguments and evidence (*confirmatio*) in favor of the major proposition are set forth. After that, the speaker proceeds to dismantle the arguments of the opponents (*confutatio*), followed by a closing statement (*peroratio*).

At the very outset of his *narratio*, Melanchthon explains why the Lutherans and the Roman party arrive at opposite positions on the matter of justification: "in order both to substantiate our confession and to remove the objections that the opponents raise, we need first to say a few things by way of a preface in order that the sources of both versions of the doctrine, the opponents' and ours, can be recognized" (Ap 4.4; p. 121). Melanchthon then points out that there are two basic teachings in the Bible, namely, the law and the promises. He then notes, "Of these two topics, the opponents single out the law (because to some extent human reason naturally understands it since reason contains the same judgment divinely written on the mind), and through the law they seek the forgiveness of sins and justification" (Ap 4.7; p. 121). By contrast, the Lutherans choose the promise of the gospel and seek thereby to be justified.

This distinction of the law and the promises shapes Melanchthon's discussion on justification for the next four hundred paragraphs. And throughout he reminds his readers of its importance. For example, he opens the section in which he will address and dismantle his opponents' arguments by stating, "Having acknowledged the fundamentals in this issue (namely, the distinction between the law and the promises or gospel), it will be easy to remove the objections raised by the opponents. For they quote passages about the law and works *but* omit passages about the promises" (Ap 4.183; p. 149).

So the definition of the gospel as promise is central to an understanding of the Lutheran teaching on justification. And with that, it becomes key for defining the way in which Lutherans understand faith, the Word of God, and the sacraments. It provides something of a completely different paradigm than that used by Melanchthon's Roman counterparts.

I have found Thomas Kuhn's analysis of how scientific advances occur not by accumulation but by a shift in paradigms to be helpful here.[4] In studying the

4. Thomas Kuhn, *The Structure of Scientific Revolutions* (Chicago: University of Chicago Press, 1962).

history of science, Kuhn observed that both the Ptolemists and the Copernicans worked with the same data (the telescope had not yet been invented), but they accounted for that data within different paradigms. Take the retrograde of the planets. The Ptolemists accounted for it by inventing something called epicycles (Mars is doing loops around Earth). But by placing the sun at the center of the solar system, the Copernicans accounted for the retrograde by placing Earth on an inner orbit to that of Mars. It accounted for the data more simply and elegantly.

In a similar way, the Lutherans and the medieval church were working with the same data, namely, the Scriptures. And they had to account for all the data, especially the relationship between God's actions and our actions within the matter of justification. The way they dealt with that data gave rise to two different anthropological paradigms. Within these paradigms, classic biblical and theological terms related to justification such as "faith," "gospel," and "justify" are interpreted in very different ways.

The Opponents Select the Law

To appreciate the Lutheran understanding of the gospel as promise, one has to see it against the backdrop of the medieval church's position on justification. This means one needs to see it against the backdrop of issues related to anthropology. In fact, I would argue that the Reformation represents something of an anthropological turn in its focus. Whereas the ancient creeds (Nicene, Apostles', and Athanasian) focused on the Trinity and Christology, the Reformation focused on what that means for being a human creature of God. Consider the topics that dominated the discussions: original sin, free choice, faith, good works, the church, civil society, and the like.

The medieval church (at least according to Melanchthon's portrayal of it) focused on what we might call a modular or compartmental understanding of the human person. Drawing upon Aristotle (especially his *Nicomachean Ethics*), they organized the human person according to higher powers and lower powers. The higher powers consisted of reason/intellect and the will. These were seen as that which makes humans like God, or at least that which we have in common with God as those made in his image. By contrast, the lower powers consisted of passions/emotions and bodily locomotion. These were regarded as lower because they are what we have in common with the nonhuman creatures we see in the world around us.

The central issue revolved around the proper functioning of these components in relationship to each other. Ideally, the intellect would inform the will about the right thing to do in order to elicit that action (an act of love) from the will. The will in turn would keep the passions in check and control the actions of the body. The passions were not seen as sinful, but were regarded as somewhat unruly. The ideal understanding of the human life would be a life lived according to reason rather than one controlled by the passions (we see this also today—consider the psychology of the stock market). So how does this play out theologically?

We humans were created with a built-in tension between our higher powers that drew us toward God and our lower powers that drew us toward the world. The key to being righteous or unrighteous lay in the will. The choices that we make matter. They determine the type of person we will be. The passions or emotions were regarded as somewhat neutral. They did not make us righteous or unrighteous until we acted upon them. And so Melanchthon charges, "In the schools, however, they have taken over from philosophy the completely alien notions that our passions make us neither good nor evil, neither praiseworthy nor contemptible. Again, they say that nothing is sin unless it is voluntary" (Ap 2.43; pp. 118–19). So the will is key to the human person. This made a good deal of sense when considered within the horizontal sphere of life (namely, our relationship with others in this world) with which Aristotle was concerned. I am considered a good father or good citizen if I live that way throughout my life.[5]

So how does this apply to righteousness and justification? The narrative begins in Eden. God, who is love, created Adam and Eve, who would love him in return. After God created Adam and Eve, he gave them an additional gift of grace (*donum superadditum*) that might be likened to spiritual steroids. That is to say, it enabled the proper functioning of the human powers so as to love God completely. When Adam and Eve fell, they lost this grace and, with it, their balance. It might still be possible to love God with all one's heart (in the view of the *via moderna*), but it is incredibly difficult to do so (Ap 4.9; pp. 121–22). Christ reacquires this grace (*habitus*) that "inclines us to love God more easily" (Ap 4.17; p. 123), which is then poured or infused into a person so that the person can once again perform acts of love for God. This sets one on the road to becoming a righteous person by attaching oneself to God while limiting one's attachments to this world or anyone or anything within it.

5. Steven E. Ozment, *The Age of Reform, 1250–1550: An Intellectual and Religious History of Late Medieval and Reformation Europe* (New Haven: Yale University Press, 1980). See also Ozment, "Luther and the Late Middle Ages," in *Transition and Revolution: Problems and Issues of European Renaissance and Reformation History*, ed. Robert M. Kingdon (Minneapolis: Burgess Publishing, 1972).

Within this anthropological conception of the human creature, Melanchthon's opponents located faith within the human intellect. As a result, faith alone cannot save inasmuch as it is not located in the will. Corresponding to this, the gospel was defined as the biography of Christ. So the gospel is the story about Jesus. It informs reason of what God has done in Jesus. Faith (located in reason), then, is nothing other than believing that the facts of the story are true. This is why Rome could not go along with "faith alone." They immediately recognized that this would imply that the devils and certain unbelievers could be saved as well! After all, even the devils believed that Jesus was the Son of God and was raised from the dead. But this does not save them! The real difference between believers and unbelievers was love (located in the will).

This does not mean that faith is unimportant. One could not be saved without faith. It is the starting line that sets one on the road to righteousness. Faith, believing the gospel, is inspired to love God in light of what he did. And thus faith would elicit acts of love or devotion from the will. These voluntary acts are what ultimately led to justification or becoming righteous.

In responding to these arguments, Melanchthon often expresses frustration. This is why he often complains that his opponents misunderstand justifying faith, for they define faith as nothing other than "historical knowledge." As a result, they limit it to human reason, which, within their paradigm, is not where righteousness takes place. So much of what then takes place, I sense, is Melanchthon's attempt to convey what Lutherans mean by translating it into another paradigm. You can sense this at one point where his frustration seems to boil over and he basically says, "Fine, if it will help you understand what we mean by faith, we will locate faith in the will since it means to desire the promise of the forgiveness of sins." He writes, "Instead, he [God] regards a person as righteous through mercy because of Christ, when anyone clings to him by faith. Therefore faith can be called righteousness because it is that which is reckoned as righteousness (as we say with Paul), regardless in which part of a person it may finally be located. For this does not prevent divine reckoning, even if we locate this faith in the will. For faith is the desire for and the reception of the promise of Christ" (Ap 4.305A; p. 165). Of course, even this does not convince the opponents, and I suspect is not what Melanchthon would prefer to do. These are simply two very different anthropological paradigms.

Melanchthon's opponents are working within a modular or compartmentalized understanding of the human creature whereas Melanchthon and the Lutherans are working with a holistic and relational understanding of the human creature. In other words, they are not so much concerned about how the individual components of a person are functioning in relationship to each other in order to produce acts of love toward God as they are concerned about how the whole person is oriented to God and related to God. One is related to God either rightly or not rightly. That now brings us to the Lutheran paradigm of promise and faith.

Lutherans Choose the Promise

The gospel, for Melanchthon, completely changes the way in which human anthropology is conceived.[6] Neither Luther nor Melanchthon is concerned about how the various powers or faculties relate to each other within a human person. They are no longer concerned about where to locate faith or love within those faculties.[7] Instead, they are concerned about how the *whole* person is *related* to God. In light of Luther's understanding of the righteousness of God in Romans 1:17, the gospel is set forth as a promise of forgiveness. So what are the basic features of the gospel as promise, and why do Luther, Melanchthon, and others within Lutheran tradition argue for them?

Gospel = Story + Promise

For Melanchthon, the reason his opponents failed to grasp why Lutherans insisted on salvation by faith alone is that they misunderstood justifying faith. And the reason they misunderstood the definition of justifying faith is that they misunderstood the nature of the gospel itself. They understood the gospel to be only the historical account of who Jesus is and what he did during his life prior to his ascension. Thus faith could be nothing other than the knowledge or conviction that all of this was true.

For Melanchthon, the startling thing about the gospel is that it is much more than historical information. It is a gracious promise. Now, Melanchthon did not discount the historicity of Jesus or the reality of his work. It's just that limiting the gospel to such knowledge does not answer the "so what?" question. Or to be more precise, it does not answer the question about the purpose of Christ's work. That's where the gospel as promise comes into its own and becomes key for a Lutheran understanding of faith, and with it justification, not to mention the vitality of faith for driving sanctification.

6. See Robert Kolb and Charles P. Arand, *The Genius of Luther's Theology: A Wittenberg Way of Thinking for the Contemporary Church* (Grand Rapids: Baker, 2008).

7. One can see this in Melanchthon's description of faith as the desire to receive the forgiveness of sins, or embracing the gospel, etc. These do not fit neatly into reason, will, or passions. They pertain to the orientation of the entire person toward God.

Melanchthon makes clear what he means by the promise by referencing the forgiveness of sins in the third article of the Apostles' Creed. "Thus it is not enough to believe that Christ was born, suffered, and was raised again unless we also add this article, which is the real purpose of the narrative: 'the forgiveness of sins'" (Ap 4.51; p. 128).

Melanchthon brings this out vividly in the third article of the Augsburg Confession, on Christology. There he quotes the Apostles' Creed and inserts into it the purpose of the narratives. Thus, after the words "crucified, dead, and was buried," Melanchthon inserts "in order both to be a sacrifice not only for original sin but also for all other sins and to conciliate God's wrath" (AC 3.3–4; p. 38). After the words "is sitting at the right hand of God," Melanchthon inserts "in order to rule and reign forever over all creatures, so that through the Holy Spirit he may make holy, purify, strengthen, and comfort all who believe in him, also distribute to them life and various gifts and benefits, and shield and protect them against the devil and sin" (AC 3.4–6; p. 38).

Excursus: The Unity of Scripture

For Melanchthon, the gospel as promise brings out the unity of the Scriptures. A person might ask, If one has the New Testament, why does one need the Old Testament? Doesn't the new replace and supplant the old? Or from a Lutheran view of law and gospel, it has not been entirely uncommon or unusual to see the Old Testament as law and the New Testament as gospel. Even speaking of the gospel as "good news" has its unintended consequences. For example, it can come off sounding as if the Old Testament is bad news and the New Testament is good news.

By focusing on the promise, Melanchthon can highlight both the continuity and the discontinuity of Scripture. God is a God who makes promises all through the Scriptures. He highlights this unity of Scripture by observing that Scripture communicates the promise concerning Christ, "either when it promises that Christ will come and on account of him offers the forgiveness of sins, justification, and eternal life, or when in the gospel itself, Christ, after he appeared, promises the forgiveness of sins, justification, and eternal life" (Ap 4.5; p. 121). The discontinuity enters with respect to the time frame. In the Old Testament, that promise is given in view of the Christ who would come; in the New Testament it is made in view of the Christ who has come.

Melanchthon's emphasis on promise shows that this was God's one and only plan of salvation given from the very beginning. This promise was given to Adam, and then the patriarchs, the prophets, and finally in Christ (Ap 12.53; p. 195). The law was never given for the purpose of rescuing us from sin or acquiring salvation, or retaining salvation once it had been acquired (see FC 4). His opponents "choose the law" and seek to be justified by it because natural reason somewhat understands it, as it was written into human hearts at creation. It was prelapsarian.

So what was the purpose of the law if not for salvation? To borrow a definition from the Formula of Concord, the law simply reveals or shows us what life as a human creature looks like as God envisioned it and then created us to be in our thoughts, attitudes, and deeds (as a whole person). This is what the life of Adam and Eve looked like before they fell. This, after all, is what it means to be righteous. It is to be the human creature that God envisioned us to be when he created us. Or put another way, it is to be conformed to the design specifications of our creation.

And what were those design specifications? In brief, to live with God (*coram Deo*) by faith and to live with our neighbors and creation (*coram mundo*) by love. The former deals with an identity given us by God as creatures and then as his children. The latter deals with the living out of that identity within the world. The latter depends upon the former. For this reason, Lutherans speak of two kinds of righteousness (as Melanchthon tirelessly does).[8]

A Wedding Analogy

This shift in understanding the gospel as promise led to a shift in the focus on anthropology. Instead of conceiving of how grace assisted the various powers of the human person to function properly so as to do righteous acts before God, the focus now shifts to viewing the human person holistically and relationally. In other words, how does the whole person relate to God? How is the person oriented to God? Here we might borrow from the marriage analogy that Luther used for talking about the happy exchange (*fröliche Wechsel*) in order to explore the various facets of the gospel as a promise and the anthropology it assumes.

When the bride and groom prepare to speak their vows, they stand at the altar facing each other. The focus is on how these two people in their

8. See Charles P. Arand, "Two Kinds of Righteousness as a Framework for Law and Gospel in the Apology," *Lutheran Quarterly* 15 (Winter 2001): 417–39.

entire being are oriented toward and related to each other. What exactly is going on when they speak their vows? They are making promises to each other. There are several facets to those promises. First, two people are looking into each other's eyes and making promises to each other. The promises are personal. Second, they are making a promise to each other regarding their future together, namely, that they will be there for each other. Third, the purpose of doing so is to elicit and strengthen confidence (and with it joy) in each other. Fourth, the promise and faith of each other establishes and constitutes their relationship or marriage. It establishes the nature and bounds of their marriage. Finally, the promise and faith launches the new life together that ensues.

The Promise Is Personal

While God established marriage for humankind, at this particular wedding the promises being made are between two particular people. The promises are personal, spoken from one person to another person. They are spoken face-to-face while the persons are looking straight into the eyes of each other.

The gospel as promise highlights the personal character of the gospel and, with it, the personal character of God. By contrast, the idea of news or information can carry something of an impersonal and abstract quality with it, especially in our day. We hear or see broadcast news. Or we read newspapers. Or, more likely, we get our news from social media or other online sources. In each of these cases, the news is broadcast out to everyone in general and yet to no one in particular. One can hear about the good news that a war has ended or a terrorist plot has been foiled. And to be sure, that benefits all of us. But those announcements are aimed more generally at the entire population.

To be sure, the gospel is good news for the entire world of which we ourselves are a part. But the gospel as promise goes further by bringing out the personal address of the gospel to us. It speaks to the personal relationship between the one who is making the promise and the one who is hearing the promise.[9] What I mean by that is that in the gospel, God himself is making a promise to us. It is as if God is looking a person in the eye and saying, "I prom-

9. To use Oswald Bayer's language, the gospel is personal "address." See Bayer, *Martin Luther's Theology: A Contemporary Interpretation*, trans. Thomas H. Trapp (Grand Rapids: Eerdmans, 2008), and his earlier work, *Promissio: Geschichte der reformatorischen Wende in Luthers Theologie* (Göttingen: Vandenhoeck & Ruprecht, 1971).

ise that you will be mine forever and that I will harbor no more anger toward you on account of the work of Christ."

It is for this reason that Luther and Melanchthon retained the practice of private confession (AC 11), even though Scripture does not require this particular form of it. But in retaining it they also shifted the focus away from one's confession of sins to the absolution announced, so it would be better to call it "private" or "personal absolution." Here a pastor looks into the eyes of a penitent and announces, "I by the command of our Lord Jesus Christ forgive you your sin in the name of the Father and of the Son and of the Holy Spirit. Amen. Go in Peace" (Small Catechism, par. 28; pp. 361–62). The same thing takes place in baptism—the pastor speaks for Christ by saying, "I baptize you . . ."; or in the Lord's Supper—the pastor says the blood is "shed for you for the forgiveness of sins."[10]

The Promise Is Future Oriented

The promises made between a bride and a bridegroom do not only (or even primarily) pertain to the present. More importantly, they are about their future life together. They may not know what the future holds, but they are making a promise to face it and go through it together.

Again, it is worth noting that Melanchthon rarely renders the term "gospel" as "good news." Though it is certainly proper to render *euangelion* as good news or good tidings, there is a sense where it can still carry too much of a historical ring to it—even in our day. In other words, when we think of news, we think of something that happened yesterday or last week. It is information about the past. It's like hearing about what the stock market did last week or what a politician said on the campaign trail yesterday. Now I have to decide what to do with that knowledge. Do I buy or sell? Do I vote for this candidate or for someone else? So even if the news is good, it is still only information. I must decide what to do with it.

By contrast, the gospel as promise is future oriented. To be sure, it is rooted in what has happened in the past, but based on that past it declares to us what the future now holds for us. In the case of justification, the gospel becomes a promise by which God says to us: "Our future is secure. We will

10. See Phillip Cary's argument that Luther's theology of promise requires an understanding of the "Catholic notion of sacramental efficacy." Phillip Cary, "Why Luther Is Not Quite Protestant: The Logic of Faith in a Sacramental Promise," *Pro Ecclesia* 14, no. 4 (Fall 2005): 455.

pass through the final judgment and be received into the new creation." With regard to forgiveness, it is as if God is saying, "I will not let the past determine or dictate our future together."[11] This feature points to the eschatological character of the promise.

The Promise Seeks Faith

In a wedding, the groom promises to be there for his bride in sickness or in health, in wealth or in poverty. Why does a bridegroom make such a promise to his bride? He seeks to give her confidence that he will be there for her and only her, no matter what. The whole purpose of making that promise is to instill confidence and joy in his bride—not just in her intellect but in her entire being.

The understanding of the gospel as promise redefines faith for Lutherans. News seeks to inform. A promise seeks faith. But it seeks a particular kind of faith, a faith that is confidence and trust. A good example of this can be found when Melanchthon moves to the *confirmatio* section of Apology 4, in which he must argue for faith alone. He begins with the definition of faith itself. He opens that section by stating that it is not simply historical knowledge that could be acquired by one's own powers[12] or that would allow moral sin to coexist with it.[13] To the contrary, faith is to "assent to the promise of God, in which forgiveness of sins and justification are bestowed freely on account of Christ." He goes on to insist that to avoid the misunderstanding that it is merely knowledge (residing in human reason), "we will add further that to have faith is to desire and to receive the offered promise of the forgiveness of sins and justification" (Ap 4.48; p. 128). In the German translation, it speaks of faith as "embracing" the promise. I particularly like that language, as embracing includes both the idea of taking hold of an idea in the mind and making it personally one's own.[14]

11. I am indebted to my colleague Joel Okamoto for this fortuitous way of expressing it.

12. Such faith resided in the intellect and could be acquired apart from grace (*fides acquisita*). "Acquired faith refers only to the objective factuality of God's revealing acts in history." Heiko Oberman, *Harvest of Medieval Theology* (Grand Rapids: Eerdmans, 1967), 73. In his *Loci Communes*, Melanchthon criticizes the "herd of sophists" sharply for defining faith as assent to evangelical histories (175).

13. "Sola fides, all agreed, was a *fides informis*, even a *fides mortua*—an unformed, dead faith which even the demons could have. Faith needed to be informed by love, for love, not faith, was the religious glue." Ozment, *The Age of Reform*, 242.

14. One finds similar language for faith throughout Luther and Melanchthon. Faith means to cling to the promise, take hold of it, hold on to it and the like.

For Melanchthon, Paul testifies that righteousness thus depends "'on faith, in order that the promise may . . . be guaranteed.' He realizes that the promise cannot be received in any other way than by faith" (Ap 4.50; p. 128). Promise and faith are corollaries. It is the very nature of a promise that it seeks faith. The whole point of making a promise is to elicit faith or create faith in the person to whom you are making the promise. The focus of each is upon the promise that each other has made and not on whether or not the other believes.

The Promise Elicits the Faith It Seeks

When the groom makes a promise to his bride, the last thing he wants to hear upon making his promise is for her to laugh and say, "I don't believe you." So why does the bride not laugh at him (at least I'm not aware of any bride doing so)? Because his promise elicits the very confidence that it seeks. Another way of saying this is that the promise creates the very faith that it seeks! Why? Because the bride knows her groom. She knows his character and trustworthiness.

Melanchthon brings out this point on why the promise of the gospel elicits and creates faith and why faith in turn can count on the promise. He inserts (perhaps at the suggestion of Luther) into the second edition of the Apology one of the Lutheran reformers' favorite passages about Abraham. Melanchthon points out that "'Abraham believed God, and it was reckoned to him as righteousness,' that is, Abraham realized that he had a gracious God only on account of God's promise. He assented to the promise and did not allow himself to be pulled away from it, even though he saw that he was unclean and unworthy. He realized that God keeps a promise *on account of his faithfulness* and not on account of our works or merits" (Ap 4.58A; p. 129 [emphasis added]). In other words, the promise is sure because God is faithful.[15] He speaks the truth. Phillip Cary rightly observes the following about Luther: "God is sure to be true to his word, whether we believe it or not. Hence the certainty of faith is rigorously objective rather than subjective, in the sense that what makes faith certain is not the activity of the subject of faith (the perception, reasoning, intuition or experience of the believer) but the faithfulness of the object of faith (the fact that God keeps his word). The certainty of Christians is not based on

15. See David Steinmetz, "Abraham and the Reformation," in *Luther in Context* (Bloomington: Indiana University Press, 1986), 32–46.

their faith but on God's faithfulness."[16] The promise of God elicits faith because God himself is trustworthy. He has remained faithful to his promises spoken through the ages. In a sense, God says, "You have my word on it!"

Excursus: The Promise Becomes Good News—the *Verba Dei* and *Opera Dei*

We need to distinguish law and gospel as theological topics or loci (the *verba Dei*) and law and gospel as the two works of God (*opera Dei*). The former deals with the content of law and gospel. The latter deals with its impact upon the hearer.

In the opening of his *narratio* in Apology 4, Melanchthon states that all "Scripture should be divided into these two main topics: the law and the promises. In some places it communicates the law. In other places it communicates the promise concerning Christ" (Ap 4.5; p. 121). Then in Apology 12, which deals with repentance (where justification hits the road in practice), Melanchthon shifts to focus on the effects of law and promises when he writes, "The entire Scripture is divided into these two works. One part is the law, which reveals, denounces, and condemns sin. The second part is the gospel, that is, the promise of grace given in Christ" (Ap 12.53; p. 195).

Melanchthon does not make this distinction to provide systematic categories by which a theologian can organize all of theology, as if in volume 1 you put all the law statements (imperatives) and in volume 2 all the gospel statements (indicatives). The church has other organizational categories such as the one provided by the creeds (and Melanchthon's ordering of the Augsburg Confession). Instead, Melanchthon makes this distinction in order to demonstrate the source of both positions on justification. But, that having been said, one can certainly say that law and gospel are pastoral categories for *applying* or *addressing* theology to people so as to produce contrition or awaken and strengthen faith.

In Apology 4, Melanchthon expounds law and gospel as two theological topics, whereas in Apology 12 he then utilizes them as categories for speaking about the two works of God (*opera Dei*).

The Formula of Concord (1577) brings this distinction out nicely in two paragraphs that provide the most succinct summary of law and gospel within the Lutheran Confessions. The law "is a divine teaching in which the righteous, unchanging will of God revealed how human beings were created in their nature, thoughts, words, and deeds to be pleasing and acceptable to God." Then it shifts

16. Cary, "Why Luther Is Not Quite Protestant," 450.

to the effects worked by the law. "This law also threatens those who transgress it with God's wrath and temporal and eternal punishments. For, as Luther stated against the nomoclasts, 'Everything that reproves sin is and belongs to the law. Its proper function is to reprove sin and to lead to the knowledge of sin'" (FC SD 5.17; p. 584).

The gospel, by contrast, shows what God does for us. It "teaches what people should believe, namely, that they receive from God the forgiveness of sins; that is, that the Son of God, our Lord Christ, has taken upon himself the curse of the law and borne it, atoned and paid for all our sins; that through him alone we are restored to God's grace, obtain the forgiveness of sins through faith, and are delivered from death and all the punishments of our sins and are saved eternally" (FC SD 5.20; p. 585). Then again it shifts to the effects worked by the gospel. "For everything that provides comfort—everything that offers the favor and grace of God to those who have transgressed the law—is and is called the gospel in the strict sense. It is good news, joyous news" (FC SD 5.21; p. 585). Note how the first part of the definition focuses on its content (*verba Dei*) while the second part shifts to its work or effect (*opera Dei*).

The law can become bad news for me by addressing me in such a way as to accuse me, crush me, and kill me. By contrast, when the gospel is addressed to me as such, as one who has been crushed and killed, it produces a gospel effect (*opus*) in my conscience, namely, peace and joy.

The Promise Says "For You" and Faith Says "For Me"

Upon hearing the promise of her groom, the bride says, "I believe you." She embraces it with her entire being. But what does that mean? It means that she knows that he will be there for her in sickness and in health. He will always be there for her. He will never leave her.

Lutherans have classically expressed this corollary of promise and faith with the prepositional phrases "for you" and "for me." The promise states that Christ died "for you." Christ rose "for you." The addition of that prepositional phrase brings the language of the promise to the foreground. This is the language of the gospel. By the same token, faith then responds with the prepositional phrase "for me." With the "for you" of the promise and the "for me" of faith, it is important to keep in mind that the focus of faith is not on the activity of believing, but upon the object of faith. The emphasis is not so much on me as it is on the gift promised to me.[17] The focus is on the external word (*externum verbum*) by which his work incorporates me into his story.

One of the best examples of this "for me" of faith can be found in Luther's explanation of all three articles of the Apostles' Creed in his Small Catechism. In each case he avoids falling off the road either by turning faith exclusively into an intellectual activity of the head (*fides quae creditur*) or by turning faith into exclusively a matter of the heart (*fides qua creditur*). Instead he holds them together. He does this first by speaking of God not in terms of propositions to be believed but in terms of God's activity for us within this world. Second, he focuses faith's attention not upon itself, but upon the works and gifts of God. God created me, preserves me, provides for me, protects me, defends me, redeems me, purchases and wins me, calls me, enlightens me, sanctifies me, keeps me, forgives me, and will raise me from the dead.

The Promise Holds Faith Captivated

Notice what the bride focuses upon when she hears her groom's promises. Is it the activity of her believing? No. She focuses on her bridegroom and the content of the words he speaks to her. That is all she can think about. It is him and his promise that fill her heart. When they are not together, it is the promise that keeps her close to him. She is, to borrow a line from the musical *Grease*, "hopelessly devoted to him."

Analogously, when it comes to the promise of the gospel and faith, we can say that the promise holds faith captivated and enthralled. It keeps our hearts focused upon our bridegroom, Jesus Christ. Look who he is! Look what he has done! This is what he has done for me in life and death. He is now mine forever! I think this is captured nicely in Luther's treatment of the second article of the Apostles' Creed: "I believe that Jesus Christ . . . is my Lord." And a little later in that same explanation, he declares that Jesus has done all this "that I may belong to him, live under him in his kingdom, and serve him in eternal righteousness, innocence, and blessedness" (*BC*, 355). And faith clings to how this is free and undeserved. How did I ever deserve such love? I didn't!

We get a sense of this also in Luther's discussion of the sacraments in the Small Catechism. Luther had emphasized the importance of faith over and against Rome's view *ex opere operato* of the sacraments in the early 1520s.

17. For a helpful discussion of this, see Cary, "Why Luther Is Not Quite Protestant," 447–86.

But by the late 1520s, Luther's attention turned toward Zwingli and the Anabaptists. Over and against this wing of the Reformation, he now had to stress the objective efficacy of the promise. And so in both baptism and the Lord's Supper, a strong emphasis is placed upon the word (command and promise) by which God works in water, bread, and wine. This is what faith focuses on.

Promise and Faith Form the New Relationship

This brings us to the final characteristic of the marriage analogy. The promise and faith bind each to the other. The pastor declares, "I now pronounce you husband and wife." Here, Luther draws upon German marriage law that what is legally the groom's now becomes the bride's, and what is legally the bride's comes into the groom's possession.

In the case of the promise and faith, our sin and death become Christ's; Christ's righteousness and life become mine. This is Luther's joyous exchange! And so because faith is the reception of a personal promise, it constitutes a new relationship of righteousness.

This is precisely what Roman Catholic theologians considered offensive. How could the pure and holy Christ unite himself with a prostitute? In 1526, Jacob Hochstraten, the Dominican inquisitor of Cologne, contended,

> What else do those who boast of such a base spectacle do than make the soul . . . a prostitute and an adulteress, who knowingly and wittingly connives to deceive her husband [Christ] and, daily committing fornication upon fornication and adultery upon adultery, makes the most chaste of men a pimp? As if Christ does not take the trouble . . . to choose . . . a pure and honorable lover! As if Christ requires from her only belief and trust and has no interest in her righteousness and the other virtues! As if a certain mingling of righteousness with iniquity and of Christ with Belial were possible![18]

Of course, that was exactly the point for Luther. Luther expresses this nowhere more winsomely than in the final thesis (28) of the Heidelberg Disputation: "The love of God does not find, but creates that which is pleasing to it."[19] In

18. Steven Ozment, *A Mighty Fortress: A New History of the German People* (New York: HarperCollins, 2004), 84.

19. *LW* 31:41.

other words, we are not loved by God because we are so lovable; we are lovable because we are loved by God!

And this is what Melanchthon drives at when he speaks of justification both in terms of God declaring us righteous in the gospel and in terms of God making us righteous. Now this was perhaps seen in Catholic-Lutheran bilateral dialogues as a place where they could find agreement.[20] But such an opinion ignores Melanchthon's conception of the promise. For Melanchthon, God's word does what it says. When it declares us righteous, it makes us righteous. That is, it bestows upon us the righteousness of Christ. A new relationship now exists. And it is a genuine relationship.

By contrast, Melanchthon's opponents viewed the gospel information upon which you had to act with the help of grace. Once you have received an infusion of grace, you may go on to perform works of love with the assistance of grace. Hopefully, by the end of your life you have developed the *habitus* of being a righteous person, a loving person. At this point, God's word of justification becomes a descriptive word; it describes what someone has become with the assistance of God's grace. At times, Roman Catholics will regard the Lutheran view of justification as a "legal fiction." God says we are righteous, but we really are not. But that misses the point of what Lutherans mean by the promise or the word.

For Lutherans, the promise of the gospel, to borrow from contemporary linguistic theory, is a performative word. That is to say, it does what it says. Because it is God who is speaking, the word actually accomplishes its purpose. Here the Creator is speaking, the very one by whose word creation comes into existence. Now the Creator speaks again, this time by bringing righteousness into existence for the sinner, or better, by bestowing the righteousness of Christ upon the sinner.

Promise and Faith Embark upon a New Life

After speaking their promises to each other and being declared husband and wife, the bride and groom go running or skipping joyously down the aisle, out

20. See *Confessing One Faith: A Joint Commentary on the Augsburg Confession by Lutheran and Catholic Theologians*, ed. George Wolfgang Forell and James F. McCue, in cooperation with Wenzel Lohff and others (Minneapolis: Augsburg, 1982). This joint commentary was written partly in response to a suggestion by Cardinal Joseph Ratzinger that Rome might be able to recognize the Augsburg Confession as a genuine Christian confession.

of the church, and embark upon their new life together. It is a life that spills outward toward others around them (especially children).

For the Christian, faith makes alive and gives new spiritual impulses (Ap 4; pp. 120–73). It inaugurates a new life. And in this new life, faith is irrepressible in its activity. The Formula of Concord quotes Luther as describing faith in precisely that way. "It is a living, busy, active, mighty thing, this faith. It is impossible for it not to be doing good works incessantly. It does not ask whether good works are to be done, but before the question is asked, it has already done them, and is constantly doing them" (FC SD 4.10; p. 576). So one no longer needs the law? This is where the Lutheran debate over the third use of the law enters the discussion.

I would contend that, in the Formula of Concord, the third use of the law primarily functions to *channel* a believer's energies in a constructive and positive direction (think of super-active children whose energies need to be channeled in positive directions). So faith arises and says, I want to serve God! What can I do? The old Adam will immediately arise and say, "You want to do good works? I've got some really good works for you to do. Go on a pilgrimage, buy some relics, etc." At that point, the law in its third use enters to channel our energies in directions that lead us to be the people that God created us to be and now has re-created us to be.[21]

The Gospel as Promise

The promise of forgiveness is key for defining the content of the gospel and the goal of the gospel in terms of awakening new life and, with it, peace and joy. It is also key for speaking about the nature of faith, as a corollary to the promise, as involving the whole person (and not just the intellect), for its focus on the external word, and for the effect of the new life that it produces. The promise of the forgiveness of sins on account of Christ is central to any discussion of the gospel on the part of Lutherans.

21. In other words, human creaturely life looks like this and not like that. For this reason, article 6 of the Augsburg Confession states that faith ought to produce good works *as God has commanded.* And article 6 of the Formula of Concord consistently contrasts the self-chosen works of the monks with those commanded by God (FC SD 4.3, 20; pp. 587, 590). And in the Large Catechism Luther frequently contrasts the Ten Commandments with the vows of the Carthusian monks.

Chapter 4

The Gospel in the Reformed Tradition

Scott R. Swain

Reformed dogmatics has much to say about "the gospel of the glory of the blessed God" (1 Tim. 1:11) because Holy Scripture has much to say about this topic. The gospel begins and ends with "the blessed God," who alone possesses the fullness of being in and of himself in the happy fellowship of the Father, the Son, and the Holy Spirit. The gospel concerns the "glory" of this blessed God: the external manifestation of his intrinsic radiance in the sending of the Son and the Spirit to redeem and sanctify his elect children in order that they too might share in the beatitude of his triune life (1 Tim. 3:16; Titus 2:13; 3:4–7). The gospel concerns the manner in which—at great and gracious cost to himself—the blessed Trinity makes us blessed through the incarnation, death, and exaltation of Jesus Christ to the praise of his glorious grace.

The vocation of dogmatics relative to the gospel is to provide a conceptual representation of biblical teaching about the good news of Jesus Christ, attentive to both the matter and scope of that teaching, as received and confessed by the church, and oriented to the church's edification in the knowledge and love of God. To speak faithfully of the gospel in a Reformed key is to speak of the mystery of the Son of God manifested in the flesh for us and our salvation, a mystery whose meaning exhibits itself in relation to and distinction from the law of God and, more fully, in relation to the triune God and his works in the economy of nature, grace, and glory.

What follows is a dogmatic sketch of the gospel in the form of five theses, which seek to summarize and commend, for the sake of fraternal dialogue, the teaching of Holy Scripture as confessed by the catholic church of the Reformed confessions.

Thesis 1: The Gospel

> The gospel is the word and work of God in Jesus Christ the Son of God who became incarnate to redeem sinners from their guilt and misery that they might receive the gifts of righteousness and eternal life in and through him to the glory and praise of God.

a. The gospel is the work of God in Jesus Christ. In briefest form, the gospel is the announcement "that Jesus Christ has come in the flesh" (1 John 4:2). In more extensive form, as narrated in the Gospels and proclaimed in the apostolic writings in accordance with the Old Testament Scriptures, the gospel is the entire sequence of events that constitute the Son of God's incarnate mission to save sinners: from his conception and birth, through his public ministry, culminating in his death on the cross for our sins, to his resurrection on the third day, ascension, and enthronement at the Father's right hand, to which we direct our minds in eager expectation of his return. The Heidelberg Catechism recognizes the second article of the Apostles' Creed as a faithful summary of God's redeeming work in and through his incarnate Son (HC 24) and expounds the significance of that work by means of commentary upon the various titles, events, and saving benefits attributed to the Lord Jesus Christ therein (HC 29–52). Though less explicitly tied to the language of the Apostles' Creed, a similar summary and exposition of the person and work of the Redeemer appear in the Westminster Standards (WCF 8; WSC 21–28; WLC 36–56). According to these descriptions, the objects of Christ's redeeming work in the gospel are elect sinners, guilty and miserable.[1] The benefits secured by Christ's redeeming work are the gifts of righteousness and eternal life, enjoyed through filial union and communion with Jesus Christ, to the glory and praise of God (John 1:12–13; Rom. 5:21; HC 1–2; WCF 8.1; WLC 59; 65–83).[2]

As the preceding discussion suggests, the central subject matter of the gospel is Jesus Christ and his redeeming work, *historia salutis* rather than *ordo salutis*, redemption accomplished rather than redemption applied. According to Zacharias Ursinus, the gospel is "the doctrine which reveals, describes, and

1. The scope of my present assignment does not permit engagement with differing views regarding the nature and objects of Christ's satisfaction in Reformed theology. On this topic, see Richard A. Muller, *Calvin and the Reformed Tradition: On the Work of Christ and the Order of Salvation* (Grand Rapids: Baker Academic, 2012).

2. *SPT* 22.20–21, 23.

offers him [the Mediator] unto us."[3] Similarly, according to the Leiden Synopsis, "the gospel is entirely occupied with telling about his redeeming work, his satisfaction for our sins, and his other benefits."[4] The identification of the person and work of Christ as the central subject matter of the gospel does not intend to separate Christ from his benefits or to divide redemption accomplished from redemption applied. According to the Reformed confession, the latter follows the former by God's design as Christ in his kingly office applies the benefits of the gospel to the elect by means of the ministry of Word and sacrament, through which the Holy Spirit awakens repentance and faith in obedience to the gospel. However, the latter work of applying the benefits of redemption, as well as our embrace of Christ and his benefits through faith and repentance, are "the proper effect" of the gospel,[5] not its central subject matter, as we will see more fully below.

b. The gospel is the Word of God in Jesus Christ. Jesus Christ is not only the central subject matter of the gospel. As the consubstantial Son of the Father, he is also the sole author of the gospel (Heb. 1:1–4). The great work of salvation accomplished by the Lord was "declared at first by the Lord" and later attested by "those who heard" (Heb. 2:3) in keeping with what God had "promised beforehand through his prophets in the holy Scriptures" (Rom. 1:2). In addressing the question of how we come to know the redeeming work of Jesus Christ, Heidelberg Catechism 19 responds: "the holy gospel tells me." The catechism acknowledges the instrumentality of patriarch and prophet, and of old covenant sacrifice and ceremony, in revealing the gospel, but it identifies God as the primary author of the gospel: "God began to reveal the gospel already in Paradise; later, God proclaimed it by the holy patriarchs" and so forth; "finally, [God] fulfilled it through God's own dear Son." The gospel is the Word of God alone, neither from man nor by man, though witnessed by prophets and apostles (Gal. 1:12).

The Reformed emphasis upon the divine authorship of the gospel is not meant to undermine or qualify Holy Scripture's status as the Word of God (WCF 1). Nor is it designed to delegitimize the gospel ministry (WCF 15.1; 25.4; 28.2; 30.2; WLC 63; 176; 191). It is meant rather to characterize the nature of biblical revelation with respect to the gospel. While much of Scripture is devoted to rehabilitating the knowledge of God otherwise available to creatures

3. Ursinus, *Commentary on the Heidelberg Catechism*, trans. G. W. Willard (reprint, Phillipsburg, NJ: Presbyterian and Reformed, 1852), 101.

4. *SPT* 22.19.

5. *SPT* 22.26, 32–33.

through general revelation but despoiled through idolatry and sin (see, for example, Rom. 1:18–32), the biblical revelation of the gospel concerns things "not known naturally" but "divinely revealed to the Church alone through Christ, the Mediator."[6] From the beginning to the end of the world, "The gospel is . . . the doctrine which the Son of God, our Mediator, revealed from heaven," the doctrine "which he brought from the bosom of the Eternal Father."[7] In this respect, the Leiden Synopsis describes "the Father as the foremost author of the gospel, since it is from his bosom that it is said to have proceeded (John 1:18)," "the Son as the most trustworthy ambassador of the Father, who earnestly declares that the words he brings forward are not his own but those of his Father (John 14:10, 24)," and "the Holy Spirit as the most closely related interpreter of the Son's words, since Christ says that the Spirit would declare nothing new to the apostles, but that he would announce the same things that they had heard from himself (John 16:13, 14)."[8] From and through and to the triune God alone come the word and work of the gospel.

Thesis 2: Law and Gospel

> The relation and distinction between law and gospel, which constitute the twofold administration of the covenant of grace, provide the immediate context for understanding the Word and work of God in Jesus Christ.

a. The Word and work of God in the gospel are closely related to the Word and work of God in the law.[9] According to the apostle Paul in Romans 1:1–2, "the gospel of God" was "promised beforehand through his prophets in the holy Scriptures." Later in the same epistle the apostle declares that "the Law and the Prophets"—Pauline shorthand for the Old Testament writings—"bear

6. Ursinus, *Commentary*, 104.

7. Ursinus, *Commentary*, 101.

8. *SPT* 22.11.

9. For more extensive treatment of the place of the law in Reformed theology, see Michael Allen's essay in the present volume, along with Brenton C. Ferry, "Works in the Mosaic Covenant: A Reformed Taxonomy," in *The Law Is Not of Faith: Essays on Works and Grace in the Mosaic Covenant*, ed. Bryan D. Estelle, J. V. Fesko, and David VanDrunen (Phillipsburg, NJ: Presbyterian and Reformed, 2009), ch. 3; and Mark Jones, "The 'Old' Covenant," in *Drawn into Controversie: Reformed Theological Diversity and Debates within Seventeenth-Century British Puritanism*, ed. Michael A. G. Haykin and Mark Jones (Göttingen: Vandenhoeck & Ruprecht, 2011), ch. 8.

witness" to the righteousness of God revealed in the gospel (Rom. 3:21). From one vantage point, therefore, the ἐπαγγελία of Old Testament law is merely a different dispensation of and preparation for the εὐαγγέλιον of the New Testament (Gal. 3:8, 18). "The law was given through Moses; grace and truth came through Jesus Christ" (John 1:17; HC 19).

From another vantage point, Holy Scripture presents the Word and work of God in the law in sharp antithesis to the Word and work of God in the gospel. The one performs God's work of "killing," the other God's work of "making alive" (Deut. 32:39; 2 Cor. 3:6). The same apostle who proclaims the coordinated testimony of Old Testament ἐπαγγελία and New Testament εὐαγγέλιον declares that "by works of the law no human being will be justified in his sight, since through the law comes knowledge of sin" (Rom. 3:20). And he proclaims that in the gospel of Jesus Christ "the righteousness of God has been manifested apart from the law" (Rom. 3:21). From this vantage point, the law of God only makes me know my "miserable condition" (HC 3). It belongs to the gospel to make me know "how I am set free from all my sin and misery" (HC 2, 19).

b. The covenant of grace explains, at least in part, how Reformed theology understands the relation and distinction between law and gospel. In terms of their positive relation, the Westminster Confession of Faith describes law and gospel as two temporal administrations of one covenant of grace: "This covenant [of grace] was differently administered under the time of the law, and in the time of the gospel" (WCF 7.5). Nevertheless, "there are not . . . two covenants of grace differing in substance, but one and the same under different administrations" (WCF 7.6). Within this redemptive-historical scheme, "law" refers to the Mosaic covenant, which was the initial, typical fulfillment of the Abrahamic covenant and which also served to govern the kingship under the Davidic covenant (Deut. 17:14–20) until the coming of the new covenant, which rendered the Mosaic covenant, as an administration of the covenant of grace, obsolete (Rom. 6:14; 7:1–6; 2 Cor. 3:11; Heb. 8:13). Under this aspect, the law adumbrates the grace of God in Jesus Christ as the ἐπαγγελία of the εὐαγγέλιον.

In terms of the antithesis between law and gospel, "law" refers more specifically to the "moral law." In the beginning, the moral law is written on the hearts of Adam and Eve in the garden and published in the covenant of works. Later, in the Mosaic administration of the covenant of grace, the moral law is republished in the Ten Commandments at Sinai. Finally, the moral law is written anew on the hearts of believers within the context of the new covenant (WCF 19). The moral law thus binds all human beings, regenerate and unregenerate. Among its diverse functions across the economies of nature and grace, the moral law (i) indicates the path of perfect obedience that leads to eternal life, (ii) exposes and condemns sin, (iii) demonstrates fallen humanity's need for the perfect obedience and satisfaction of Jesus Christ if we are to enjoy the blessings of righteousness and eternal life, and (iv) directs the redeemed sinner in the life of gratitude (HC 3–11, 114–15; WCF 19.6).

It is in the second aforementioned sense that the moral law constitutes the Mosaic covenant a letter that kills and a ministry of death (2 Cor. 3:6–7). This is not because the Mosaic covenant *qua covenant* is a republication of the covenant of works (Gal. 3:21; WCF 7.5; 19.2). Rather, it is due to the weakness of fallen human nature and to the fact that the Mosaic covenant publishes the moral law only "on tablets of stone" and not "on tablets of human hearts" (Rom. 8:3, 8; 2 Cor. 3:7, 9). For these reasons, the Mosaic covenant brings about the knowledge of sin and condemnation: "For all who rely on works of the law are under a curse; for it is written, 'Cursed be everyone who does not abide by all things written in the Book of the Law, and do them'" (Gal. 3:10; Rom. 3:19–20; 5:13; HC 3–11).

c. The relation and distinction between law and gospel, as comprehended within the covenant of grace, further enhance our understanding of Christ's incarnate mission. With respect to the relation, under the ἐπαγγελία of Old Testament law Christ both signifies beforehand and bestows efficaciously to old covenant saints that which he reveals more clearly and bestows more efficaciously under the εὐαγγέλιον of the New Testament (1 Cor. 10:1–4; 12:13). The law's "promises, prophecies, sacrifices, circumcision, the paschal lamb, and other types and ordinances delivered to the people of the Jews" all signified beforehand "Christ to come," and "were for that time sufficient and efficacious, through the operation of the Spirit, to instruct and build up the elect in faith in the promised Messiah, by whom they had full remission of sins, and eternal salvation" (WCF 7.5).[10] Though Christ comes in the flesh *after* the law to fulfill the law, by virtue of his eternal appointment as mediator of the covenant of grace he also comes *before* the law and performs his ministry through the law among his people as the one who, in the fullness of time, will come in the flesh (WCF 8.1). There is but one redeemer and one work of redemption under both Old and New Testament dispensations (WCF 8.6).

With respect to the distinction between law and gospel within the covenant of grace, the law reveals our need for Christ, defines the work of Christ,

10. Contra the standard Roman Catholic view, recently summarized by Thomas Joseph White, *Exodus*, Brazos Theological Commentary (Grand Rapids: Brazos, 2016), 99–103.

and guides us in the new life brought into effect by the work of Christ. What the law cannot accomplish due to the weakness of fallen human nature, God does in Jesus Christ, the mediator of the covenant of grace (Rom. 8:3; Heb. 9:15; HC 18; WCF 8.1–3; 21.2; WLC 32–42). The law reveals God's righteous will, which the children of Adam cannot fulfill (Rom. 8:8), and therefore sentences the children of Adam to misery and death (Rom. 3:19–20; 6:3; 1 Cor. 15:56). In his incarnate mission, the Son of God redeems the children of Adam, making them children of God and heirs of eternal life (Gal. 4:4–7), by fulfilling the righteous requirement of God's law (Matt. 3:15; Rom. 5:12–21) and by bearing the curse of God's law on their behalf (Gal. 3:13; Heb. 2:10–18; 1 Pet. 2:24). Thus Johannes Wollebius: "The gospel is the good news, or teaching concerning the Son of God, who was sent into the world so that, after assuming our nature, he might undergo the curse of the law in our place and by his perfect obedience to it earn eternal life for us."[11] As a consequence of Christ's redeeming work, "the righteous requirement of the law" is now "fulfilled in us, who walk not according to the flesh but according to the Spirit" (Rom. 8:4). "Because I belong" to Jesus Christ, the mediator of the covenant of grace, Christ by his Spirit "makes me wholeheartedly willing and ready from now on to live for him" (HC 1, 2, 91–115).

As the preceding discussion indicates, the law not only plays various roles within the one covenant of grace, illumining the nature of Christ's person and work in the gospel. The law also plays contrasting roles in the prelapsarian covenant of works and the postlapsarian covenant of grace. In the former, the moral law functions as the covenantal condition for inheriting eternal life (WCF 7.2; 19.1). In the latter, the moral law points to our need for a mediator to fulfill that condition on our behalf and to bring about our evangelical obedience through union and communion with him (HC 12–18, 114–15; WCF 8.4–5; 19.6–7). Ursinus draws the contrast well in his Larger Catechism. Question 36 asks: "What is the difference between the law and the gospel?" The answer:

> The law contains the natural covenant, established by God with humanity in creation, that is, it is known by humanity by nature, it requires our perfect obedience to God, and it promises eternal life to those who keep it and threatens eternal punishment to those who do not. The gospel, however, contains the covenant of grace, that is, although it exists, it is not known at all by nature; it shows us the fulfillment in Christ of the

11. Johannes Wollebius, *Compendium of Christian Theology*, in *Reformed Dogmatics*, ed. and trans. John W. Beardslee III (Eugene, OR: Wipf and Stock, 2009), 85.

> righteousness that the law requires and the restoration in us of that righteousness by Christ's Spirit; and it promises eternal life freely because of Christ to those who believe in him.[12]

By its reference to creation, human nature, and the natural covenant instituted by God with humanity in the beginning, Ursinus's statement suggests that, although the postlapsarian dynamics of law and gospel are integral to a Reformed account of the gospel, they do not exhaust that account. To appreciate the full scope of Reformed teaching about the gospel, therefore, we must locate that teaching within a broader context.

Thesis 3: The Triune God, the Works of God, and the Gospel

> The triune God and his works in the economy of nature, grace, and glory provide the broad context for understanding the Word and work of God in Jesus Christ.

a. The gospel is the Word and work of the triune God, from whom and through whom and to whom are all things (Rom. 11:36). Accordingly, when speaking of the gospel, Reformed dogmatics follows a method of "reduction," tracing the gospel not simply to its immediate principles and causes within the historical economy of salvation but ultimately to its deepest principles and causes within the blessed Trinity. Following this method, Reformed dogmatics identifies the triune God as the supreme author, end, and subject matter of the gospel.

As noted above, the triune God is the supreme author of the gospel insofar as the gospel is a Word authored by the Father, communicated by the embassy of the Son, and interpreted by the Holy Spirit. According to the Leiden Synopsis, the triune God's authorial relation to the gospel encompasses not only the publication of the gospel in time but also the planning of the gospel in eternity.[13] "God, the Father, Son, and Holy Spirit" is "the principal efficient cause" of his eternal, evangelical purpose for creation: the summing up of all things under one messianic head in Jesus Christ (Matt. 11:27; Eph. 1:10; 3:9–11).[14] Moreover, the "impelling cause" of this eternal, evangelical purpose for

12. Ursinus, The Larger Catechism, question and answer 36, in Lyle D. Bierma, *An Introduction to the Heidelberg Catechism: Sources, History, Theology* (Grand Rapids: Baker Academic, 2005).

13. *SPT* 22.7–11.

14. *SPT* 22.7–8.

creation is nothing but "God's unrestricted mercy and goodwill with which he purposed to embrace the wretched human race that had fallen into sin by the guilt of Adam."[15] The giving of the Son to be the redeemer and head of God's elect and the giving of the elect to be his seed flow solely from the sovereign, gracious good pleasure of God (WCF 3; 8.1; WLC 30; 32).

As the gospel is from the triune God, so also it is to the triune God. The triune God is the supreme end of the gospel in two senses. The triune God is the supreme end of the gospel in that "The ultimate goal of the Gospel is the glory of God, to whom praise of his highest mercy and justice is ascribed in this Gospel's testimony, because he did not spare his own Son, our surety, but gave him up to an accursed death on the cross for us, in order that he might reconcile us to himself for ever, freed from the curse of the law."[16] The triune God is also the supreme end of the gospel because the gospel's ultimate blessing for elect sinners is that, having been "taken up to meet our Lord Jesus," "we shall ascend with him far above all the heavens, so that in his Father's house we shall have the joy of beholding him close and in full, and we shall have blessed communion in eternity."[17] The chief end of the gospel is that we might forever glorify and enjoy the triune God through union and communion with Jesus Christ (HC 1; WSC 1).

The triune God from whom and to whom the gospel flows is, furthermore, the supreme subject matter of the gospel. Although the mystery of the Trinity was adumbrated in the Old Testament,[18] "God was pleased to delay the full and complete revelation of this profound mystery until the coming of the Messiah."[19] In manifesting the mystery once hidden but now revealed in the gospel, Jesus manifests not only the *purpose* of the triune God for his creation, the summing up of all things under one messianic head: "All things have been handed over to me by my Father." Jesus also manifests the *persons* of the triune God to his elect siblings: "no one knows the Son except the Father, and no one knows the Father except the Son and anyone to whom the Son chooses to reveal him" (Matt. 11:27). "No one has ever seen God; the only God, who is at the Father's side, he has made him known" (John 1:18). Because it stands at the apex of gospel revelation, the doctrine of the Trinity "is the core of the Christian faith, the root of all dogmas, the basic content of the new covenant."[20] This is eternal

15. *SPT* 22.12.

16. *SPT* 22.23.

17. *SPT* 22.29.

18. *SPT* 7.39–48.

19. *SPT* 7.38.

20. Herman Bavinck, *Reformed Dogmatics*, vol. 2, *God and Creation*, trans. John Vriend (Grand Rapids: Baker, 2004), 333.

life: to know the only true God through Jesus Christ, whom he has sent, in the fellowship of the Spirit (John 17:3; 1 John 4:13; HC 1).

b. Given its supreme position among gospel verities, the doctrine of the Trinity provides the ultimate framework within which all Reformed teaching, including Reformed teaching about the gospel, receives its meaning and import (HC 24, 26–64). As tempting as it may be to make the gospel, or the distinction between law and gospel, the foundation and critical principle of Christian theology, Reformed dogmatics acknowledges that this privilege belongs to the triune God alone. The Trinity alone is the author and end of all things, including theological knowledge.[21] Robert Jenson rightly asserts: The doctrine of the Trinity "must have explanatory and regulatory use in the whole of theology." The doctrine of the Trinity "is not a separate puzzle to be solved but the framework within which all theology's puzzles are solved."[22]

Following this rule (as well as the examples of Luther and Melanchthon),[23] the Heidelberg Catechism appropriates the works of nature, grace, and glory, as summarized in the three articles of the Apostles' Creed, to the persons of the Father, the Son, and the Holy Spirit, respectively. This is not because God's external works are divided among the persons of the Trinity: *omnia Dei opera, quae ad extra vocantur, sunt indivisa.*[24] The economy of nature is appropriated to the Father, the economy of grace to the Son, and the economy of glory to the Spirit, insofar as one considers in them the *ordo personarum agentium*, "the order of the acting persons."[25] According to this scheme, the sum of Christian teaching concerns "God the Father and our creation," "God the Son and our redemption," and "God the Holy Spirit and our sanctification" (HC 24).

Although the second article of the creed summarizes the gospel in the strict sense, in a broad sense the entire creed summarizes "all that is promised us in the gospel" (HC 22). What is the relationship between the gospel in the strict sense, as encapsulated in the second article of the creed, and the gospel in the broad sense, as encapsulated in all three articles of the creed? A Trinitarian

21. See John Webster, "*Rector et Iudex Super Omnia Genera Doctrinarum?* The Place of the Doctrine of Justification," in *God without Measure: Working Papers in Christian Theology*, vol. 1, *God and the Works of God* (London: Bloomsbury, 2016), ch. 11.

22. Robert W. Jenson, "Karl Barth," in *The Modern Theologians*, ed. David F. Ford, 2nd ed. (Oxford: Blackwell, 1997), 31.

23. Lyle D. Bierma, *The Theology of the Heidelberg Catechism: A Reformation Synthesis* (Louisville: Westminster John Knox, 2013), 27–28.

24. *SPT* 10.8.

25. *SPT* 7.26.

framework illumines the relationship between God's work in the gospel and God's works in nature and glory by enabling us to see God's work in the gospel as the means whereby "grace restores and perfects nature."[26] By virtue of the triune God's sovereign and gracious purpose, the work of God the Son in the gospel restores God the Father's good purpose for creation and brings creation into glorious perfection in God the Holy Spirit.

Thesis 4: The Gospel and Creation

> God the Son's work in the gospel realizes God the Father's good purpose for creation.

a. The Father's good purpose for creation is realized in the Son's work in the gospel. In speaking of the mystery of the gospel, Jesus blesses his Father as "Lord *of* heaven and earth" because the mystery of the gospel realizes his Father's sovereign purpose *for* heaven and earth (Matt. 11:25). In similar fashion, the apostle Paul declares that "the plan of the mystery hidden for ages in God who created all things" is "realized in Christ Jesus our Lord" (Eph. 3:8, 11). According to the gospel, Jesus Christ is the second Adam who, by virtue of the Father's eternal, sovereign appointment, stands in a relationship to God's elect within the covenant of grace that is analogous to the first Adam's relationship to all human beings within the covenant of works. Where the first Adam failed to bring human beings into their God-appointed glory, the second Adam succeeded. By virtue of Christ's fulfillment of the Father's will, we may receive the blessing of eternal life promised in the covenant of works by means of a covenant of grace (Rom. 5:12–21; 1 Cor. 15:47; WLC 22; 31).

Note well: The relationship between God's works in nature, grace, and glory is not constituted by God's works themselves. Grace and glory presuppose nature, but nature does not entail grace, and grace does not entail glory. As Ian McFarland rightly observes, God's works of "redemption and glorification are not the outworking of the creature's own capacities, but gifts of divine grace added to rather than demanded by the grace of creation."[27] The relationship between God's works of nature, grace, and glory derives not from God's works themselves but from God's eternal counsel and decree, his plan

26. *SPT* 11.11.

27. Ian A. McFarland, *From Nothing: A Theology of Creation* (Louisville: Westminster John Knox, 2014), 107.

for the fullness of time to sum up all things in heaven and earth under one messianic head (Eph. 1:10).

b. With this point in place, what may be said of the relationship between God's work in the gospel and God's work in creation? We have already seen that, according to Reformed teaching, the law's entrance into the world is a prelapsarian rather than a postlapsarian phenomenon. Chapter 4, paragraph 2 of the Westminster Confession of Faith describes two functions for the law of God in the state of nature. According to its first function, the law is constitutive of human nature: "God . . . created man, male and female, with reasonable and immortal souls, endued with knowledge, righteousness, and true holiness, after his own image, having the law of God written on their hearts, and power to fulfill it." To be human is to stand, by nature, in an ordered relation to God and neighbor, an ordered relation whose imperatival force is summarized in the twofold love command of Matthew 22:37–40: "You shall love the Lord your God with all your heart and with all your soul and with all your mind. . . . You shall love your neighbor as yourself" (HC 4). The law of God, according to this understanding, is not an external or arbitrary rule, imposed upon the human being from without, to which the human being must struggle to conform an otherwise contrary nature. The law, according to this understanding, is the law of human nature, the natural condition in which the whole human person, body and soul, exists and flourishes to the glory of God: the law of the Lord revives the soul, makes wise the simple, rejoices the heart, and enlightens the eyes (Ps. 19:7–8).

According to its second function in the state of nature, the law of God comes to Adam and Eve from without as loving divine address, directing them upon the path of happy fellowship with God and of peaceful rule over other creatures: "Beside the law written in their hearts, they received a command not to eat of the tree of knowledge of good and evil; which while they kept, they were happy in their communion with God, and had dominion over the creatures" (WCF 4.2). The confession later adds that walking upon the path opened by God's loving address would lead, by God's gracious appointment, to eternal life (WCF 7.2). As noted above, this promised state of glory will follow the state of nature not by virtue of the power and merit of human nature but by virtue of the "voluntary condescension" of God (WCF 7.1) exhibited in God's "special act of providence" in the covenant of works (WSC 12). The reward promised in the covenant of works does not follow from either condign or congruent merit, but from merit "*ex pacto*," from God's loving, covenantal beneficence. That said, the promise of eternal life does require Adam and Eve to enact their natures intelligently and freely in obedience to God's law—which is the law of their being—if they are to have "fruition of him as their blessedness and reward" (WCF 7.1). After all, the *perfection* of human nature promised by God in the covenant of works is the perfection of *human nature*, a perfection that graciously crowns and fittingly realizes human nature as defined and directed by the law of God for happiness in God.

c. The preceding suggests several implications regarding the kind of creature that God makes, the kind of creature that God redeems, and the kind of redeemer God provides to secure his creature's redemption. These implications help us better appreciate how, according to the Reformed confession, the grace of God in the gospel restores and perfects our creaturely nature.

With respect to the kind of creature that God makes, in the state of nature there is no intrinsic conflict between heteronomy and self-realization, between a *verbum externum*, which addresses us from without, and our identities as "dependent rational animals,"[28] who determine ourselves from within by means of rational deliberation. In fact, it is precisely because the human being is the kind of creature it is that God moves this creature to its divinely appointed end of communion with himself, not only by an interior motion of providence that enables the human being to enact its deliberate, rational nature, but also by an external loving address in the covenant of works.[29] On this understanding, human beings flourish as they discover and enact the correspondence that exists between God's Word and human nature. Human beings flourish as they answer God's Word by means of a rational act of worship (Rom. 12:1). We will return to this point below.

We discuss now the kind of redeemer that God provides. As a consequence of our first parents' sin, human beings are born in a state of guilt and misery, alienated from the life of God and also from their own nature (Rom. 1:26; 5:12; Eph. 4:18; WCF 6.2). In his infinite mercy, God has appointed the Lord Jesus Christ to be the redeemer of a sinful people (HC 18). In fulfilling the office of redeemer, Jesus Christ pays a twofold debt to God's law, a debt that miserable sinners cannot pay (Ps. 49:7–8; HC 13): he is born "under the law" (Gal. 4:4) to fulfill the righteous requirement of the law on our behalf and to bear the curse of the law in our place (Gal. 3:13). Fulfilling his office vis-à-vis God's law, moreover, requires that Christ "be made like his brothers in every respect" (Heb. 2:17), for he does not come to help "angels" but to help "the

28. To borrow the language of Alasdair MacIntyre, *Dependent Rational Animals: Why Human Beings Need the Virtues* (Chicago: Open Court, 1999).

29. The Reformed emphasis upon "external" and "internal" in God's providential movement of the human being has deep roots in the Augustinian theological anthropological tradition.

offspring of Abraham" (Heb. 2:16), those whose natures can only be realized in relation to God's law. A perfect redeemer for human beings must be a perfect human being, body and soul (WSC 22), contra the errors of docetism, Apollinarianism, and monothelitism. Accordingly, the Son of God takes upon himself "man's nature, with all the essential properties and common infirmities thereof, yet without sin" (WCF 8.2). As the Danielic "Son of Man," he repudiates the beastly character of human existence east of Eden and, by his perfect human obedience and sacrifice, brings his human siblings from the state of nature into the state of glory (Heb. 2:10; 12:2).[30] Christ the redeemer assumed our nature, miserable because of sin, not to destroy human nature but to bring it—and to bring us in and with him—into its divinely appointed perfection at the Father's right hand (1 Cor. 15:49; 1 John 3:2; HC 49; 52; WCF 8.3; WLC 82–90).

And what kind of creature does God redeem? In the state of nature, God addresses human beings through a *verbum externum* in the covenant of works. In the state of grace, God addresses human beings through a *verbum externum* in the covenant of grace:

> "Come now, let us reason together, says the LORD:
> though your sins are like scarlet,
> they shall be as white as snow." (Isa. 1:18)

The law that exposes our sin and enjoins our repentance and the gospel that promises forgiveness and renewal for Christ's sake are, according to the theological anthropology of the Reformed confession, humanizing words. The law in its pedagogical use declares that sin is contrary to nature, irrational, futile (Rom. 1:18–32), while the gospel announces the healing of human nature, not through any system of self-improvement, or even on the basis of our faith and repentance, but solely on the basis of the finished work of our brother and redeemer, the Lord Jesus Christ (compare Mark 7:18–23 with 7:24–30; Eph. 2:8–9; Col. 2:20–3:4; WCF 11.1). Through the preaching of law and gospel, God addresses us not as "senseless stocks and blocks" but as the kind of creatures we are, thereby remaking us "fully alive" through the powerful operation of the Holy Spirit (WCF 10.1–2). Moreover, because the grace announced in Jesus Christ restores and perfects human nature, the creature justified, adopted, and made alive by the gospel (WCF 10–12) is also made lawful by the gospel (Eph.

30. On the developmental character of Christ's human nature according to Reformed theology, see Michael Allen, *The Christ's Faith: A Dogmatic Account* (London: T. & T. Clark, 2009).

2:10; Rom. 8:4; HC 86–91; 114–15; WCF 13; 19.7; WLC 75; WSC 35). The glory of God is the human being fully alive, and, given our nature, lawfulness is the proper form of human aliveness. Furthermore, lawfulness is the path upon which we walk—if only in the smallest "beginning of this obedience" (HC 114), toward the promised form of human perfection that will be granted us in and through Jesus Christ at his return (Rom. 8:4–14; Heb. 12:14; 1 John 3:3; WCF 13.1).

Thesis 5: The Gospel and the Application of Salvation

> God the Son's work in the gospel results in God the Holy Spirit's gift of eternal life.

a. Having realized his Father's good purpose for creation, Jesus Christ ascended to the right hand of the Father in order to fill his people with the fullness of blessing procured for them by him through his redemptive work (Eph. 1:20–23). As the head of the church, Christ pours out these blessings upon (and through) his church through the person and work of the Holy Spirit: "But when the goodness and loving kindness of God our Savior appeared, he saved us, not because of works done by us in righteousness, but according to his own mercy, by the washing of regeneration and renewal of the Holy Spirit, whom he poured out on us richly through Jesus Christ our Savior, so that being justified by his grace we might become heirs according to the hope of eternal life" (Titus 3:4–7; HC 1). In applying the redemption planned by the Father and procured by the Son, the Spirit brings God's good purpose for creation to its goal in the gift of eternal life. In this regard, "the application of salvation is no less an essential constituent of redemption than the acquisition of it."[31]

b. The saving transfer of the elect from "the domain of darkness" into "the kingdom of [God's] beloved Son" (Col. 1:13) through the powerful operation of the Holy Spirit is "the proper effect" and "goal of the Gospel."[32] This saving transfer occurs in two stages: "in the first one we are led, in this age, into the kingdom of grace."[33] This saving transfer "happens by God's ordained purpose and through the gift of being called to faith, of being justified through faith, and

31. Herman Bavinck, *Reformed Dogmatics*, vol. 3, *Sin and Salvation in Christ*, trans. John Vriend (Grand Rapids: Baker Academic, 2006), 523.

32. *SPT* 22.25–26.

33. *SPT* 22.27.

of being made holy by faith that gives evidence of itself through good works."[34] In the second stage "we are carried up into the kingdom of glory in the age to come."[35] This saving transfer "will take place by the gift of being glorified" and will be consummated in "blessed communion" with the triune God "in eternity."[36] The members of Christ's body thus "enjoy union and communion with him in grace and glory" as a consequence of the Father's purpose and of the Son's redeeming work (WLC 65; 69–90).

c. According to the Heidelberg Catechism, the three articles of the Apostles' Creed enumerate "all that is promised us in the gospel" (HC 22). The preceding paragraph illustrates how we might conceive of the blessings summarized in article 3 under the heading "God the Holy Spirit and Sanctification" as the proper effect and goal of the work summarized in article 2 under the heading "God the Son and Our Redemption" (HC 24). However, a few clarifications must be made regarding the relationship between articles 2 and 3 if we are to understand the nature of the gospel according to the Reformed confession.

The missions of the Son and the Spirit are both integral to the realization of "the mystery hidden for ages in God who created all things" (Eph. 3:9). But they are integral in distinct ways and for distinct reasons. As vital as it is to relate the work of the Father's two hands, "nothing can be more unscriptural in itself, or more pernicious to the souls of men," James Buchanan asserts, than to confuse the work of the Father's two hands.[37]

How should we coordinate and distinguish the works of the Son and the Spirit vis-à-vis the gospel? The consensus response of the Reformed is to say that the Father's evangelical purpose for creation is *accomplished* by Christ's gracious work *for us*, whereas his evangelical purpose for creation is *applied* by the Spirit's gracious work *within us*.[38] This means that, while all the blessings of redemption flow to us on the basis of "the sacerdotal work of Christ," none of them depend upon the gracious work of the Spirit within us.[39] "The Spirit is life *because of* righteousness," the apostle Paul proclaims (Rom. 8:10). Affirming this point does not make the Spirit's work irrelevant to the gospel, but it does properly locate it. According to Buchanan, "The work of the Spirit is

34. *SPT* 22.28.

35. *SPT* 22.27.

36. *SPT* 22.29.

37. James Buchanan, *The Doctrine of Justification: An Outline of Its History in the Church and of Its Exposition from Holy Scripture* (Edinburgh: Banner of Truth, 1997 [1867]), 387.

38. Consider the title of John Murray's book on this topic: *Redemption Accomplished and Applied.*

39. Buchanan, *The Doctrine of Justification*, 387–88.

not the cause, but the consequent of our redemption."[40] Buchanan continues: "Accordingly, so far from leading us to rest on his work *in* us, as the ground of our acceptance with God, that work itself mainly consists in applying to us the redemption which was procured by Christ—by convincing us of our need of it,—by revealing its all-sufficiency,—by 'making known to us the things that are freely given to us of God,'—and disposing, and enabling, us to trust in Christ alone."[41] As the consequence of Christ's redeeming work, the necessity of the Spirit's work "*consists* in deliverance from the power and practice of sin, as well as from its guilt and punishment, and is designed, not only to give us a title to eternal life, but also to 'make us meet for the inheritance of the saints in the light.'"[42]

The Gospel according to the Reformed Confession

The Reformed confession of the gospel seeks to provide a faithful summary of biblical teaching that can guide the reading and proclamation of Holy Scripture, the administration of the sacraments, and the witness of the church to the nations, for the sake of Jesus's name. In expounding this confession, Reformed dogmatics sounds a number of distinctively Protestant notes, particularly with respect to the relationship between law and gospel, even as it seeks to locate law and gospel within the broader catholic context of the triune God and his works in the economy of nature, grace, and glory, as summarized in the Apostles' Creed. Though one cannot and should not ignore the legitimate theological differences that color Lutheran and Reformed accounts of the gospel, on this topic at least, it is right to expect many opportunities for concord, and even consensus, among Lutheran and Reformed theologians who share the catholic faith of the evangelical confessions. This expectation too is one of the proper effects and goals of Christ's work in the gospel.

40. Buchanan, *The Doctrine of Justification*, 395.
41. Buchanan, *The Doctrine of Justification*, 398.
42. Buchanan, *The Doctrine of Justification*, 399–400.

PART III
Law and Gospel in Theology and Ministry

Chapter 5

The Law-Gospel Distinction in Lutheran Theology and Ministry

Steven Paulson

The tip of the iceberg linking Lutheran and Reformed teaching of the law is naturally the third use of the law. Denominations, traditions, and movements among Protestants could be placed on a sliding scale as to how primary or tertiary the third use was. But before the third use was even a germ in the curious mind of Melanchthon, Luther had already thought the impossible: Christ had an unexpected effect on the law. He not only fulfilled it, but ended it. This struck down not only semi-Pelagian notions of good works, but also the most sacred and sticky assumption of theology—that law is eternal, and thus cannot be distinguished from God. Aquinas gives us our definition: "that the whole community of the universe is governed by Divine Reason. Wherefore the very idea of the government of things in God the Ruler of the universe has the rationale of a law. And since Divine Reason's conception of things is not subject to time but is eternal . . . therefore it is that this kind of law must be called eternal." If nominalists make any changes on this rule, it is only to say that God's will is the law and always was, absolutely, even before we knew what legal code he would ordain for us. It did not take long for Reformed orthodoxy to readopt this rule that made God into law and law into God.[1] The

1. Aquinas, *ST* I-II, q. 91, a. 1, reply ob. 3: "The law implies order to the end actively, in so far as it directs certain things to the end; but not passively—that is to say, the law itself is not ordained to the end—except accidentally, in a governor whose end is extrinsic to him, and to which end his law must needs be ordained. But the end of the Divine government is God Himself, and His law is not distinct from Himself. Wherefore the eternal law is not ordained to another end." That nominalists prefer the law to be the will of God before, or along with, reason does not change their assumption of God as law but rather intensifies it. But the most interesting thing for our purposes is that, as Lutheran and Reformed Orthodoxy developed into the seventeenth century, the same assumption governed all theology; see, e.g., Caspar Brochmann (1585–1682), *Universae Theologiae Systema* (1633): "By the Law is to be under-

eternal law has a magnetic pull for sinners, as if it were the source, foundation, future, and essence of law that theoretically precedes and supervenes Luther's introduction of "uses" of law (*usus legis*). The idea that the law is the essence of God is so attractive that it produces in us the unhappy habit of turning gospel into law, which ruins preaching and theology altogether in what we call the legal scheme that forms the depth of the iceberg linking even Reformation theologies beneath the surface.

The difficulty of preaching is also that of doing theology. Sinners want to have direct, immediate contact with God's hidden essence, apart from Christ's cross and forgiveness's preacher. They think they can find this essential righteousness of God, untouched by sin or even Christ, in the law. They do not want to let God be God; they do not want to have a God rather than be a god, they do not want to have a crucified God, and they especially do not want their God in a little word of absolution. This unholy drive is so ingrained and intense (indeed, it is original sin) that it will do anything to have the hidden, unpreached, naked God in majesty rather than the lowly, preached God hiding under the sign of his opposite in the cross and delivered to us through an earthly preacher. In short, humans hate Christ and so spend their time looking for ways to change the gospel into the law, especially by explaining *ad nauseam* how much we really love Christ—or could if we tried harder.

This unholy alchemy separates law into two kinds, one that attacks and kills, and one that inspires and gives life. While Law I hurts, Law II awakens. Yet, while this dream of finding Law II never happens, just as lead will not become gold, it still has deadly consequences. It imagines the theological project to be equating God and law, which, in turn, requires a special theological calculation that abuses Aristotle's essence/accident categories in order to claim that God's eternal, objective, righteous essence is none other than a graceful, nonthreatening, ordered, beautiful, eternal law as the thing that unites the complicated contradictory attributes of mercy and justice. If we could find this Law II, so the story goes, we would immediately love it, and if we loved the *lex aeterna*, we would love God where it counts—in God's self. Sin would then be conquered, and we would no longer be mere creatures, but would participate immediately in God's righteousness as once Adam and Eve luxuriated in the law before the unfortunate incident with the tree. Suddenly, theology becomes romantic recovery of an imagined past and supernatural stretching to the preferred eternal future of our divinization. Regrettably, the greatest

---

stood the eternal and immutable wisdom and decision of God concerning those things which belong or do not belong to *a rational creature*, as such, *united with His will*, that they may or may not be done."

transformers of gospel into law are Lutherans, who had the gospel's birthright by primogeniture, before selling it for pottage.

The Light and the Sowing

When students first heard Luther teach, they experienced something dramatic—the living distinction of law and gospel that opened Scripture before them. The Luther effect continued into the second generation of Lutherans, when Jakob Andreae described what he heard as dazzling enlightenment in the Formula of Concord's fifth article: "The distinction between law and gospel is an especially brilliant light which serves the purpose that the Word of God may be rightly divided." Here we have the Reformation's true bequest, and Andreae wanted the third and subsequent generations of Lutheran/Reformed to cherish it: "we must therefore observe this distinction with particular diligence lest we confuse the two doctrines and change the gospel into law." Therein lies the stumbling block for evangelicals—changing gospel back into law. Why is this herculean task so tempting—especially when one realizes that it is impossible, even for God? Why is it that, upon receiving the free inheritance of the gospel, one wants immediately to hock it for the old prison of law?

Consider the story of the farmer who came sowing seed (Luke 8). Whether by necessity of the method or pure recklessness, the seed went hither and yon, some falling where it was snatched up, some withering in the heat of the day, some reproducing excessively in good soil. Yet to this story Jesus added a threat: "He who has ears to hear, let him hear!" Now, either Jesus inordinately mixed his metaphors, or ears are not a metaphor at all. The parable is a *mysterion* that some catch and others do not. But how come those ears? Are ears signs pointing to an act of will that corresponds to God's act of grace (Erasmus)? A natural or infused grace? Are they doing your best, God will do the rest (nominalists), or perhaps the *obex* idea, that if you cannot accept—at least present no obstacle and refrain from rejecting?

When you are soil, this musing over ears is disastrous because you do not know what kind of soil you are. Am I good or bad? Is Christ scolding or commending me? Indeed, the very sign of bad soil is being turned inward, and never being sure: Do I have the ears, or not? What is worse, Christ's little story gives you no hope for transformation of soil types. How do I cease being rocky or weedy soil, and become good soil? Such questions, however, are not neutral inquiry by a scientist about oneself or God. They are the very symptoms in sinners that the law's principal use is at work. The law is not there to give ears, but to take them away. It does not give, but removes faith in God's word. Worse, the law is there to kill sinners wherever it finds them. Suddenly it dawns on you that soil does not have free will! It cannot change itself. I'm stuck, and can't get out! So, Christ threw his hearers back upon themselves and surgically removed whatever certainty they had.

When the law is at work, bad soil panics, and begins interpreting everything internally, attributing to itself the cause (efficient and final) of everything, especially faith. It thinks of itself as a user of the law. It looks, in particular, to its power of reason as the one unbroken link to the inherent will of God, which is another name for the law. Consequently it twists Scripture into tropology, interpreting Jesus's words as threatening proverbs that hold clandestine moral instructions to direct creatures to what pleases God. This self-protective scheme uses the law as its object, or form of righteousness, since it senses that survival depends upon fighting death with the only tool it finds—the very law that threatens. It takes the gospel seed and turns it into self-transforming soil.

This Unhappy Habit

This unhappy habit is very deep indeed; it enters the conscience's inner ear, and turns Christ's words into suggestions, demands, or accusations. Like a black hole, it sucks everything into its scheme and reads all as a sign of some gnostic instruction that, if decoded, could guide one out of sin and back to God. The conscience first metaphorizes (*this* must mean *that*), then translates "that" to mean a law. Conscience becomes a machine tirelessly manufacturing laws for itself in its pursuit of comfort, or as Luther liked to say: *cor fingens*—the heart is a fabricator.

Indeed, if you could somehow hold to the literal word momentarily, soil has no ears. It is unable to hear what is being said from outside: "he who has ears, let him hear." Soil can be changed from the outside with fertilizer, but it cannot change itself from the inside. Indeed, the insane notion of active soil takes control of the seed and transforms it into its own image—smothering, choking, refusing, and translating everything into its own idiom. Here I lie, I can do no other: "Oh, wretched man that I am, who will deliver me from this body of death?" (Rom. 7).

But then, for a select, little group ("And when his disciples asked him what this parable meant . . ." [Luke 8:9]), Jesus stopped speaking in parables and preached directly in the form of a promise. He used the proper application of the pronoun: "*To you*, it has been given to know the secrets of the kingdom of God, but for others they are in parables, so that 'seeing they may not see, and hearing they may not understand.'"

The difference between a parable and a promise now emerges: the promise is "to you," and is in the form of a gift, according to which even the parable takes on a whole different light. Jesus did not tell them what they were to do, but what he was doing for them. The parable moves from soil to sower—and that sower, we find to our horror and delight, is precisely not law. Christ is not the law! There is no *Lex Christi*, and Jesus is no new Moses.

In truth, the law must be fulfilled, but it cannot tell you who will fulfill it.[2] Christ's stories like this one are always about divine election; accordingly the parable means one thing when you are a hearer, and another when you are a preacher. Hearers wait; preachers act—spontaneously, freely, and unaware. So the preacher says: this is what Christ did: he came into the world and sowed seed wildly—unconditionally—upon the good and bad. We killed him for this, but the Father raised him. Now this Christ has something to say to you. You were hard, indifferent, thorny, superficial, and too busy changing gospel into law to notice, but nothing hindered Christ from preaching recklessly—not even your hatred of him and the law's condemnation of you.

In this way Christ's word is dispersed and accomplishes what he wants it to, never to return to him empty. This is the true mystery and the secret of Scripture—the power is in the seed, not the soil. All that Christ wants is for his preachers to give these two words as unconditionally as he did, regardless of the unlikely outcome, thus leaving to the Holy Spirit to give ears where and when it pleases him.

Consequently, what was a moral tale of impossible alteration suddenly became a freeing gospel to those who had procured a preacher. Preaching is not explanation or meaning. It is a particular, divine doing, and the disciples whom Jesus had chosen were given the courage to sow this seed without any concern about the status or preparation or righteousness of the hearers, and without a single reward for themselves.

2. This became one of the crucial points in Luther's later *Antinomian Disputations*, as the way to counteract both the misled antinomians, like Agricola, and nomio-philes (including many of Melanchthon's students): "The law says to a certain person: 'Render what you owe; God has given the law that you might fulfill it, yet you have not fulfilled it, therefore you have an irate God and strict Judge.' Meanwhile the law does not say in what way or by whom that person can fulfill it. It cannot show him who fulfills it, until the gospel comes and says: Christ has done it." Martin Luther, *Solus Decalogus est Aeternus: Martin Luther's Complete Antinomian Theses and Disputations*, trans. Holger Sonntag, ed. Paul Strawn, Cygnus Series (Minneapolis: Lutheran Press, 2008), 51.

Preachers Distinguish, Speculators Separate/Combine

This sort of proclamation was the kind that enlightened Luther's students. They no longer merely talked *about* things, but *did* something with the thrill of changing the world. They were like Christ's amazed disciples who came back from their first attempt to preach and had to tell Jesus about everything they had done. The word worked—not only when Jesus said it but also when they did!

Admittedly, it is more than a little strange that Protestants find such delight in exercising a *distinction* rather than explaining a *thing* (*res*), especially a distinction between two common words. On other occasions I have paused at this point to note that *distinction* of law and gospel is meant neither to confuse nor separate the two, and how the antinomian controversies of the sixteenth century joined with the controversies over the necessity of good works to produce the fifth article of the Formula of Concord.[3] From the beginning of the Reformation until now, separators and confusers have abounded. It is not easy to be a proper distinguisher, since the unhappy habit is to explain rather than give the text.

Bible explanation has two common ruts. On one hand, explaining attempts a unity of law and gospel in the Neoplatonic fashion of putting Humpty Dumpty—the original pattern of God's wholeness—together again. Among reformers, this is often done by saying God has one word, which can be distinguished in the two categories of law and gospel. But God's original unity (or single word) is always assumed to be a universal, eternal, divine law. This becomes the common archetype that turns gospel into law, or Christ into a better Moses. The law is taken to be the form of the will or mind of God (or in extreme cases, like Meister Eckhart, god beyond god), and so we mold our god into the shape of our happy law, and we, his faithful citizens, live in joyful obedience and sweet compliance with a law in which we finally delight. The law is one, and it is God's simplicity.

On the other hand, explanations often attempt to separate law and gospel so that preachers do not have to bother with the law, but can simply dole out a gospel antinomian-style. This is because preachers like to be liked, and also want God to be liked—why else would one go into the churchly business? But in reality preachers use this desire to protect themselves from the consequence of their own preaching. They do not want to die by preaching. These preach-

3. Steven D. Paulson, "Law and Gospel: Separators, Confusers, and Preachers," in *Preaching and Teaching the Law and Gospel of God*, ed. Carl E. Braaten (Delhi, NY: ALPB Books, 2013), 49–54.

ers work overtime to keep themselves from falling victim to law's judgment, and seek to remove judgment from any struggling person seeking their help. Although it is counterintuitive, the secret of antinomian separation is not to evacuate the law, but to turn the gospel back into the law.

The attraction of the eternal law turned the earliest evangelical theologies into a struggle between confusers and separators of law and gospel: nomiophiles and antinomians. Just prior to the great period of Protestant orthodoxy in the seventeenth century, the second generation of Lutherans, led by the inimitable "second Martin," Chemnitz, transferred the system of merit from sinners to Christ, saying it was not our merits, but Christ's, that justified. Especially in the fight against Osiander, the human nature was highlighted (which Osiander had discarded in his notion of Christ's indwelling), precisely so that the system of merit could be retained christologically rather than anthropologically. But by introducing the category of "the righteousness of Christ's human performance," Chemnitz "did not clearly develop Luther's emphasis on the necessity of death for sinners, rather than the necessity of satisfying an eternally existing law." It is one thing to recognize that Osiander had ruined the public word of absolution with his theory of Christ's indwelling in the divine nature, but it is quite another for Chemnitz to say that God, who is the "freest of free agents" (*agens liberrimum*), chose the norm of righteousness precisely because that "which is revealed in the Law is the eternal, immovable, and unchangeable will of God."[4]

The Visitation and the Antinomians

When properly distinguishing law and gospel, the crucial moment comes with how or when the law actually ends. *Finis legis* requires addressing the impact Christ had on the law, and vice versa. A universal and eternal law cannot be historicized, and so cannot be done unto or caused to suffer. Modern theology has spent its whole wages on the ability of God to suffer, but the real issue is whether the law can suffer. Indeed, the law utterly changes with Christ. Luther is very precise on this matter. Christ's crucifixion and ministry do not abolish the law (*Christus non tollit legem*); he fulfills the law (*Christus implet legem*).[5] But

4. Robert Kolb, "Human Performance and the Righteousness of Faith," in *By Faith Alone: Essays on Justification in Honor of Gerhard O. Forde*, ed. Joseph A. Burgess and Marc Kolden (Grand Rapids: Eerdmans, 2004), 133.

5. Luther, *Solus Decalogus est Aeternus*, second disputation, twelfth argument, 187.

fulfilling is not the moment the law hands out its prize. Christ's unexpected fulfillment of the law on the cross has a most dramatic effect on the law, evacuating or emptying it, *lex est oratio vacua.*[6] As Scripture says, "For Christ is the end of the law" (Rom. 10:4), and the great promise of a prophet like Moses—"whose words the Lord will avenge" (Deut. 18:18–19)—demotes Moses and raises up God's Son. So also Christ said, "The Law and the Prophets were until John" (Luke 16:16; Matt. 11:13). Put simply, the law killed Christ, and yet on the third day he was raised, but the law—unexpectedly—was not honored with the feat, was emptied, having nothing more to do. What do you do as law if there is no more sin but that nailed to Christ's cross and dead in his blood? You do not continue in a new form as Law II with no accusation—you become dumb.

The end of the law is the negative way of declaring the bright light: Christians are free! Free from sin, wrath, death—and even God's law, which becomes for the saints "an empty matter when it comes to our paying back."[7] But as freeing as this is, the end of the law is also a threat to order in this world, which is the most important ingredient to earthly survival. The rule of law is the basis for political life. The threat is just as acute when we consider church order, since the peril to harmony, tranquility, stability, method, institution, regularity, and the like is truly catholic—always and everywhere the same. The minute you have established a true church from preaching, it is immediately infiltrated with clandestine, fanatic preachers just as Paul found in his churches of Galatia. For this very reason, Elector John the Steadfast wrote to Luther on June 24, 1524, suggesting a visitation of his churches: "May God hear our complaint, but there are too many enthusiasts, and these are causing us plenty of trouble up here." But along with the fur came the pests. Once the evangelicals started their visits, Luther could not help but cry: "Dear God, what misery I beheld! . . . They live like simple cattle or irrational pigs, and despite the fact that the gospel has returned, have mastered the fine art of misusing their freedom."[8]

Melanchthon's response to the iniquity and stupidity of the churches became typical. The misuse of freedom was due to something that we call today "cheap grace," and the answer was to lay out the pattern of the Christian life in a threefold way: repentance, followed by faith in forgiveness, followed by doing good works. The catechism was then laid out in eighteen points or orders that were meant to lead churches through this penitential process. To put it bluntly, the free and merry gospel is blamed for the failures of church order.

6. Luther, *Solus Decalogus est Aeternus,* second disputation, third argument, 161.

7. Luther, *Solus Decalogus est Aeternus,* second disputation, third argument, 163.

8. Martin Luther, Small Catechism, in *BC*, 347–48.

Luther had agreed to the visitations, but quickly corrected the outline for catechism—which was not given as parts of the whole Christian life shaped in the pattern of repentance, faith, and good works. Instead, Luther did as he had done ever since his return from Wartburg. He used the proper distinction of law and gospel: first comes knowledge of the law (in the most usable form of Moses's Decalogue), and then hearing the gospel in the creed. The law, until Christ. Everything in the Christian life is distinguishing between these two: what we are to do (and do not); and what God does for us despite the law's accusation. Melanchthon fought the fanatic abuse of freedom with the *loci* and visitation articles—Luther by unfettered preaching of law/gospel, naming the person, place, and circumstance in which the law comes to an end—and sowing freely.

Meanwhile, Agricola smelled a rat in the Saxon visitation articles and circulated his supposedly anonymous theses (1537) that objected to Melanchthon's approach, as with the last thesis: "As soon as you think, Thus and thus things should be in Christendom, there should be decent, honorable, holy, chaste people, you have already missed the gospel, Luke 6."[9] But Agricola's own understanding of the gospel had collapsed already in this first thesis: "Repentance is to be taught, not from the Decalogue, or any law of Moses, but from doing violence to the Son through the gospel." Gospel and law are epochs, which change at the moment of the incarnation. Since we are now in the new epoch, God's wrath and the law are to be communicated through the cross, not Moses. The carrot is to replace the stick—yet (and here is the sticking point) the goal remains the same. Agricola's own position was lifted from a comment in Luther's preface to James: instead of making people better by *harping on the law—stimulate people to love!* Antinomianism is a worthwhile dream, but as Luther pointed out, it is always a drama played before an empty theater. No one is stimulated by crucifixion. People hate Christ as much now as they did when Adam and Eve found themselves east of Eden.

So it was that Luther's bright light distinguishing law and gospel was snuffed out as quickly as it came. By now most of us know the litany of woes concerning the distinction of law and gospel.

1. It once worked in the sixteenth century because people felt guilty then; but today no one feels guilty.
2. Sin among white men in power positions could accurately be described as "pride," but now the marginalized, such as women and people of color, do not need scolding; they need empowerment.

9. Luther, *Solus Decalogus est Aeternus*, 31.

3. The law/gospel distinction is anti-Judaic and antigentile at once, since it does not understand the difference between entering a covenant and staying in—the one being the gift of the law as grace, and the other the covenant of works aided by grace.

Two Trees: Adam and the Cross

In each case the objections to Luther's law/gospel distinction are replaced with images of the gospel in the form of the law. Theologians then fixate on two trees, the one in the center of paradise, the other the one on which Christ was hung. When gospel is being made into the law, speculation first focuses on the tree of knowledge given to the sinless Adam and Eve by means of which an implication can be made. With the tree came a command (Do not eat!), and a threat (Lest you die!), but then speculators wonder, does this not imply the existence of a prelapsarian, prehistorical law that was not inherently oppressive? Is this primitive law not actually a type that promises life—indirectly for sure—hidden behind the threat of death, if the command should ever be fulfilled? Consequently, there must be a "primal," prelapsarian law that not only does not oppress, but empowers creatures to do what it asks. Conclusion: law at its most basic level is actually grace, gift, and empowerment. If such a thing once existed before the Fall, then even after sin, there must be a pathway back to such a gracious law. Is Christ not the guide for just such a journey?

Here, then, comes the other tree. The preacher wants to protect Christ from blame and present Christ as desirable to an audience in the form of glory rather than the cross. This means that the relation between Christ and the law is doctored to protect the supposition of a gracious law. Atonement must heel to the order of this prelapsarian law if it is to be beneficial. Herein lies the source of atonement theories that interpret the cross by the law, not vice versa—whether Anselm's, Abelard's, or Irenaeus's. Churches have repeatedly failed to preach purely and boldly at the precise point of the impact of the law on Christ, and Christ on the law, that Scriptures typically picture as the difference between Christ and Moses: "For the law was given through Moses; grace and truth came through Jesus Christ" (John 1:17). Specifically, Christ's cross must either pay a debt, attract by love, or establish a victory that restores the eternal, objective order of Eden.

The problem is evident in public preaching, whose primary failure comes in the word "love." Indeed, before and after Luther, the way love is portrayed is precisely the devil's confusion of law and gospel. So the sermon *du jour* has three parts: First, the preacher proves *God is love* (in essence) if you only get to know him a little—which proof is what Scripture is supposed to provide. Second, God's inner love goes out (*ad extra*) and is revealed to you. So the preacher adds the pronoun: *God loves us all* (despite some unlovable qualities), as God showed in creating us so well as to leave a pleasant *imago Dei* that endures despite our (somewhat dubious) blame due to Adam's fall that is shown especially in Jesus's benevolent Sermon on the Mount and his self-sacrificing cross. Third, the preacher adds the admonition that after so much grace, it surely would not be too much to ask for you to *return a little of this love*—without which, the grace would be cheap, and the neighbor would not be helped. In sum, God is love, he loves you, so love each other. Christ does not end the law, he makes it possible for us to fulfill it, and enjoy the law while we do, giving us pleasing structure. The secrets for accomplishing this are doled out in the church, if you should only enter therein.

God Is Not Law

Speculation about these two trees softens and universalizes law all in one fell swoop. It was the very attraction of this bad preaching of love, especially perfected by the Franciscan monks, that originally provoked Luther to seek a gracious God—a Big Lover up above to replace the awful Judge below. Luther set out on his pious journey to find a law somewhere that did not accuse, condemn, indict, allege, fault, reproach, censure, denounce, inculpate, or lay blame, but the search came to a precipitous halt in *Anfechtung*. Luther said it was like falling in a dream, only this time he did not wake up before hitting bottom. He had fallen into the greatest of all theological conundrums via Augustine, who calculated what Paul meant by distinguishing letter and spirit (2 Cor. 3). How could the law be a ministry of death, when law is what we all are searching for? And how could the Spirit be a ministry of life, when "by grace" means that *God chooses whom he will*? But Luther went to the root of the problem. Preaching is what elects, and that divine choice is not universal and abstract, but particular and accidental. One gets a preacher, the other does not—who can deliver me from this body of death?

The gospel is precisely the opposite of a nonthreatening, nonaccusatory law. Gospel is not faith clinging to God's word of law as God's freely chosen order, even if that word were to condemn you. That is the most profound way of making gospel into law ever tried. But, as Luther found, the gospel is no law at all. It is a word of God uttered apart from, and in opposition to, law. It is simply the end of all law, especially the eternal law. The law's word, or voice, is empty. All the schools, monks, and mystics had agreed on one point, and Luther broke free from it. God is not law! But how can you know that as long as you are trying to turn everything said on earth and in heaven into the law?

Nominalist Nicodemus

If you fail to make the distinction between law and gospel, you are left to make all your distinctions under the law alone. One of the classic examples is the man Luther was closest to, and most obviously broke with, Gabriel Biel, the last of the scholastics. Biel followed Duns Scotus and Occam in the famous nominalist distinction of two divine "orders" or forms of law: *potentia absoluta* and *potentia ordinata*. When one does not distinguish law and gospel, another distinction within the law alone is the only option. On one hand, God's absolute potential is to choose from among all possible laws. Who knows which law God would choose? On the other hand, God's ordained potential is that he not only can choose, but has chosen, a particular law without the necessity of the truth of one form of law imposing itself on God's original freedom. Law is not necessity of being—eternally the way things are, even for God. Instead law is *this* law, given to creatures as God's free gift.

Biel used Nicodemus to show this gift of the law that works sweet compliance.[10] Thus, Nicodemus came to Jesus at night, a *viator*, seeking the truth of God's beneficial law (or more exactly, he sought the proof that he was on the right path already). But since that divine law is abstract, the one thing Nicodemus could not provide for himself was assurance of his own acceptance by God according to this law. That means that in order to be given a reward or merit, his good works must fit into God's ordained order, or chosen law (*in opere*). Not only must the works be there, but they must be done with the proper disposition (*in operante*). Finally, God seals the pact by accepting the proper works (*acceptatio*). Accordingly, when Nicodemus said, "Rabbi, we know you are a teacher come from God," he meant that Christ had the means of revealing whether or not his deeds were acceptable to God.

10. Gabriel Biel, *Canonis misse Expositio*, Lectio 18G, 1.157.4; Lectio 34L, 2.10.22. Discussed in Heiko Oberman, *The Harvest of Medieval Theology: Gabriel Biel and Late Medieval Nominalism* (Cambridge, MA: Harvard University Press, 1963).

But instead of accepting his *old* deed, Christ gave Nicodemus a *new*, unexpected deed: be baptized with water and spirit! Suddenly, Nicodemus was translated from God's absolute law (which is frightening) to the new, ordained law, which is the church's law that at least has the virtue of being simple. For Nicodemus, this was initially confusing, but even for the relatively free nominalist, *contingent* is not fickle or arbitrary (without order)—it simply points out that things are unpredictable until the new law is finally revealed. Yet, unpredictable law is still very much law, and once it arrives with Christ it is no longer unpredictable.

So from that historical moment in which Nicodemus arrived to Jesus, God's new law had become the order of the day: baptism saves children. This is a sweet law, Biel thought, a happy obedience, once you get accustomed to it and live into the culture of Christendom. It was not as if Nicodemus had come naked, without law. It was only that he was operating under the old law of the Jews. So, Biel thought, there and then Nicodemus had proof that the *absoluta*, including his old law of circumcision, *was* true, but *is* no longer. The man stood at the crux between absolute and ordained legal orders.

For Biel, Nicodemus's night explains why revelation is historical. It was one way up to Nicodemus's visit to Jesus, then afterward it is always another way. In this way the law concerns history, not metaphysics—the great nominalist discovery. Who knew that the law, which is very much still presumed to be eternal, is nevertheless received not as abstract and universal, but rather as something particular, historical, and contingent? Yet even as history, law remains the thing by which God stabilizes life, limits uncertainty, and saves those who repent and accept what God has accepted. Only after Nicodemus's faith has accepted God's chosen order of baptism can a theologian (arriving after the fact like Biel) point out the *ratio de congruo* (reason that goes along with God's plan). Thus Nicodemus merited his justification (to some extent) by corresponding hand in hand with God's new law.

Evangelical Nicodemus

But evangelicals consider Nicodemus differently than Biel. Biel made two distinctions within the law (abstract and objective); evangelicals distinguish between law and gospel. For Biel, a liberal man like Nicodemus knows that law can change over time. The teacher comes to Jesus looking for acceptance, but finds to his chagrin that Jesus is no traditional rabbi. Nicodemus knows enough of the law to know that whatever Jesus is saying is different. Still, it seems to be coming from God—even though it is not legal. Yet, what else can one get from God but a better law, or *acceptatio* for the law one already has?

Here Jesus changes the game: "unless a man is born again, from above, anew—he cannot see the kingdom of God!" Nicodemus translates everything into legalese—that is, how his deeds correspond to God's decisions and meet approval. What is he supposed to do with this new law of being born? Indeed, even in his first birth Nicodemus had never been consulted. How would it be different in the second? So Nicodemus replies: What does this mean? How can I turn birth into something I do? Can I crawl back into my mother's womb? Won't she have something to say about that? So, he ends with a *reductio ad absurdum*: you have given me a law that is impossible to do. But Jesus simply adds fuel to the burning pyre: "Unless a man is born of water and the Spirit he has no chance. What is born of flesh is flesh, and of spirit is spirit. Don't be surprised when I say you must be born from above. What do you expect? The Spirit, like the wind, blows where it wills, it comes and goes, and you don't know where it comes from or where it goes" (John 3:5–8).

This word is not a new law. It is how one is born of the spirit. Nicodemus keeps pushing this word back into the same box the nominalists were in: How is baptism *potentia*? I could take either absolute or ordained law, but at least give me some *possibility for doing*! How can you, a rabbi and a spiritual man, say these things that are directly opposed to spirit *as law*? What in the world can we do with anything like baptism? How can that be relevant? Then Jesus gives the *coup de grace*: "You are a teacher in Israel and you don't know these things?" Where have you been, Nicodemus? What in the world do you think Israel's long history has been about?

Nicodemus is pushed into something he could not do, namely, fulfill baptism as a law. His potential, his free will, is being withdrawn from him. He is being put to death, and can only wait for a preacher to preach to him. Furthermore, his preacher will have to give him something entirely different than a work or *acceptio Dei*. Nicodemus needs a promise that comes out of nowhere. Currently, people love words like "difference," the "other," and the "new"—until it comes to the gospel. In John's Gospel it takes the whole remainder of the story of Christ's crucifixion and resurrection, with the giving of the keys to the kingdom, before there is even the slightest hint that Christ could finally preach to him: "I forgive you." This is not acceptance, but death and resurrection.

So Nicodemus waits to hear that the Spirit has blown to him and for the preacher to say: "I am here to get you." "No one," Jesus said, "has gone up to heaven except the one who came down from heaven, the Son of man who is in heaven, and the Son of man must be lifted up as Moses lifted the serpent in the desert so that everyone who believes may have eternal life in him."

Meaning versus Use in Paul's Spirit and Letter

One aspect of this evangelical teaching is to say that it is not the *meaning* of words, but the *use* of them, that is key for distinguishing law and gospel. This distinction of meaning and use comes from the most important biblical source of the distinction of law and gospel in 2 Corinthians, where Paul contrasts letter and spirit. Unfortunately "letter" has come to mean something quite different than what Paul intended, since the word is now synonymous with explanation. Consequently, the letter itself was presumed to be dead, and the expositor, who alone was presumed to be alive, was required to resurrect a dead letter by making the thing relevant or meaningful in what is considered a new "context"—literally an addition to the text. And what addition do you suppose the expositor inserts? The legal scheme, naturally, which assumes eternal law as God's essence—that is the abstract idea you must make concrete in your own place and time.

Now, why was the letter considered dead? Because it was stuck in time—in mortality—and had to be made into something outside of time—immortal. This assumption reads everything as law; yet, as anyone under the law can tell you, law is always liable to corrosion or irrelevance. That is why law always needs progressive legislators. Law, stuck back in time, is dangerous, as we find with the growing pains of modern Islam. We call such old law "tradition" or "ceremony" since it attacks us, and we need to be free from it.

The law discovered in the text of Scripture is dead, mortal, discardable letter. Thus, if law were to have any import in the present, it must be extracted from its defunct location and time, and made *immortal*—statuesque. It must be made *new* law that applies in all places and times. So the Jewish law must be made universal in a way that includes gentiles, if not by way of entry, then by way of remaining in God's people. So, letter became local, traditional law (positive). Its counterpart was taken to be spirit—which then came to denote the eternal, universal law. So literal legalism is hated; eternal legalism is touted as the great refuge of humankind—and so becoming a universal lover is the stuff of preaching in the present.

However, when Paul said "the letter kills and the spirit gives life" (2 Cor. 3), he was very specific, including illustrations! He did not say the law is dead. He said the letter kills. The problem Paul had with the law is the same that you and I have: it kills us in whatever form it comes—ceremonial or moral—and we don't want to die. It does not make us righteous; it condemns. This is no mistake or by-product of pleasant law; law kills neither because it is misused (though we certainly do that), nor because we have not fulfilled the law (though we certainly have not), but because God gave the law for this one and only purpose: to threaten us with death, and carry out the death wherever there is sin. Likewise, Paul's "the letter kills" is no mistake. It is the act of God in the law, and God intends to finish the job come hell or high water, which point we state dogmatically as God's *proper work of the law*. The law is the active one here, or better yet, God is truly the actor using the law precisely when it is not pleasant to us.

This realization attacks our reason, which is our most preciously guarded human commodity. God's use of the law to kill us attacks our dream of free will. The theory of the free will is not an inductive inference from our daily experience, but is a last-ditch effort to defend ourselves from the very Creator who seems to turn against us just because we do not want to have him preach to us, and so this God seems to want nothing but to be our Destroyer. The letter, in short, is neither a neutral thing (which may mean one thing or another depending upon the interpreter), nor is it a sign pointing to something else. Letter is a thing, sent by God; indeed, it is the divine will of God, and this thing is out to get us! It wants sinners dead! Moses learned the truth on the first night of his new calling, when God suddenly tried to kill him in the middle of the night, and would have were it not for Zipporah's quick thinking and a sharp flint (Exod. 4). Law's object, goal, and use cannot be stopped by thinking it away. It cannot be deflected by assigning it a different meaning. Nor can it be explained as a part of the natural cycle of life, or by some other psychological explanation like those of the Stoics or Epicureans. Law is certainly not God giving us a warning, or providing a direction or guide in life; nor is it establishing a certain order of things to which we must either hail—sweetly and kindly—or perish.

The law is grace, no doubt, and so even "gift" in the common language of modern French anthropology. It is certainly part of the all-working of God. But it is not gospel—it is not good news; it is very bad news indeed. The law is out to get you, and it never misses in the end.

It was Luther who simply took the literal letter literally. First because he lived it. Second, as he said, he attended to what Paul was actually saying in the words rather than what Occam or Aquinas was saying. Third, there simply was no other way. The law was a fake gospel that ended in literal death. But this also meant that Luther took spirit literally—not as a failed form of traditional law, but as the person who resurrects the dead, and does it in the only way the

Spirit wants to do anything since he always blows where he wills through a preached word that is opposed to the law as gospel.

Gospel does not describe God's essence, but gives the one thing sinners can actually use: the forgiveness of sins. Likewise, the only thing dead people can use is the resurrection from the dead. The Spirit resurrects the dead through a preacher recklessly giving a new word that counteracts the law. That is why Paul talks so much about his ministry, since the preaching (or ministry) of Moses and the preaching of the Holy Spirit are total opposites. What the preacher says is not an explanation—especially not the modern form of explanation called "theodicy" (i.e., why a person imagines a good God could allow evil). Instead, what the preacher says is a deed, that is, a doing rather than an explanation, a thing, not a sign. What is done with the Spirit's word cannot be done with anyone else's word: God covers sin with the blanket of Christ. He ignores it. This is not a legal fiction that needs to become a legal reality; it is the end of the law. Therefore, it is not the uniting of mercy and justice as attributes in the being of God, but is God forgetting something out of mercy that overcomes justice:

> Remember not the sins of my youth or my transgressions;
> according to your steadfast love remember me,
> for the sake of your goodness, O LORD! (Ps. 25:7)

The word of law and gospel comes out of the mouth of a single preacher, but what law and gospel accomplish is separated as far as the East is from the West.

The New Antinomian Pests

Here we come to a crucial matter in distinguishing law and gospel. Before the freedom is felt, the gospel first offends. It is not that good news starts off being bad; it starts off being hated. We could take any one of the examples from John's Gospel (or from a letter of Paul) such as Nicodemus, or the woman at the well, or, more profoundly, Mary and Martha at the death of Lazarus. The thing that ultimately kills the very best and highest of our old selves is the unleashed, unconditional, absolute gospel itself. The unfettered absolution of sinners, while they are sinners, does not fit the pattern of the law. Here God goes rogue, operating *ex lex*—outside the law.

Those who are most offended by it are the best at keeping the law, since they have the most to lose. Christians in particular, though Jews and Muslims (and even an observant Buddhist or committed secularist, communist, or capitalist) would have to agree—they do not want the gospel to be absolution. They do not want their election to come by means of a meager, accidental preacher.

Consequently, the most contested matter theologically regarding law and gospel, especially by Lutherans, is the end of the law (Rom. 10:4). Can the law actually end, if it is the will of God, or God himself, or at least is the structure set up by God from the beginning for human flourishing, which is what we mean by "being" and "ontology"? Is the law not in fact eternal, and pleasant, just as God is? If not, is freedom not simply chaos, anarchy, and unrest? Isn't preaching precisely antinomian, concentrating only on Christ without any mention of the law?

Here the second fight over the law occurred among Lutherans, culminating in the Eisenach Synod of 1556, which came to be known by its victors pejoratively as the extermination of "second" antinomians. But just as the church was reduced to three people after Nicea, Athanasius being one, so the church was reduced here to a few pastors, Poach, Neander, Otho, and Musculus, who refused all Lutheran varieties available at the time—Philippist and Gnesio alike. Their thesis was simple, but upsetting: *The New Man is totally free from the law; the Old Man is totally under the law.* Their banner replaced the old Augustinian thesis that gospel was the "new law" in the form of the *power of grace to fulfill the law*. Instead, the law is ended by Christ. The baptized, then, must be distinguished as two, the old and the new—and each total, each having the opposite relation to the law. The new is not guided by law, but is already beyond it, so that law is not yet to be done but is already finished.

This antinomian controversy—one generation following the first—revealed a systematic problem that Lutherans had with Luther and Scripture, since they knew the law had to end, as they put it, *practically* because Paul said it must. But this made their heads hurt. Reason and will require that God's way of thinking and choosing is rational. Consequently, the victorious Lutherans limited the end of the law to psychology—as the end of the law's effect as accusation, or the feeling of guilt. That is what they meant by "practically" ending. So that if at a future date a whole generation said they didn't feel guilty anymore, then there was no work of the law—not because Christ ended it, but because psychology did.

For systematic, ecumenical purposes, and because the participants feared "cheap grace," Eisenach made a lamentable distinction: while the law ended practically, it must continue theoretically/abstractly forever. If the law were not theoretically eternal, it would imply an end to God himself.[11] Theoretical, eternal law had to be inferred from the two trees: Adam's tree and Christ's. In the garden, law must have been there to provide an opportunity for humans to be eternal, though we shall never know certainly because of the turn of events. Thus, this is hypothetical. Then, subsequently one could measure Christ's merit on the cross as sufficient payment, implying that the operating assumption of the crucifixion is God finding a clever way of maintaining justice by means of law despite the universal fall of humankind. Accordingly, they speculated that the law once carried the water of salvation theoretically. If Adam and Eve had completed it, it would have been rewarded with eternal life. But once sin entered, the cross was needed to bring God's fractured attributes of mercy and justice, grace and law, into one simple union. God needed the cross to unite himself.

So God's gospel is made to fit within the universal, eternal, infinite, objective, rational order of the divine law—since God's theoretical essence is law. Whether we speak of Flacius Illyricus's distinction between God's *essential* righteousness and the *function* of the law among us, or Chemnitz's distinction between the divine and human performance of Christ in the cross, or the attempts of Melanchthon's students to find a third use of the law that does not accuse Christians *qua* Christians—the pattern was set for the seventeenth century to bring in an orthodoxy whose first principle was the eternal law of God.

Admittedly, it is very hard to distinguish God from the law—and precisely impossible if the Spirit gives no ears. Why is it so hard to stop making the gospel into the law? In actual experience, and in the highest form of human thought, the law is the best thing we have. Law is, as Luther famously put it in the first article of his Heidelberg Disputation—"the most salutary doctrine of life." Plato, for example, could never quite tell the difference between God and law—even though he realized that he could not determine if law were something like the best idea God ever had, or if God had the idea of law because it was the best thing ever. Was the law *extradeical* or *intradeical*?[12]

Aquinas could never differentiate between justice and God, but since the law is imposed on everyone, he figured God must be the one on whom it

11. The argument is described and opposed by L. Haikola, *Usus Legis* (1958), and its opposition is presently carried on by Nicholas Hopman in two essays: Steven D. Paulson and Nicholas Hopman, "Christ, the Hated God," *Lutheran Quarterly* 30, no. 1 (2016): 1–27, and Nicholas Hopman, "Luther's Antinomian Disputations and *Lex Aeterna*," *Lutheran Quarterly* 30, no. 2 (2016): 152–80.

12. H. Wolfson, "Extradeical and Intradeical Interpretations of Platonic Ideas," *Journal of the History of Ideas* 22 (1961): 3–32.

is not imposed because it *is* him eternally, at least his practice.[13] Even when nominalists, like those who taught Luther, are blamed for destroying the church's received tradition merely by implying that law and gospel are "essentially different,"[14] and who therefore stripped the "new Law" (gospel) of its legal character, we should be reminded of what Biel actually did with the distinction. He simply received the whole tradition from Origen up to his own day—including Aquinas and Occam—that assumed that the distinction of law and gospel found in Paul or Augustine was a minor event theologically—not worth mentioning. It is not what makes the two *different*, but what makes them the *same*, that really mattered to Biel and every theologian prior to him, with some exceptions applied to Augustine.

Two Breasts and Loss of Law/Gospel

Indeed, what makes law and gospel the same for Biel is that they are both law. The law is the law, whether given by Moses or Jesus. True, Moses's *form* is the "old law," and nominalists were perhaps more willing than most to say that such an old law is more malleable than God's own eternal life is, but nevertheless it is the law after all, and the law is what leads to righteousness. There is no qualitative difference between Christ and Moses because the difference between law and gospel is not of kind, but of degree. The gospel is the law like Moses's—only more so—that is, a new, better law.

In fact, Biel's favorite depiction of law and gospel is *duo ubera* (twin breasts). Now, a person can manage with one, but two is better. And who cares if the breasts are not identical? The main thing is that they are both there and both promoting the same goal: to get unrighteousness to become righteousness. In short, the law of Christ is the perfection of Moses. Moses could only direct us to the goal, and so required exterior acts and ceremonies like Passover or Booths to be forced from the outside. Christ sheds the exterior acts (ceremonies and even judicial laws like an eye for an eye) and gives to us the heart's dearest desire—interior acts that are not forced but voluntary. So, the gospel is an interior, unimposed law, which was taken by Biel (and all of Christendom) as Paul's distinction between letter and spirit.

For Biel, the difference between law and gospel is that between *lex timoris* (inspiring fear like Moses) and *lex amoris* (inspiring love like Christ). That is

13. *ST* I-II, q. 91, a. 1.

14. See Georg Ott's argument in Oberman, *Harvest of Medieval Theology*, 117n90.

why Agricola wanted to get rid of the law in preaching. He thought anything Christ said was the gospel, even when Jesus gave a command. So, the new dispensation that began with Christ's teaching of repentance should give the gospel in the form of inspiring love. Antinomian aspirants are always nomians in the end, of the Jesus persuasion. Likewise, in Bonaventure, law and gospel are an accusing law and an encouraging law. Nevertheless, though the old law is thought to scare one into taking a better path (toward love), and Christ's new law of love attracts everything into itself—in the end it is all law. This result is not peculiar to nominalists; for Thomas too, the cradle of the old law was fear, just as the cradle of the new law is love.

These are all psychological distinctions within the metaphysical category of law, and have nothing to do with what Luther discovered. The great distinction of all theology is not between what we fear and what we find attractive, but between God preached and God not preached—which leads to an experience, no doubt, but is something that for once is truly theological. Luther especially concerned himself with what God is doing, not what we are feeling.

Everything in Christendom's doctrine and life—whether works, merit, faith, grace, gospel, law—can be plotted on the law's map. Accordingly, Christ is alleged to give us a law that we do not fear but attracts us by love. Both the original antinomians and the students of Melanchthon agreed on this matter. Jesus says in John's Gospel: "A new law I give you . . . that you love one another." This was taken to be identical to Paul: "By works of the law shall no one be justified" (Gal. 2:16), as if this meant precisely what nominalists imagined—that the *old* law will not justify; only *new* law will. So it went down the years with the distinction of law and gospel reduced to an asterisk, a dangerous subcategory of theology. Paul and Christ must mean something like: eschew the exterior and embrace the interior, or do not incite fear but promote love. This is why Agricola would later realign with the papal party in ecumenical discussions.

And so even the great comfort of Christ, "Come to me, all who labor and are heavy laden, and I will give you rest" (Matt. 11:28), was interpreted by Biel as part of the legal scheme. What is this "rest" of which Christ speaks? It is the infusion and preservation of grace—as a free gift—in the form of a command to love that comes not from Moses but from Christ. This new law awakens what is already within us to prepare ourselves (or, as later Protestants prefer to say: we *respond* to the gospel), which registers the conditions attached to such a promise as "I will give you rest." We conclude that rest is fine, but it takes a little work eventually! Grace is a free gift, but gifts imply response. Grace does not save unless it is infused so that it enlivens the heart in such a way that a person finally fulfills the law. Of course, in all this figuring of law and human righteousness, the forgotten man is Jesus Christ—especially that Christ actually ended the law.

So, as Bartholomaeus von Usingen, disciple of Biel and Luther's teacher, insisted—Christ redeems us by faith (so far, so good) from the bondage to sin and the power of the devil, but Christ does not save anyone *from* the law. Instead, Christ delivers you *into* the law of love.[15] The law as love is both gift and command—since no gift comes without a response. But the good news, according to the legal scheme, is that you may rest assured that somewhere—probably in the mouth of Jesus—there exists a command that does not accuse you, but attracts you. When you find that nonaccusatory law, as when you hear these words: "Love, as Christ first loved you," it will not hit you as an onerous task. You will have joy, and the law's work will finally be pleasant obedience. Of course, you have to be prepared for this; it doesn't happen magically. Baptism doesn't seem to work when it comes to this disposition, so that something more needs to be added—but to believe otherwise would be sacramentalism, wouldn't it? But when you tune your ear to Christ, then the law changes. When Moses says, "Do this," we chafe, but with the proper preparation—as when Christ says: "Do this"—it sounds sweet to our ears.

The Tragelaphus

This search for a nonaccusatory law had to end, and it did, abruptly for Luther: "A law that does not condemn is a fake and counterfeit law, like a chimera or a tragelaphus (half goat/half stag)."[16] But not many have followed. Paul says, "you have died to the law," and by law he did not mean ceremony—excluding the moral or love. He meant the whole shooting match. Not a part, but the whole of law. Not law, except for the way law is eternally God's essence as justice (and only so, mercy). But isn't the law given by God? Yes. And if it is given by God, must it not, by logical deduction, be given to people who can do it, as ought implies can? And isn't this "can do" an implication that God gave the law to make us righteous? And in making us righteous, is he not uniting himself to us—immediately—so that we are like him, participate in him, and indeed are gods ourselves? We simply must find the right law, or the right Legislator who gives us a law with no finger pointing to accuse us, but only to guide us. Then, on that great day, we will naturally (or supernaturally) desire, want, crave, long

15. Oberman, *Harvest of Medieval Theology*, 118.

16. Luther, *Solus Decalogus est Aeternus*, 375.

for, yearn, need, aspire to, covet—and be set free by that very command. The joy of obedience, the pleasantness of law, is our aim in life. Consequently, theology repeatedly overlooks Christ, and especially eschews his offensive death.

The command to love, *lex charitatis,* is the likely place to look for this pleasant law, and so it is not surprising that sermons become the love covenant. However, this is not the gospel, and is not even close to fulfilling the law. Thus, "Whatever the Antinomians say about God, Christ, faith, law, grace etc. they say without understanding, like a parrot his 'hello.'"[17] The reason is, they adopt a legal scheme and mash everything by means of this sieve. But as far apart as they were on the use of law in repentance, antinomians and nomio-philes continued their common work of turning gospel into gracious, pleasant law, and the Christian life into joyous obedience.

But to all this we say no. That is the first part of the evangelical discovery, which, of course, is the most fearful thing of all: "The law of God, the most salutary doctrine of life, cannot advance humans on their way to righteousness, but rather hinders them." When Luther spoke at the Augustinian society in Heidelberg (1518), he had not grasped the second part, or gospel itself. Soon, he found that what one said after the end of the law (the "no") was the great "yes" of the promise of forgiveness in the absolution. But at least in Heidelberg he knew righteousness would not be a new, better, perfect law. That search for the goat/stag was over. He knew that if one tried to describe God's essence apart from forgiveness, what he got was God = law, which is God in naked majesty without any gospel, and that the end of that quest was death.

Unfortunately, the scramble to be the first actual antinomian, and so the first ever to exist, is what constitutes most Christian theology. In fact, this is typically what existentialism means. It turns the gospel into the law. Law and gospel are not even close to being a pair of breasts—as not only Biel, but theologians everywhere, were attempting to assure was the case. Nor are law/gospel two opposing powers, or epochs, as the remainder of failed theologians like Mani and Marcion assumed. But the distinction does mean that God never did give the law to make anyone righteous—not to Christ, not to Moses, not to Paul, and not even to Adam and Eve. Indeed, Paul said it directly: the law was given not to reduce sin, but to increase it (Rom. 5:20). Nor is law the first step on the way to gospel. Most importantly, the otherwise endless search for a particular kind of law that will not accuse, the Tragelaphus, is cut off.

Of course, everyone is afraid to say that there is no eternal law because that would cut the root of human reason: from eternal law comes natural law, from

17. Luther, *Solus Decalogus est Aeternus,* 375.

natural law (whether ten commandments, or Christ's *lex charitatis*) comes *lex gentium*, and thus comes positive law, etc. What would happen to a world that is already spinning out of control if this ended? What would happen if we lost the single thing holding existence together: the law of love!

Yet, in the face of this fear, we hold these two contradictory things at the same time: law is the most salutary doctrine of life, and law hinders righteousness. Likewise, we can say law is pure gift, and yet has nothing to do with justification. Furthermore, we say the Golden Rule, even if given by Christ, is not the gospel and does nothing to save you—or anyone else. Christians need no guide, unless one is not speaking of the Christian, but of the old sinner. By the time the guide is there, the good is already done, without guide or law.

The law is not the heart or will of God. Order or structure is not what the word *hesed* really means, and mercy certainly is not an idea or thing of itself, a soul, animal, structure, plan, idea, organization, or scheme for some divine architect to build the cosmos. Luther is the only one who has given you such an audacious slogan—the law, until Christ! The law is not a dream, especially not the dream of finding a nonaccusatory, uncritical law, or even nonthreatening law that empowers rather than oppresses. In heaven, thank God, we do not return to Adam and Eve's original position with the requirement of choosing better than they did. Eternal, divine law that is the mind or will of God that attracts and empowers Christians is not only a Pyrrhic search; it is a lie. It is a stag-goat (*hircocervis*), a South Dakotan jack-alope, a northwestern yeti, or Southern Sasquatch or Fouke Monster. Unfortunately, but predictably, Protestants unwittingly took up the search for the nonaccusatory guiding law that already made the distinction of law and gospel seem beside the point for either nominalists or old Catholics, turning it into the endless search for the third use. But the consequence of that was the same as it was prior to Luther—the distinction of law and gospel was subjugated to the unity and goodness of the one, divine law, who is God himself. Of course, we know the direction that attempt took from the minute it was first floated in Melanchthon's classroom. Logically and practically, the third use had to become the primary use, and the primary use equated with the mind and will of God himself. Thus, reformers end up saying the same thing the nominalists and scholastics did, with the anti-Pelagian proviso that law is not fulfilled with good works unless God gives them.

But even more subtly, the Lutherans resurrected (metaphorically) the notion of the eternal law that Luther had discovered was a Babylonian captivity. The subtlety that was spun at the Eisenach Synod demoted *lex aeterna* to the subcategory of a theory instead of a reality. The form of a theory is the way law's origin and purpose must have occurred to Plato—that my mind and desires all seem to point to it and demand it. If I don't have a hypothetical legal scheme, then nothing makes sense to me, and I go about my life as if I were Abraham, who was given a promise one day only to have God demand he kill the promise the next. But surely God is not the kind who would ask of us the obviously antimoral, like killing a son. Where is the order, reason, love, and justice in that? In that case love would be so free that it would be absolutely frightening, mostly because we don't think we would actually produce any love in the moment it was demanded. And if somehow I, as a baptized Christian, managed to produce love for the neighbor, I would not even be informed about it so that I could claim credit. In that case, I would end up saying exactly what every firefighter or police officer says: "I was just doing my job." I wouldn't have any idea whether or not my loving act fit into God's divine plan for me or the cosmos, and I would be bereft of any certainty as to whether the deed did any good for me or not. But Luther just plowed ahead: "It further follows from this that a Christian man living in this faith has no need of a teacher of good works, but he does whatever the occasion calls for, and all is well done."[18] That is not fanaticism; it is the only way to fight a fanatic.

Such a life with the eternal law behind me, emptied of its content and form on account of Christ who fulfilled the law for me, would mean I would never know where I fit on the divine chart of good works. Worse yet, it would be impossible for me to sin, no matter how hard I tried. Despite myself, good works would come pouring out despite my feeling that it was all too much to believe, and that the consequence was finally my own death as an old Adam. I would be good soil on account of the seed sown, not on account of my deeds or my character.

What, then, would happen to teaching classes on morality? What would happen to preachers like me? I would no longer be explaining things; I would be doing something. I would take Christ's words literally that he has given me the keys to the kingdom of heaven. No more: "God is love. He loves you, so love one another." Instead, I would sow recklessly, lawlessly, trusting that whatever I said last would hold forever—and that would be one of two words, the law or the gospel: "You have not done," or "I forgive you."

18. This is the conclusion of Luther's *Treatise on Good Works* that is otherwise often claimed as Luther's positive use of the Decalogue precisely for Christians. *LW* 44:26.

Ten Theses on How to Stop Making Gospel into Law

1. God gave the law to creatures, but God is not the law.
2. The law has two "uses," both used by God, one that fosters and preserves life in the old world, and the other that makes a person run from God's threat/wrath to the mercy of Christ's promise.
3. The law always accuses, in both its uses, which is the essential or constant voice of the law.
4. Christ alone fulfills the law, and so is the point, the "thing" that law wants, needs, and demands—and which sinners cannot give.
5. But Christ did not take a reward from the law (even to give to sinners later), but rather bore the complete accusation of the law. He who knew no sin became sin—that is, the curse (Gal. 3:13 and 2 Cor. 5). The law attacked and killed him as the one and only sinner of the cosmos.
6. Thus, the law came to an end, *telos* (Rom. 10:4), and is not only fulfilled, where and when Christ is.
7. The law's demand is for Christ to be present and give eternal life to Adam and Eve (speaking forgiveness for sinners); the Father is not satisfied until this happens.
8. The end of law is only in Christ—not in part, but wholly, present with all he has (human and divine in complete interpenetration in himself), and conveyed to his sinners by preaching, that is, by the Holy Spirit.
9. When this happens—Christ and faith—the law is quiescent, evacuated (*lex vacua*), and stops accusing only so far as it says nothing at all (especially uttering no happy command, guide to the faithful, form or plan for sanctification, joyful obedience, or any other description of an imaginary "third" use of the law).
10. Such is Christian freedom, lived in love, given by and as the Holy Spirit, doing what the law demands and more—without the law. Look, Mom! No law!

Chapter 6

The Law-Gospel Distinction in Reformed Theology and Ministry

Kelly M. Kapic

"'Gospel' is now a dead word for you! Please stop using it." Finally reaching a point of exasperation, I let these words fly out of my mouth one day in class. While it was funny to say, I was serious. I told students they couldn't use the word "gospel" for a season of time. Doesn't that sound outrageous? Isn't that actually offensive to Christian faith and practice? Why would I ever do that? The short answer is that from what I could hear, the word "gospel" was being thrown around left and right, and it wasn't very clear that people knew what they were talking about. Divorced from biblical settings and classic Reformational understandings, this glorious and life-giving word, I worried, was starting to sound hollow.

Anecdotally, it appears to me that over the past twenty or thirty years, the term "gospel" has regained a special prominence, especially in the spheres where American evangelicals and conservative Reformed believers overlap. Budding up everywhere were *gospel* hermeneutics, *gospel* sermons, *gospel* churches, *gospel* conferences, and even a *Gospel* Coalition. Out came *gospel* study Bibles and *gospel*-centered manuals to help you discover your latent legalism. A new simple litmus test developed: "Is it gospel?" You prayed? Good. But was it a *gospel* prayer? You exegeted a passage of Holy Scripture? Good, but was it *gospel* exegesis? Simply say the word "gospel," and you instantly have a trump card: conversations cease and you win. Furthermore, "gospel" was almost always reduced to a mere equation with the idea of justification by faith alone; not surprisingly, when students would actually read their Bibles, especially the "Gospels," they soon discovered you cannot simply substitute the phrase "justification by faith alone" every time you run across the word "gospel": it creates confusion, not clarity. Let me be clear: justification by faith alone is central to the gospel, but I don't believe it exhausts the gospel. More on this point later.

Personally, I believe that in so many ways this resurgence is a genuine gift to the evangelical church. Some who were previously soaked in suffocating fundamentalism or various forms of moralism were finally receiving words of grace and hope. In that way, I don't believe you can ever have too much "gospel." Having written and participated in many of these "gospel"-branded activities and publications, I have found much of it personally helpful, and I do hope many have been encouraged and strengthened by these various efforts.

As often is the case, however, excitement about (re)discovering an idea—even a biblical truth—can unintentionally create new misunderstandings and challenges. And, as we found in the Reformation itself, handing down the truths of the gospel from one generation or leader to the next is not always easy. Assumptions once intuited—such as the legitimate place for Christian obedience to divine commands—were sometimes too easily tossed aside in the name of radical grace (cf. Synodical Declaration of Berne, 1532):[1] antinomianism is always a genuine danger (cf. Rom. 6:1–2). Sadly, in response to such misunderstandings, others are tempted to highlight God's law in a way that subtly or not so subtly makes divine grace contingent upon repentance and law keeping:[2] legalism is not simply a danger Protestants once needed to be aware of, but it remains an ever-present enticement that must be resisted.

At its best, the Reformed tradition has greatly cared about parsing out the law and gospel distinction, not because they merely enjoyed scholastic theology, but because they believed one's understanding of this relationship has massive pastoral consequences. When I asked the students to stop saying the word "gospel," it was not because I dislike the gospel, but because I *love* the gospel. I desperately wanted them to rediscover the full depths of what it means, not just theologically, but personally. Unfortunately, simply repeating

1. Jan Rohls believes Berne represents an antinomian propensity; *Reformed Confessions: Theology from Zurich to Barmen*, trans. John F. Hoffmeyer, Columbia Series in Reformed Theology (Louisville: Westminster John Knox, 1997), 197. To determine why this accusation is made, see "The Bern Synod (1532)," in *Reformed Confessions of the Sixteenth and Seventeenth Centuries in English Translation*, vol. 1, 1523–1552, ed. James T. Dennison Jr. (Grand Rapids: Reformation Heritage Books, 2008), esp. chs. 6–17 (pp. 237–45).

2. A powerful example of the subtle but deadening effects of creeping legalism and hyper-Calvinism comes in the Scottish Marrow controversy. For a brief history of the debate as well as relevant theological and pastoral reflections upon it, see Sinclair B. Ferguson, *The Whole Christ: Legalism, Antinomianism, and Gospel Assurance—Why the Marrow Controversy Still Matters* (Wheaton, IL: Crossway, 2016). A nicely edited version of the book behind the controversy (originally published in 1645), including Thomas Boston's early eighteenth-century editorial notations and extended reflections, is also now available: Edward Fisher, *The Marrow of Modern Divinity* (Fearn, UK: Christian Focus Publications, 2009).

the word "gospel" is no guarantee that you understand the good news of the gift of Christ, nor that your life is being lived in and out of that gospel reality! Much recent confusion on these matters mirrors historical challenges that occasionally arise not simply from without, but often from within the Reformed tradition itself. Let us then consider the law and gospel distinction, with specific reflections on consequences for pastoral care and preaching given most clearly at the end of the essay.

Confusion about the Law?

While it may surprise some, there is often real confusion and even debate about what one means by "the law" in Christian theology and proclamation. This puzzlement is especially strong among laity. Does law simply refer to the Levitical code? Many instantly think of the Ten Commandments and nothing else. For some, all five books of Moses come to mind, while others envisage the Scriptures in their entirety. Maybe this ambiguity is not only understandable, but not all bad. Take the Hebrew word commonly translated as law: *Torah*. One can find *Torah* used to represent God's will (e.g., Jer. 18:18) or priestly decisions (e.g., Hos. 8:12); sometimes it points to specific laws within the Pentateuch, while at other times it represents the whole of the first five books of the Hebrew Scriptures.[3] Along similar lines, the New Testament employs the very term *nomos*, or "law," in different ways as well, "ranging from law as a principle revealed in nature or reason, to the OT Scriptures as a body, the first five books of the Scriptures, or any single command of the Scriptures."[4] If one aims to reflect the biblical language of law, such flexibility must be kept in mind.[5] Yet it seems that behind these variations, there is an underlying point: these all, in one way or another, serve as part of the revelation of God. They, in some way, reveal God and his will.

Part of what makes our reading of the New Testament texts potentially difficult is that when the apostle Paul refers to the "law," he sometimes appears to have in mind what Herman Ridderbos calls "Jewish-synagogical nomism,"

3. See "Torah," in *New International Dictionary of New Testament Theology*, ed. Colin Brown, 4 vols. (Grand Rapids: Zondervan, 1975–1978), 1:70.

4. "νόμος," in *Greek to English Dictionary and Index to the NIV New Testament: Derived from the Zondervan NIV Exhaustive Concordance*, entry 3795. Cf. "νόμος," in *Greek-English Lexicon of the New Testament*, entry 3551.

5. For more on how "law" was particularly understood in the Reformed tradition, especially after Westminster, see Michael Allen's essay in this volume.

which represents a Pharisaical abuse and misuse of Israel's ordinances, an approach Paul himself had once embraced.[6] More recently, scholars like James Dunn have argued that Paul's warnings against "works of the law" are not really about earning salvation through logging merits by law keeping; rather, Paul had as his target those who made salvation somehow contingent upon a person's link to national Israel, with law keeping (esp. circumcision, Sabbath laws, and food laws) serving as an identity marker.[7] Paul is thus reacting against this kind of abuse when he speaks so negatively about the law. This would help explain why sometimes he can speak positively of the law (referring to God's intended purposes) and at other times negatively about it (referring to abuses of God's intent). Nuanced understandings like these mean that when Paul is railing against the "law," he doesn't necessarily have in mind what Moses originally intended, but rather a perverse reading and application of the law's function in some Second Temple Jewish circles. Paul thus sometimes appears to have as his target *perverse* uses of the law, not God's gift of the law rightly understood. Within the New Testament, including Paul, a right understanding of law is necessarily christocentric: serving as Prophet, Priest, and King, Jesus fulfilled the law, liberated his people from its condemning power, and gave them his Spirit so that they might now freely follow the commandments to love God and neighbor. Later I will return to contemporary Pauline scholarship when I discuss how to ground our ethics.

John Calvin long ago observed that in Paul the key was differentiating not so much between moral, civil, and ceremonial laws (although that could fruitfully be done), as between a narrow and broad use of the law. One functions destructively while the other serves a more positive purpose. In his exegesis of Romans 3:21–4:25, where Paul highlights the righteousness of God "apart from the law," Calvin reveals this distinction.[8] The *narrow* view referred to "the whole law as works," which is abolished. Unlike others (historic and contemporary), Calvin sees this approach to law in terms of a form of works righteousness, and not primarily about ceremonial fidelity. It is thus a perversion of the purposes of God's law. A narrow view of the law seeks, in whatever form—whether ceremonial or civil—to give law or works a power to make one

6. Herman Ridderbos, *Paul: An Outline of His Theology*, trans. John Richard De Witt (Grand Rapids: Eerdmans, 1975), 156, 157.

7. See J. D. G. Dunn, *Jesus, Paul, and the Law: Studies in Mark and Galatians* (Louisville: Westminster John Knox, 1990), 191–203.

8. Here I am drawing from Barbara Pitkin, *What Pure Eyes Could See: Calvin's Doctrine of Faith in Its Exegetical Context*, Oxford Studies in Historical Theology (New York: Oxford University Press, 1999), 44. Hereafter, page references from this work will be given in parentheses in the text.

righteous, and this is strongly rejected by Calvin (as he believes he is merely echoing Paul here). However, the *broader* view of the whole law still serves as a positive "expression of the will of God," which means it therefore contains "the promises" that are established in Christ (45). God's will and promises found in the law thus can speak to its continued helpful place for the Christian. God's moral law is here discovered; it raises our awareness of our sin and guilt, thus leading us to Christ; but he adds, "faith then confirms and establishes the law." He explains. Justification is not based on the law, but "in justification the exact righteousness of the law is imputed to human beings." But that is not all, since "in the process of sanctification human hearts are formed to the law" (45). In other words, when sinners attempt to use the law as a means to gain justification, they have misunderstood their relationship to the law. When saints, filled with the Spirit, listen to God's revelation in his law, they are able to glean from the law God's good promises as well as wisdom for how to now live as children of God.

Without question, the law must now always be seen in terms of the fulfillment of the messianic promises, which changes one's orientation to the law. But that doesn't annihilate the law's value. For example, Calvin elsewhere observed how in Psalm 19 David praises God's law, but in the broad rather than narrow way (100–103). By *faith* David saw the law in his redemptive-historical context in terms of the free promises of salvation that were to come. However, when Paul in Romans 1:18–23 appears to draw on texts like Psalm 19, he is dealing with opponents who are employing the law in the narrow sense; they are attempting to use law as the basis of their right standing with the God of Israel (101). They divorced law and gospel, and the result was to undermine both. Writing in a different context than David, Paul therefore warns against misusing the law (102). It was meant to point to Christ, not to serve as a substitute for him. But those who rest on the promises then seek lives of obedience shaped by God's revelation, including the law. This takes me back to a question about how we speak of the law, whether in our pulpits or personal conversations.

Is the Law Purely Negative?

Imagine that every time you hear the "law" or commandments of God mentioned from clergy, it is negative. Repeatedly we hear that the law condemns; it crushes, it judges. Christians are supposed to be people of the gospel and not of the law. Looking to the law only shows you what a miserable sinner you are, but nothing positive. It is like an unforgiving mirror that, held up before you, shows every blemish, every wrinkle, every imperfection. Again and again the listener hears versions of this, but never any positive word about God's commandments. Is that a problem?

I must be very careful here, but I have come to believe this one-sided use of the law feeds abiding confusion about the law, and maybe more significantly, stunts the experience of grace that is intended for the saints of God. For example, if one only hears how the law judges us, at some point it makes one ask if the Giver of the law is himself unkind or even cruel. And if the law has no place for the Christian, then is God now unconcerned with righteousness and obedience? How does one even define righteousness and obedience without God's revealed will? Does such one-sided emphasis also undermine any appropriate place of human agency for the Christian? Put differently, I believe that if we only speak of the condemning voice of the law and God's commandments, then we are actually undermining crucial aspects not just of the law, but of a life shaped by the gospel.

As is well known, the early reformers and creeds basically agreed that the law (in its various meanings) served at least a pedagogical role. It exposed the fallen human as a sinner who now stands exposed before a holy God. Proclaimed since our expulsion from the garden, the law of God certainly functioned well to show sinful humanity its place under divine judgment. But, is it right to speak only of the law in terms of judgment? This is especially a concern since throughout the Old Testament, God's law is something to be delighted in (Ps. 1:2), stored in your heart (Pss. 37:31; 40:8; cf. Josh. 1:7–8), and considered praiseworthy (e.g., Neh. 9:13–14). It is perfect and sure (Ps. 19:7). The longest psalm in Scripture endlessly glories in the gift of God's law (Ps. 119).

So should the Christian speak only negatively of the law? If so, I fear we can lose sight of the full power of God's grace. Let us not forget that Paul declares, "Do we then overthrow the law by this faith? By no means! On the contrary, we uphold the law" (Rom. 3:31). "The law is holy, and the commandment is holy and righteous and good" (Rom. 7:12; cf. 1 Tim. 1:8). While admitting a psychologically complex reality, whereby obedience remains a struggle for him, Paul nevertheless declares, "For I delight in the law of God, in my inner being" (Rom. 7:22). He may not always follow it, but he knows it presents God's character and is meant to protect and promote love (cf. James 2:8–12). Jesus is clear: he did not come to abolish the law, but to fulfill it (Matt. 5:17). John puts it this way: "the law was given through Moses; grace and truth came through Jesus Christ" (John 1:17). Might it be that this grace and truth—this person—is what John imagines liberates a believer from the law's curse? Once liberated, saints are enabled to hear wisdom and purpose in the law, rather than merely judgment and death. We are never to return to a Mosaic dispensation. But that doesn't mean the law is now merely negative or irrelevant. Why? Because the law is now seen in light of Christ and the indwelling presence of his Spirit in the believer.

What Grounds Your Ethics?

We must stop imagining that Paul advocated for divine grace whereas his fellow Jews rejected grace. John M. G. Barclay makes this abundantly clear in his recent magisterial study entitled *Paul and the Gift*: how Paul's opponents employed the idea of grace was just different from Paul—creating profound implications.[9] Paul was especially provocative in how he highlighted the *incongruity* and *superabundance* of God's grace, whereas they were drawing on other "perfections of grace," thus creating a chasm between the two perspectives.[10] Rather than imagining that Paul believed in grace and many of his Jewish brethren didn't, we must recognize that the two were functioning with different concepts of grace. To speak anachronistically, Paul's emphasis on the incongruity of God's grace is roughly what Luther and the reformers (re)discovered and desperately wanted for the church catholic again.

Yet this focus on the incongruity of the divine gift—which is at the heart of the gospel—also played into the different conception Paul had for the believer's relationship to the law. Many Second Temple Jews appeared to embrace what has been called "covenantal nomism," whereby grace is extended specifically to Israel by God's establishment of his covenant; law keeping was accordingly essential *not to enter* the covenant, but *to stay in it!* Paul, however, radicalizes this idea by consistently carrying out the emphasis on incongruity: there is nothing one can do to prepare oneself to be worthy of receiving God's great gift (*charis*), nor to stay in God's grace. It is grace upon grace, from first to last. Grace gets one in and grace keeps one in. God freely gives, even outrageously to the unworthy gentiles who were normally deemed unfit to receive such divine favor. Having received the Christ-Gift, Paul called the saints to joyfully respond to the gift freely given, believing the gift of Christ established a new relationship.

Barclay's research into the discipline of anthropology proves illuminating. It is arguably a very modern notion that for something to be a "pure" gift, rather

9. John M. G. Barclay, *Paul and the Gift* (Grand Rapids: Eerdmans, 2015).

10. On various "perfections" of grace, begin with Barclay, *Paul and the Gift*, 66–78; cf. 562–74.

than merely a transaction, there can be no sense of expectation of return. That is to misunderstand gift giving and social relations. Put simply, gifts are often given with the purpose of establishing or strengthening a relationship. Obviously this can be and has been abused: gifts have been used to manipulate, put people in debt, etc. The gospel is radical because a person did not need to be "fitting" to receive this gift, nor is the relationship based upon reciprocation. However, Barclay and Peter J. Leithart rightly conclude, this does not mean there is no sense of reciprocity in divine gift giving as portrayed in the biblical and Christian tradition.[11] God's gifts are freely given and freely received by faith, but this does not mean that God has no expectation of return: all things are from him, through him, and to him (Rom. 11:36).[12] His gift establishes and maintains the relationship, but it is with the expectation of a real relationship, which thus expects response.

For Paul, personal obedience to God's law was not meant to function as the means to get in or to stay in, but that didn't mean that God's law was of no value to those living under the blessings of divine favor. Navigating through this complexity, Paul, following Jesus, does not advocate for hatred of the law, but believes the only way to rightly understand the law now is through the lens of the Messiah's advent, death, and resurrection: the gospel! With the coming of the Messiah, it makes sense that distinctions within the law (e.g., civil, ceremonial, and moral) could legitimately make sense.[13] How does the coming of the Gift of God fulfill, inform, and transform the law's place and purpose?

Talking about the law and gospel distinction, Karl Barth asked a related question: What grounds Christian ethics? Here we might advance the conversation. Drawing on Zwingli and then later Calvin, Barth believed these reformers recognized that one needed to ground their ethics, not on the law, but upon grace.[14] This distinction is subtle but crucial. Whether or not it is historically fair, Barth imagined that early Protestants had two main options to ground their ethics: "faith" or "grace." In Barth's reading of the material, Luther and

11. Peter J. Leithart, *Gratitude: An Intellectual History* (Waco: Baylor University Press, 2014).

12. Cf. Kelly M. Kapic, *God So Loved He Gave: Entering the Movement of Divine Generosity* (Grand Rapids: Zondervan, 2010).

13. While this threefold division of civil, ceremonial, and moral has fallen on hard times, see a recent robust defense of this approach by Philip S. Ross, *From the Finger of God: The Biblical and Theological Division of the Law* (Glasgow, UK: Mentor, 2010).

14. Karl Barth, *The Theology of the Reformed Confessions*, translated and annotated by Darrell L. Guder and Judith J. Guder, Columbia Series in Reformed Theology (Louisville: Westminster John Knox, 2002), 87.

many in the Lutheran tradition answer "faith," while those following Zwingli and Calvin answer "grace." Obviously both speak of the vital importance of faith and the unquestionable dependence we have on God's grace. This is not faith versus grace. But, what Barth suspected he found—and I leave the historical accuracy of this assertion to historians for now—was that each tradition did actually put the weight on a different piece of the puzzle. *Faith* was the key in Luther's conception of the Christian life, and thus it served as the foundation for his understanding of Christian ethics. A detectable shift from faith to grace as that foundation appears in the early Reformed leaders. Whether or not this is fair to the Lutheran tradition, I am not qualified to know. My reading of Luther and Melanchthon has been hugely helpful for me through the years, but in this context, I am not the person to answer those questions. But what I can say is that this is basically right in the Reformed tradition. Grace becomes the key to rightly framing a Christian ethic, allowing that ethic to employ the law in positive ways without becoming a slave to the law, as happens to those outside of grace.

Grace enables one to delight in God's gift of the law without being condemned by it. Drawing on Calvin, Barth argues that "He who gave the gospel also gave the law; as seriously as the gospel is to be taken in faith, so seriously is the law to be taken for the will."[15] In this context he makes what he thinks is a classic distinction: for Calvin, "to be sure, ethics is established not directly upon faith, as Luther attempted to do, but upon grace." Once this subtle but critical distinction is made, he continues: "the law does not establish obedience, as little as the gospel itself establishes faith. Rather, both obedience and faith are established through the grace of the Holy Spirit, and as the gospel sets the direction there, now the law does so here."[16]

Obviously this then relates to one's conception of the will. Early on in the Reformed tradition, strong emphasis was given not merely to the catastrophic effects of sin on the natural-born human, but also to the life-giving power of the Spirit. Sin remains a real problem for believers, but by the Spirit, they are called not merely to see how bad they are, but also to find joy in the resurrection life they might now participate in even this side of glory. Drawing on Bullinger, Barth freely admits that indwelling sin remains a problem, but by the Spirit, "the human person should know that through grace he has really been put on

15. Barth, *Theology of the Reformed Confessions*, 101.

16. Barth, *Theology of the Reformed Confessions*, 101. Barth's concern is partly that "faith" can reduce the importance of this question to the "specifically religious sphere"; he sees the "problem of human life in its totality," and thus stresses the need to better see what it means to love God in all of life, following him in a "universal way" (101).

his feet in order to *walk*."[17] Put differently, the redeemed sinner—brought to life by the Spirit and secure in Christ's atoning work—was not made alive in order to become a passive rock: no, she was called to live, to love, and to serve. Guidance for this new life comes from God's revealed will, including his law.

Zwingli and the Positive Role of the Law

As early as the 1520s Zwingli was already noticing this potential problem when he observed that those who spoke of the abolition of the law did so in a "wholly clumsy fashion."[18] His concerns are biblical, theological, and pastoral. I will draw on Zwingli here to show that, from early on, Reformed instincts were not to trash the law once the Messiah had come, but to recognize that the gospel revolutionizes a person's relationship to the law. It still has value for the Christian, so that one might still even dare praise God for his holy ordinances.

Zwingli is one of the early people to recognize that "law" cannot simply be put in a negative manner, because it was meant originally as a gift from God. As early as 1523 Zwingli defined it this way: "the law is nothing but a manifestation of the will of God."[19] What he has in mind here is the eternal will of God, and so his focus is on the law "which is *conducive* to the godliness of the inner person."[20] With this turn toward the heart, rather than mere ritual or external obligation, he sees the law as positive rather than negative. Notice his language of "conducive." Zwingli will establish a view that becomes key to rightly understanding a Reformed approach: "laws do not have the power to make a person godly or righteous; rather, they point out only how a person should be if he wants to live according to the will of God, become godly and come to God."[21] Others after him will further develop and clarify this intuition.

Even early on one can see the idea emerging that *the law serves more like a map than like an engine*. It was *never* made to empower, but only to guide (cf. Acts 13:39; Rom. 2:13). When a person tries to turn the law into an engine, such as when a sinner tries to use the law to justify himself before God, insurmountable problems arise. It was never intended to serve that capacity.

17. Barth, *Theology of the Reformed Confessions*, 92.

18. Huldrych Zwingli, "A Short Christian Instruction . . . ," in *Huldrych Zwingli Writings: In Search of True Religion; Reformation, Pastoral, and Eucharistic Writings*, trans. H. Wayne Pipkin, vol. 2 (Allison Park, PA: Pickwick, 1984), 63.

19. Zwingli, "A Short Christian Instruction," 53.

20. Zwingli, "A Short Christian Instruction," 53 (emphasis added).

21. Zwingli, "A Short Christian Instruction," 53.

But when the believer, filled with the power of the Spirit, looks to the law for guidance, it is a great gift.

Like a map—think here of a GPS that speaks while you drive—the law rightly judges you when you are lost and going the wrong way, but also has the capacity to point you in the right direction. On its own the law doesn't take you anywhere, but it does give you instructions. One might think here of the Old Testament language of the law's role as announcing blessing and cursing (e.g., Josh. 8:34). The law does not make one blessed or cursed, but it lets one know where one stands in relationship to God's will. What the law cannot do, nor was ever meant to do, is be the power to get you to where you need to go. And given the reality of sin, we have no such natural power available to us. We are absolutely dependent upon God's grace and provision. Apart from his grace we are dead in sin (Eph. 2:1). Born under sin's curse and effect, we stand only lost and under judgment. We see on the map how far off the target we are, and we realize we have no energy or ability to correct the ship's course. Having the map alone will not save us. What we need is wind; what we need is the life-giving breath of the Spirit of God.

Simply put, the law ably shows us how far short we come of God's will: we do not love God and neighbor with our whole hearts, souls, and strength. Jesus makes it clear: this is what was always at the heart of the law.[22] He is not adding this to the law; he is simply amplifying (think Sermon on the Mount) the law's original purpose to guide and shape our loves (e.g., Gal. 5:14). All sinners who stand before the law apart from Christ stand judged. We do not love as we ought. Hence, God's gift/grace becomes our life-giving link: here we meet Christ and enter into the gospel. In his brief work "Divine and Human Righteousness," Zwingli highlighted his christological focus: "you learn through the word of the divine will what a great treasure God is. For the goodness which he prescribes for us, he is in himself and he conducts himself as he bids us to do; for he is not at all like the tyrants who devise superb laws which they themselves never keep."[23] Thus, all must be viewed as a "free gift" from God in Christ. Receive this gift, stand in awe of the treasure, and then follow

22. Zwingli draws on Luke 16:16 and following, noting how the law and prophets served Israel until John the Baptist, but now Messiah has come. The law lasted until John, but nevertheless, even after John it also did not become void. Fully aware how contradictory this sounds to us, Zwingli argues the law comes from God himself, so we must follow carefully the implications. Accordingly, he first observes that all the ceremonial laws of the Old Testament served as a shadow of Christ, and when the light itself comes, the shadow disappears (cf. Heb. 10:1). These observances, unfortunately, were often treated merely at the external level, rather than dealing with the inner man.

23. Huldrych Zwingli, "Divine and Human Righteousness," in *Huldrych Zwingli Writings*, 2:8.

your new King. His gift does not make obedience insignificant; it just means it is not the basis of the new relationship. But as a good king, his laws are and remain good. Rightly understood and applied, the moral law is "a good thing in itself," for the law "shows the will of God."[24]

Zwingli employs theft as an illuminating example. The law clearly calls us not to steal. Jesus makes it clear that this law was always intended to point both to actual physical robbery and to greedy hearts. This law judges our thoughts, motives, and actions, ably showing us our need for a sinless Savior. As Messiah, Jesus perfectly fulfilled the law: not only did he avoid theft, he gave everything he had to those in need. Consequently, we who are now united to Christ by the Spirit are set free from the law's condemning power. Forgiven, we are no longer judged for our act of theft (cf. Heb. 10:17). In this way, the law has lost its power over us. There is therefore now no condemnation for those who are in Christ Jesus (Rom. 8:1). Nevertheless, Zwingli clarifies: to imagine that it is irrelevant whether a *Christian* steals or not—whether a Christian is greedy or not—is to misunderstand both the law and the gospel. Of course Christians should not steal, and they learn this from God's law. And in Christ, the flip side of the coin is powerfully portrayed. Obeying this command meant extending generosity, not just avoiding robbery. He gave everything he had, including his own life! It is along these lines that the Westminster Larger Catechism provides hermeneutical guidance on applying the Decalogue: "where a duty is commanded, the contrary sin is forbidden; and where a sin is forbidden, the contrary duty is commanded" (WLC 99.4). Jesus embodies faithfulness to God's commandments, and now his people are those in whom he dwells, by his Spirit. It makes sense, therefore, that as his love is spread abroad in their hearts, they would now seek to imitate their Lord's sacrificial love.

Free to Obey

Paul announces that "the law of the Spirit of life has set you free in Christ Jesus from the law of sin and death" (Rom. 8:2). Free in Christ. Because Christ became a curse for us, we are free from the curse of the law (Gal. 3:13). But does this mean that the Torah (in all its varied uses) is no longer of value? Is this not what causes some to believe that the Old Testament is no longer genuinely relevant? Does the Decalogue, which is implied and applied throughout the Old Testament and New Testament, not have abiding value for Christians

24. Zwingli, "A Short Christian Instruction," 62.

even as they are set free from the law's damning power? Let's look at this in a more positive light.

It is *loving* to teach saints the will of God as found in his moral law, so that they might know how to live *freely* as his kingdom people. Freely, because sin tends to enslave and pervert. Gospel freedom is not merely freedom *from* the law's judgment, but also freedom *to* joyfully seek to follow the triune God's desires. Breaking God's commandments tends to push us back toward feelings of suffocating entanglements to sin (Heb. 12:1); we are people who have been set free from that prison of judgment, so why act like we are still in jail? We praise God for his law, not merely because it shows us our sin, but because it guides us in our Christian freedom. Christian freedom is never about doing whatever we want or think is right apart from God's revelation. Christian freedom is the liberty to follow Christ, not because we dread punishment, but out of gratitude and love for our Lord. We are free to love God and neighbor.

Zwingli's long 1523 *Exposition . . .*, after again making it clear that the law no longer condemns the believer, adds, "not that that which God bids and wills should no longer be done."[25] You who were swindlers, swindle no more. Yet freedom and grace shape this obedience, since now this obedience "is kindled increasingly more by the love of God" as one discovers with increasing measure divine grace and "friendliness." "The greater this love, the more one does what God wills."[26] Love, not guilt, compels one to seek to follow God's revealed law, a moral law that promotes "doing good." Here is his defense against both legalism and antinomianism. Legalism is ruled out because the law, which has been satisfied by Christ, no longer condemns the believer. No one can nor should seek to secure God's favor through law keeping. Antinomianism is ruled out because of love: those who have experienced God's love and grace—or better, those in whom God now dwells by his Spirit—are motivated to follow his commandments rather than disregard them. Motivated "out of love," the believer seeks to obey, but never in his own strength. "Rather, God effects in him love, counsel and works," so that "where God is," as he noted earlier, "you need not have to worry how to do good."

John Calvin demonstrated similar assumptions when he described the "pious mind" of the believer. Here is a mind persuaded that God is "good and

25. Huldrych Zwingli, *Exposition . . .*, in *Huldrych Zwingli Writings: In Defense of the Reformed Faith*, trans. E. J. Furcha, vol. 1 (Allison Park, PA: Pickwick, 1984), art. 22, p. 189.

26. Zwingli, *Exposition . . .*, art. 22, p. 189. The following quotes in this paragraph also come from this article.

merciful," a person who does not doubt God's loving-kindness.[27] A godly person "deems it meet and right to observe [God's] authority in all things, reverence his majesty, take care to advance his glory, and obey his commandments."[28] Her motivations are not to earn God's favor, but as one who stands secure in her Father's delight. Accordingly, Calvin contrasts this "pious mind" with the impious mind that only fears God for his potential punishments and thus has not learned to obey God out of love. Calvin paints the picture vividly: "this [pious] mind restrains itself from sinning . . . because it loves and reveres God as Father, it worships and adores him as Lord. Even if there were no hell, it would still shudder at offending him alone."[29] As a father might remind his children of ancient and wise instructions for life, so Christians are taught the moral law in hopes that they might express their love and gratefulness to God by seeking to follow his commandments.[30] Similarly, the 1559 French Confession of Faith argues that we "must seek aid from the law and the prophets for the ruling of our lives, as well as for our confirmation in the promises of the gospel."[31] Honestly looking at the law, we see not only our sin but also the glory of all that Christ has fulfilled on our behalf. Looking then at the law, in light of union with Christ, offers the chance to live under God's grace and wisdom, seeking faithfulness in response to divine forgiveness and grace.

For the Christian, the law is still not power, but rightly employed, it is a trustworthy map on what it means to follow after God. The power, however, is supplied by the triune God himself: known and called by the Father, cleansed in the atoning blood of the Son, and enlivened and kept in the sanctifying fellowship of the Spirit (cf. 1 Pet. 1:2; Jude 2; 2 Cor. 13:14; Heb. 9:14). This is what it means to enter the grace of God.

27. John Calvin, *Institutes of the Christian Religion*, ed. John T. McNeill, trans. F. L. Battles, Library of Christian Classics 20 (Louisville: Westminster, 1960), 1.2.2 (p. 42).

28. Calvin, *Institutes* 1.2.2 (p. 42).

29. Calvin, *Institutes* 1.2.2 (p. 43).

30. See Zwingli, "A Short Christian Instruction," 63.

31. "French Confession of Faith" 23, in *The Evangelical Protestant Creeds*, vol. 3 of *The Creeds of Christendom*, ed. Philip Schaff (Grand Rapids: Baker, 1983), 372–73. Rohls, who also quotes this memorable portion from the French Confession, nicely summarizes the Reformed conclusion: "The law thus also applies to the justified, serving as a standard of orientation for sanctification" (Rohls, *Reformed Confessions*, 201).

Law and Gospel: Advice for Ministers

It is now time for us to put some of the puzzle pieces back together. I would like to conclude this essay by providing some reflections more explicitly aimed at helping those who minister to God's people. This is because discussions about the relationship between the law and the gospel were never meant to be merely academic, but always reflect abiding pastoral concerns. Whether in the counseling chamber or preaching from a podium, pastors must employ wisdom, joy, and hope as they bring the good news of the gospel to their listeners. With this particular audience in mind, I would like to close with three final reflections.

- First, don't pit love against the law.
- Second, differentiate between union and communion.
- Third, finish the sermon!

Love and Law

John Murray, writing in 1935, found himself dealing with early forms of sentimentality that seemed to skew more classic Christian conceptions of law and gospel. Some Christian voices were pitting God's moral law against love. Since Christians were under grace and gospel, it was believed, the law had no place in their lives: to value the law was to devalue love. Murray, following his Reformed tradition, reframed the situation: "we are not saved by obedience to the law, but we are saved unto it."[32] This is based on his view that the law of God is not arbitrary, but rather points to or reflects God's own nature, in his purity and holiness.[33] If God's character does not change, then there must be abiding relevance of the law for the believer. We can never forget the various ways Torah is employed. Obviously one must take into consideration progressive revelation, redemptive historical developments, etc., always with Christ as the focal point. But to fail to see any abiding significance for the "law"—which would include the moral law—risks saying very problematic things about the God who gave the law. Such deficiencies, for example, are manifested when ministers shy away from regularly preaching from the Old Testament. Rather

32. John Murray, "The Sanctity of the Moral Law," in *Collected Writings of John Murray*, vol. 1 (Edinburgh: Banner of Truth, 1976), 199.

33. Murray, "Sanctity," 196.

than God's love serving as the fulfillment of the law, Murray's opponents were at risk of making love and law enemies. And here Murray dissects the heart of the problem.

> What our modern apostles of love really mean is the very opposite of this: they mean that love fulfils its own dictates, that love not only fulfils, but that it is also the law fulfilled, that *love is as it were an autonomous, self-instructing and self-directing principle*, that not only impels to the doing of the right but also tells us what the right is. This is certainly not what Paul meant when he said, "love is the fulfilling of the law [Rom. 13:10]." He tells us not only that love fulfills, but also what the law is which it fulfills.[34]

According to Murray, this moral law was most markedly and simply laid out in the Decalogue. If this clear expression of God's will is negated or belittled, people try to look inside rather than outside of themselves to know the good, the true, and the beautiful. Love is now determined solely by one's intuitions, rather than by any explicit guidance from a transcendent God. David Brooks's recent volume has ably demonstrated this modern turn toward the inward, observing the social and personal consequences this shift creates.[35] But the Christian concern here is not so much about a vague notion of character, but about living in joyful communion with God and others.

While the conscience is used by God, with sin exerting its destructive inward bent, the conscience alone is simply not strong enough to provide consistent truth. It needs both cleaning and education.[36] According to Melanchthon's mature thought, "a third use of the law is necessary," as it serves "to inform the good conscience and encourage it to obedience."[37] It should not surprise us, then, that the young, budding French theologian John Calvin appears to pick up this distinction, employing it in his first institutes.[38] Jan Rohls recognizes how this dynamic informs the Reformed view of freedom: "the conscience is free only when God is the sole Lord of the conscience, and this means that

34. Murray, "Sanctity," 199 (emphasis added). He later adds, "The directing principle of love is objectively revealed statutory commandments, not at all the dictates which it might itself be presumed to excogitate."

35. David Brooks, *The Road to Character* (New York: Random House, 2015), esp. 3–15, 240–70.

36. J. W. Gladwin, "Conscience," in *New Dictionary of Christian Ethics and Pastoral Theology*, ed. David J. Atkinson et al. (Leicester, UK: InterVarsity, 1995), 251–52.

37. Timothy J. Wengert, *Law and Gospel: Philip Melanchthon's Debate with John Agricola of Eisleben over* Poenitentia (Grand Rapids: Baker, 1997), 205.

38. Wengert, *Law and Gospel*, 206.

the law as God's unsuperseded goodwill is also valid for Christians who have been redeemed and set free from the law's curse."[39] This is why many, even Melanchthon, might rightly speak of a favorable third use of the law.

Jesus does not leave the concept of love up to our imaginations—he knows we are too self-deceptive for that. He is clear: "If you love me, you will keep my commandments" (John 14:15). "Whoever has my commandments and keeps them, he it is who loves me. And he who loves me will be loved by my Father, and I will love him and manifest myself to him" (John 14:21). This commandment keeping is ultimately linked to the incarnate Son's obedience to his Father, who sent him in the power of the Spirit. "If you keep my commandments, you will abide in my love, *just as I have kept my Father's commandments and abide in his love*" (John 15:10). The divine mission was not meant to eliminate God's moral concerns, but in love to answer them. Along these lines, Murray was right to fear the sentimentalizing of love when it waged war against the moral commandments of God. Christians live by faith in the grace of God in Christ, but this is a life still governed and guided by God's revealed will, rather than one free from it. Or, put more favorably, the Christian is the one who is liberated to enter into communion with the triune God. This communion includes the liberty to obey the Spirit's motions and movements as the believer seeks to follow the Son in his love of the Father and neighbor.

Union and Communion

For those outside of the Reformed tradition, how we are able to value both law and gospel is often a mystery. But central to this approach is the distinction between *union* and *communion*. Personally I also believe this strikes at the heart of pastoral challenges and possibilities. Two biblical truths are upheld rather than conflated. On the one hand, through union those who are made alive by the Spirit of Christ are made sons and daughters of God. Here is a position of security, comfort, and rest. On the other hand, the actions of saints remain relevant to God, and therefore obedience to God's law, summarized as loving God and neighbor, has genuine consequences for the believer's *experience* of communion. So how does one uphold the latter without making void the former? Let us look at the pastoral importance of these truths.

Our obedience never was nor can ever be the foundation of the Christian life. Christ, and Christ alone, is that foundation. He was and must always

39. Rohls, *Reformed Confessions*, 200.

remain our security and salvation. This truth is celebrated in the doctrine of union with Christ. In the Reformed tradition, this reality is established by the Spirit, who unites us to Christ and thus liberates us to enjoy fellowship with God. Union is not the goal of the Christian life, as it can appear in some Christian traditions, but rather it's the starting point. There is no Christian life—there is no fellowship with God—apart from this union to our Mediator. Wonderfully, this union does not ebb and flow like the tides of the ocean, but remains always full. In other words, a believer's behavior cannot affect this union, because the union was established objectively by God's grace; it was not based on our obedience to the law. What a great comfort union with Christ is to struggling believers, as they realize that their lapses have not compromised God's love and commitment to them. God does not love them less or more today because of their obedience or lack thereof. They are secure in his Fatherly love. We would think ill of an earthly father who legally adopts a child, but then after witnessing numerous outbursts of disobedience, disowns the youngster, sending the child back to the orphanage. How in the world could we imagine our heavenly Father disowning us after he has called us his children and given us his Spirit? It can never be. Why? Because we have been united to Christ, and this provides genuine security.

Once born again, believers find themselves looking to their heavenly Father. As Karl Barth notes, "This same God [of gracious regeneration] also makes man obedient for his service."[40] Because believers are his newborn children, it would be appropriate for them to love to know their Father's wishes, to know what is good and best. Proverbs again and again calls for wise children to live under their parents' love, a love that includes keeping God's commandments, commandments that are meant to foster shalom (Prov. 3:1; 4:4; 6:20; 7:1–2; etc.). Here then comes God's law—framed in light of Christ crucified and risen—as a gift to help guide the children's responsive obedience. How can one call a child disobedient if there is not clear indication of what it looks like to live as a beloved child?

40. Barth, *Theology of the Reformed Confessions*, 148. Under the covenant of grace, the law "materially" remains in force, but its function has now been changed: "it is no longer a means of justification, but rather a standard of sanctification." As Rohls concludes, "The third use of the law (*tertius usus legis*) consists of justified sinners showing gratitude in the form of obedience to the law for the justification that has occurred" (Rohls, *Reformed Confessions*, 202). In his well-crafted book, Wengert argued that Melanchthon "wanted desperately both to defend the Reformers from the charge that they denied the necessity of good works and at the same time to avoid robbing the conscience of the gospel's consolation. So he devised a way to speak of the necessity of works for the believer by excluding their necessity for justification" (Wengert, *Law and Gospel*, 188).

As the holy and good heavenly Father, his love for his children never grows nor diminishes based on their obedience. However, the Christian's experience of intimacy with God is often helped by acts of repentance and obedience, or hindered by acts of neglect and disobedience. This is not about legalistic law keeping nor empty rituals; this is about communion with God. God is not interested in whitewashed tombs. But he is interested in communion. If one spouse neglects another, a husband and wife may still be united in marriage, but their intimate communion is not fostered. Similarly, while we are secure in our union to Christ, our actions still have consequences. Does it matter if we pray or not? Not in terms of union, but absolutely in terms of communion. Does it matter if we commit adultery or not? It does not destroy our union, but it certainly can affect our communion. As James declares, we are to be "doers of the word, and not hearers only, deceiving [ourselves]" (James 1:22). When we neglect to put into practice God's good desires for his people, we live as if we were slaves to unrighteousness. But Christians are those who demonstrate their faith by their works (James 2:14–26). Never to earn God's favor, but as a consequence of God's favor.

Here we turn to the wisdom of John Owen, who unabashedly points out that *communion* requires what he calls "mutual communication."[41] Communion is based on union, but is distinct from it. Owen explains: "Our communion, then, with God consisteth in his communication of himself unto us, with our returnal unto him of that which he requireth and accepteth, flowing from that union which in Jesus Christ we have with him."[42] Living in the now and not yet, we experience this communion as "initial and incomplete," but one day in glory it will be "perfect and complete."[43] This giving and receiving are meant to grow out of the preexistent security of God's love known and enjoyed because of union.

Ministers are therefore to hold out the security of our union with Christ to which we are called by the Father and engrafted in by the Spirit.[44] Let therefore

41. John Owen, *Of Communion with God the Father, the Son and the Holy Ghost*, in *The Works of John Owen*, vol. 2 (Edinburgh: Banner of Truth Trust, 1965), 8. For a full treatment of Owen's distinctive Trinitarian approach to union and communion, see Kelly M. Kapic, *Communion with God: The Divine and the Human in the Theology of John Owen* (Grand Rapids: Baker Academic, 2007), esp. 147–205.

42. Owen, *Of Communion*, 8–9.

43. Owen, *Of Communion*, 9.

44. For a recent, wonderful unpacking of the place of union—from a Reformed perspective—for theology and ministry, see J. Todd Billings, *Union with Christ: Reframing Theology and Ministry for the Church* (Grand Rapids: Baker Academic, 2011).

your sin, your shortcomings before the law no longer condemn you. Silence those voices of condemnation. You can rest in the robe of Christ's righteousness. Now, as do those who are secure in Christ, discover more of who this Christ is: learn of his goodness, his kindness, his compassion. These can only be fully appreciated, however, by looking at Christ in light of the law, which he fulfilled. Then, resting in the kindness of our Father, we seek to grow in our knowledge and love of our God. This means loving what God loves and eschewing what God eschews. Here the law can provide continued guidance for the believer.

Finish the Sermon

Let me now return to where I began, with potential confusion about the "gospel." The gospel is about who Jesus is and all he accomplished. He came as the Prophet, Priest, and King. Those liberated by the gospel live under our new King and Great High Priest and eagerly listen to his prophetic voice, a voice that the entire Old Testament, including the law, anticipated and promised. We long to know what it means to live in God's kingdom. This can never be about adding something to grace, but it does mean preaching the full counsel of God, Old and New Testaments. It means preaching from the law and the prophets; it means meditating on God's law and soaking oneself in his Ten Commandments. Never done apart from Christ, but now always reading these Scriptures in light of Christ, who came as the fulfillment of the law. Yes and Amen. But the abiding question is this: Do those texts have relevance for Christians besides simply saying Jesus has fulfilled them? I believe they do. I would like to explain what I mean in very practical terms by outlining how sermons are often crafted.

Moralist preachers simply use Scripture to tell stories of virtue and morality, hoping their listeners will become good citizens and family members. That is a misunderstanding of the Scriptures and the gospel to which they point. Let us always resist that temptation. However, in reaction to such reductionist preaching, I have seen a pattern in some forms of "gospel" sermons. Here is how they normally go:

- Read the passage of Scripture.
- Declare God's expectations or demands from said passage.
- Make it clear how far short we fall of living up to God's holy standard, no matter how hard we try.

- Proclaim Christ and him crucified, making it clear that Christ's perfect righteousness is ours by faith alone.
- Close in prayer

I don't think there is anything wrong with this basic outline, but I fear we abort too early. We don't finish our sermons, and in that way, we don't enjoy the fullness of the gospel for our lives. Let me explain my growing concern.

If "gospel" means that Christians should never engage their agency, that exertion of any sort is somehow inherently antigospel, then I believe we simply are not listening to Jesus. Dallas Willard put it starkly: "Grace is not opposed to effort, it is opposed to earning. Earning is an attitude. Effort is an action. Grace, you know, does not just have to do with forgiveness of sins alone."[45] I have become suspicious, on the basis of various factors, that something psychological often happens when people hear sermon after sermon that always boils down to this: you are a sinner and nothing you do can merit God's favor (true); Jesus was faithful and in him we are forgiven (true); the end (incomplete). At first this is wonderfully liberating. Praise God, my standing before a holy God is not based on my meager efforts and mixed motives. Praise him for the wideness and depth of his mercy. But over time, I often find that people begin to believe that "gospel" means that any attempt to try to follow God's commandments, any pattern of exerting effort, can only be taken as a sign of "works righteousness." If you try, it will inevitably be from mixed motives and incomplete faithfulness. Therefore, why try? If you do, you must be a legalist. Sadly, I have too often seen a combination of self-loathing and apathy develop from those consistently sitting under this pattern of preaching.

We would normally respond: "How can there be self-loathing? Look what God has done for you in Christ!" Yet, the message normally sounds like this. God demands, we fail, so God cannot stand to look upon us in our sin. But because of Jesus, the Father now sees the Son rather than us in our sin, and therefore we are loved. This is great at first, until at some point after a thousand sermons, the believer wonders: "Does God actually love *me*? Does he even know *me*? Or does the Father merely love the Son?" If the good news has been preached in a way that God the Father can't stand you, but only looking to Christ he loves you, people are in an unstable position. And this is a misunderstanding of union with Christ.

45. Dallas Willard, *The Great Omission: Reclaiming Jesus's Essential Teachings on Discipleship* (New York: HarperCollins, 2006), 61.

God loves *you*. He knows *you*. And not only does he forgive you, he also wants *you* to live. He wants *you* to receive and extend love. He wants you to be you. What does that look like? It looks like you freely obeying the triune God and enjoying communion with him and loving your neighbor. Our renewal in the image of Christ includes this liberty to imitate Christ, to enter into the movement of divine generosity, to participate in God's grace as he extends himself to sinners. We are not mere observers of that grace, but participants. Entering into God's love causes us to love. And loving God and neighbor is not opposed to the law, but what was always meant as the summary of the law.

Returning to the sermon outline, let me propose one addition near the end. After Christ crucified is proclaimed, we need to add this:

- *Christ is risen, and in him, we have been raised to life*. So *live* in him!

Too often our sermons speak in terms of the cross but neglect the promise of resurrection.[46] But this promise is not merely about a future life, it is about the present. We have been raised in him. Our life is thus necessarily a life informed and transformed by the renewing of the mind (Rom. 12:1–2), a renewal that happens by Word and Spirit. We never pit these against one another. This then includes guidance on how to live as God's people in light of the passage at hand. Such an approach allows for the positive use of the law that the Reformed tradition believes is legitimate. Law, never as a means to be justified. Law, never as a means to make oneself secure before God. But God's law does help us better understand our God and ourselves. This is the story we learn, and it is our story. These laws shape us, guide us, challenge and encourage us. Obviously these are now all understood in light of Christ, but that doesn't mean they are irrelevant now. We should flee from abuses of the law. But might it be that rightly preached and proclaimed, in light of the all-sufficient grace of God in Christ and by his Spirit, God's law is a law of liberty? Rightly understood and preached, a sermon promotes love of God and neighbor, not self-loathing or apathy.

46. To help one see how central the resurrection is to a Christian conception of ethics, see Oliver O'Donovan, *Resurrection and Moral Order: An Outline for Evangelical Ethics*, 2nd ed. (Grand Rapids: Eerdmans, 1994).

The Gospel of the Crucified and Risen Christ

I would summarize the Reformed view with this simple claim: a gospel sermon preaches Christ crucified as well as Christ risen. United to Christ by his Spirit, we rest in the love of the Father, the grace of the Son, and the secure fellowship of the Spirit. Enjoying the communion that flows out of this union, believers rightly seek to know God's will. They therefore look to God's law, not for power, but for abiding guidance. They never try to navigate the map apart from Christ, but they also recognize that without the map they can't even understand Christ himself. Nor can they fully understand what it means to live in his kingdom. The gospel means we are liberated from the law's condemnation even as we are then free to obey our Lord and Savior. Christ has died. Christ is risen. In him we now live as his people.

PART IV

Lutheran and Reformed Responses

Chapter 7

A Lutheran Response to the Reformed Tradition

Erik H. Herrmann

Like George Bernard Shaw's quip about the locutionary tragedy that is England and America, the differences between the Lutheran and the Reformed faiths are often obfuscated by a common language. There are obvious terminological continuities between the two traditions—both speak of the law and the gospel, the danger of confusing them, and the importance of distinguishing them. There are conceptual continuities so that both Lutheran and Reformed traditions orient law and gospel to the doctrine of justification *sola fide*. There are also historical continuities in which the early Reformed theologians saw themselves as heirs and beneficiaries of Luther's teaching on the matter—perhaps clarifying, deepening, or correcting—but heirs nonetheless. Yet, in spite of such affinities, there always seems to be something amiss. Lurking are suspicions of antinomianism, legalism, moralism, and libertinism. Hearing the other, one is hesitant to give a full-throated "Amen"—more often a muted "Yes, but . . ."

But in the first half of the twentieth century, the gloves finally came off. In 1935, Karl Barth launched an attack on the Lutheran distinction of law and gospel by reversing the order: not law and gospel but *gospel and law*.[1] The reaction among German Lutheran theologians was fierce, the strongest perhaps from Erlangen theologian Werner Elert.[2] Of course, both Barth and Elert are more than their respective traditions. In addition to their own creative and

1. Karl Barth, "Evangelium und Gesetz," in *Theologische Existenz heute* 32 (Munich: Christian Kaiser Verlag, 1935); Barth, "Gospel and Law," in *Community, State, and Church*, Anchor Books (Garden City, NY: Doubleday, 1960), 71–100.

2. Werner Elert, "Gesetz und Evangelium," in *Zwischen Gnade und Ungnade: Abwandlungen des Themas Gesetz und Evangelium* (Munich: Evangelischer Presseverband für Bayern, 1948), 132–69; Elert, *Law and Gospel*, trans. Edward H. Schroeder (Philadelphia: Fortress, 1967).

original contributions to contemporary theology, they are also *caricatures* of the Reformed and Lutheran traditions. I don't mean this in a pejorative sense, but merely according to the strict definition of the word—they enlarge distinctive features of their traditions so that what was once rather subtle and subdued leaps out in stark contrast. Barth's reversal, which stressed the nomistic character of the gospel and the gracious character of the law, was part of his unique answer to the modern problem of revelation. Yet his accent reflected his affinity to a theological tradition that upheld the eternity of the law and its primary use as "a rule of righteous living"—*règle de bien vivre et justement.*[3] Likewise, the sharp antagonism of law and gospel found in Elert reflected the Lutheran proclivity to speak of the law in almost exclusively negative terms, *lex semper accusat.*[4] Further, the more disputed doctrines of the reformers—the prelapsarian "covenant of works" in Calvin and the postconversion third use of the law in Luther—were stripped away by their respective positions. While Barth stressed the gratuity of God's revelation even under the form of law, Elert defined the law in the context of humanity's *Urelebnis*—the primal experience of dread in the face of finitude and death. In their extreme positions they have touched upon the skew of the two lines, the asymmetry that, though slight in the original reformers, ran along paths that grew ever divergent, leaving a wider and wider gap.

Or have they?

Even if it is a true generalization that in their distinctions of law and gospel Lutherans tilt antinomian and the Reformed tilt nomistic, what have we really said or learned? Is this a difference in substance or emphasis? Why would such a difference be present in the first place? And what are the historical-genetic factors that contribute to this difference? On the one hand, there is little doubt that, historically speaking, the originating theologians of the Reformed tradition—for example, Zwingli, Bucer, Bullinger, and Calvin—inherited the particular language and distinction of law and gospel from Luther and Melanchthon. However, their appropriation of the same was in a different context with a different set of questions. A Lutheran may demur at the Reformed exposition of law and gospel, in part because the particularities of the original intent seem obscured, lost, or somehow mishandled.

On the other hand, the genesis of Luther's reappraisal of law and gospel is not always appreciated, even among Lutherans. Luther's teaching on law and gospel is usually understood as part of his theological solution for a late

3. Geneva Catechism (1536).

4. Ap 4:285.

medieval church that obligated the pious to ritual acts within a system of merit that could also be exploited for financial gain—what Luther dubbed a religion of "works righteousness." This is indeed the *telos* of his distinction and highlights its importance for clarifying his efforts to reform Christian piety, but its *roots* are shaped by Luther's interaction with the scholastic and exegetical tradition that supported such a spirituality. It is especially the latter—Luther's work as *doctor in Biblia* in the context of the exegetical tradition—that is of particular import since the distinction of law and gospel is for Luther, first and foremost, an *exegetical* question, or to put a finer point on it, it is a question of *Pauline* exegesis. As such, it is a distinction that addresses central hermeneutical issues, especially the relationship between the Old and New Testaments. Gerhard Ebeling once observed that "the Pauline doctrine of the law must be adduced as being in actual fact the only fundamental theological indication in the New Testament as to how the question of the use of the Old Testament in the church would have to be thought out."[5] On the one hand, this seems like an obvious point: how Christianity understands the place and function of the Mosaic law—the centerpiece of Old Testament theology—is indicative of how one handles the Old Testament in general as Christian Scripture. But what Ebeling wished to underscore is that Paul's understanding of the law also *contributes* to the hermeneutical problem of the Old Testament even as it attempts to solve it.

Only in this context can one begin to understand the significance that the distinction of law and gospel had for Luther. He is wrestling with a weighty exegetical tradition in which its various attempts to solve the hermeneutical and theological problems raised by Paul's antithesis of law and faith produce even greater problems. For Luther, distinguishing law and gospel does not merely solve a single tendency in late medieval piety or theology, but it is the "two arms of the nutcracker with which Luther tries to pry open the hard shell of Scripture in order to reach the sweet kernel of meaning inside."[6] Reformed theologians are not ignorant of the Western exegetical tradition or the hermeneutical problems within it, but their interpretation of law and gospel does not arise out of this context.

5. Gerhard Ebeling, "Reflexions on the Doctrine of the Law," in *Word and Faith* (Philadelphia: Fortress, 1963), 274; "Erwägung zur Lehre vom Gesetz," in *Wort und Glaube* I (Tübingen: Mohr Siebeck, 1962), 285: "In der Tat muß die Paulinische Lehre vom Gesetz herangezogen werden als der im Neuen Testament faktisch einzige prinzipielle theologische Hinweis, wie die Frage des Gebrauches des Alten Testamentes in der Kirche zu durch denken wäre."

6. Gerhard Ebeling, "The Beginnings of Luther's Hermeneutics," *Lutheran Quarterly* 7 (1993): 452.

In my attempt to give a Lutheran appraisal of the Reformed approach to the distinction of law and gospel, I will explore three areas: the exegetical standpoint on the distinction, the relation of the law to covenant and faith, and the relation of theological method within the Lutheran and Reformed traditions.

Law and Gospel in the History of Exegesis[7]

Separatio legis et evangelii proprium et principale opus est Marcionis—"the separation of law and gospel is the proper and principal work of Marcion." So said Tertullian. Marcion, however, claimed Pauline precedent for this work, and thus began the first great conflict over the interpretation of Paul.

The significance of Marcion for the history of the church has been oft debated since Adolf von Harnack's provocative "reformer" interpretation. From the ambiguous relationship to Gnosticism to the formation of the New Testament canon, Marcion continues to remain a controversial figure among modern scholars even as his life and teaching remain shrouded in uncertainties. Yet it is rather safe to say that opposition to Marcion resulted in greater attention given to the interpretation of Paul and his teaching on law and gospel. Irenaeus himself admits as much.[8] Tertullian too recognized the Pauline basis of Marcion's theological position, noting his special affection for Galatians.[9] In fact, the dispute between Peter and Paul in the second chapter embodied for Marcion Paul's central message: the conflict between the law and the "truth of the gospel" marked a fundamental antithesis within salvation history between Judaism and Christianity, between the Old Testament and the New Testament, and between the god described in each. For Marcion, Paul's disparagement and apparent abrogation of the law necessarily entailed the abrogation of the Old Testament. Thus, in the wake of Marcion's error we may see the interpretation of Paul deepen two significant and related trends: the *continuity* of law and gospel was maintained in order to preserve the theological unity between the Testaments, and allegory became the primary means to bring hermeneutical unity to the same.

7. For a more detailed account of the exegetical tradition's interpretation of this problem, especially with respect to Galatians, see my dissertation, "Why Then the Law? Salvation History and the Law in Martin Luther's Interpretation of Galatians, 1513–1522" (PhD diss., Concordia Seminary, 2005), 14–66.

8. E.g., Irenaeus, *Adversus haereses* (hereafter *Adv. haer.*) 4.7.

9. Tertullian, *Adversus Marcionem* 1.20.

Yet this effort to focus on continuity posed a problem when interpreting Paul. Paul said things like the law could not give life (Gal. 3:21), that it could not justify (Gal. 2:16; Rom. 3:28), that the law exists only because of transgressions (Gal. 3:19) and that it came to increase the trespass (Rom. 5:20), that the passions of sin are aroused through the law (Rom. 7:5), that the law imprisons and enslaves (Gal. 3:22–23; 4:1; 4:22–31; Rom. 7:6), and that Christ has set us free from its confinement (Gal. 3:25)—indeed, he has brought the law to an end (Rom. 10:4). This certainly makes talk of continuity difficult.

In the face of such difficult words, the early exegetes of the second and third centuries limited the relevance of Paul's statements to *the ceremonial law alone.* This then preserved the moral law's goodness and its continued relevance in the New Testament. Those who made this distinction were able to limit Paul's abrogation of the law to those features that were distinctive to the life of Old Testament Israel. So, for example, when in Galatians 3:19 Paul said that the law was given "on account of transgressions," this referred to the particular transgressions of Israel at Sinai when they had bowed down to the gold calf. According to the early church, God responded by giving, in addition to the Decalogue, numerous ordinances, sacrifices, and ceremonies in order to preserve them from the idolatry to which Israel was prone.[10] This was the meaning assigned to Ezekiel 20:25, "I gave to them commandments that were *not good,* and statutes in which they could not live"—an important passage for the doctrine of the law throughout the writings of early and medieval authors.[11] Although these laws were "burdensome" (*onus*) because of the "hardness of their hearts," their purpose was ultimately benevolent, for they acted as a kind of "yoke" (*iugum*; cf. Acts 15:10; Gal. 5:1; Matt. 11:29–30), which, it was said, steered Israel away from its proclivity for apostasy and directed it to worship the true God. This then prepared the Jewish people for the coming of a "new law" (καινὸς νόμος; *nova*

10. Justin Martyr, *Dialogue with Trypho* (hereafter *Dial.*) 18.2; 19.5–6; 20–22; 46.5; Irenaeus, *Adv. haer.* 4.15.1–2; 16.5; Clement of Alexandria, *Paedagogus* (hereafter *Paed.*) 1.11.96.3–97.1; *Apostolic Constitutions* 1.6; 6.20–21.

11. See, for example, Justin Martyr, *Dial.* 21.2–4; Irenaeus, *Adv. haer.* 4.15.1; *Apostolic Constitutions* 6.20–21; Ambrose, *Epistula* 64.2, CSEL 82/2:150f.; Ambrosiaster, CSEL 50:76.16–77.13; 428.25–429.13; 469.24–470.14; CSEL 81/1:339.13f.; CSEL 81/3:326.20f.; Jerome, PL 26:369D–370C; 385B-C; 402D; Theodoret of Cyrus, PG 82:482Df.; Peter Lombard, PL 191:1399D; Peter of Poitiers, *Sententiarum libri quinque* 4.3; PL 211:1145B-C; William of Auxerre, *Summa Aurea* 4, tr. 2, c. 2; Spicilegium Bonaventurianum, vol. 19 (Rome: Collegii S. Bonaventurae ad Claras Aquas, 1985), 21, 38f.; Robert Grosseteste, *Expositio in Epistolam Sancti Pavli ad Galatas,* CCCM 130:67.513–27; 86.527–39; Robert Grosseteste, *De cessatione legalium,* ed. Richard C. Dales and Edward B. King, Auctores Britannici Medii Aevi, vol. 7 (Oxford: Oxford University Press, 1986), 1.11.2, p. 69, l. 4; and 4.7.6; p. 182, ll. 9–10; Thomas, *Sentences* IV, d. 1, q. 1, a. 5, qc. 1, s.c. 2; Biel, *Sentences* IV, d. 1, q. 3, a. 2, c. 1.

lex) and Christ, the "new lawgiver" (καινὸς νομοθέτης).[12] These ceremonial laws also benefited the Jews in that, when spiritually understood, they prefigured and pointed to Christ and the spiritual realities of the New Testament.[13] Consequently, Christians were no longer obligated to the ceremonial aspects of the law—they did not justify, they did not bring life, and they had served their historical purpose among Israel as burden, yoke, and type.

Now since, according to this interpretation, Paul was only talking about the ceremonial law, that meant that the moral law as expressed in the Ten Commandments was *not* abrogated with the coming of Christ, but continued on into the New Testament as *part of the gospel*. In a way, the gospel was seen to perfect and complete the Ten Commandments. It extended and deepened the old moral law—also as a kind of spiritual interpretation—reaching beyond the mere prohibition of evil *deeds*, and concerned itself with the inner life of evil *thoughts* and *desires*. According to this view, the "old law" merely demanded compliance to external demands and so could only produce a morality of slaves, but the "new law" of the gospel (as articulated especially in the Sermon on the Mount) was superior, for it stirred the obedience of the heart and soul and thus reflected the disposition of sons.[14] Still, continuity was maintained, for since the author of the law and the gospel was the same God, the Old and New Testaments could still find their theological unity in what was essentially the same moral law.[15]

The relationship between this view of the law and the hermeneutical problem can be understood as follows: as the law was abrogated according to the letter but continued spiritually in the gospel, so it was that the Old Testament largely lost its literal relevance with the coming of Christ, but continued as Christian Scripture when interpreted spiritually. Taking its cue from the function of the ceremonial law, this hermeneutic approached the Old Testament as a record of figures and types waiting to be filled with the spiritual content of the New Testament.

12. For "new law" see, for example, Bar. 2:6; Justin, *Dial.* 11.4 (contrasted to the "παλαιὸς νόμος" of Mount Horeb; 11.2); 12.3; cf. Ignatius, *Magnesians* 2.1 ("νόμῳ Ἰησοῦ Χριστοῦ"); Tertullian, *Adversus Judaeos* (hereafter *Adv. Jud.*) 3; 6; *De praescriptione haereticorum* 13. Justin speaks of Christ as the "lawgiver," *Dial.* 12.2; 18.3, and as the "eternal law" (αἰώνιός νόμος), *Dial.* 11.2; cf. Shepherd of Hermas, Sim. 5.6.3 (59.3); Sim. 8.3.2 (69.2).

13. Justin, *Dial.* 40–42; 44–45; Irenaeus, *Adv. haer.* 4.14.3; 16.1; 19.1; Tertullian, *Adv. Jud.* 3–6.

14. See especially Irenaeus, *Adv. haer.* 4.9.2; 13.1–4; 16.3–5; 28.2. Cf. Clement, *Paed.* 1.7.59.1–2, which describes the pedagogy of the law in the Old Testament as one of *fear* in contrast to the New Testament, which turns fear into *love*.

15. Clement, *Paed.* 1.7.58.1; Irenaeus, *Adv. haer.* 4.9.1–3; 12.3.

Among the Latin exegesis in the fourth century, the interpretation of Paul continued to be a central occupation with extant commentaries on Paul's epistles written by Marius Victorinus, Ambrosiaster, Pelagius, Jerome, and Augustine. The basic features of Paul's doctrine of law and gospel remained the same. Marcion was not quickly forgotten, especially when Manichaeism propagated similar views of the law and the Old Testament. It was the Manichaeans who sat in the crosshairs of Augustine when he wrote his early commentary on Galatians, and there he is careful to limit Paul's abrogation of the law to the ceremonial law alone.

But polemical contexts change, and Augustine would later find himself in conflict with Pelagianism. Like the tradition before him, Pelagius wanted to preserve the integrity of the moral law—in the Old Testament and in the New—especially because it supported his own doctrine of humankind's natural moral capacities and the freedom of the will over against the fatalism foundational to the Manichaean worldview. Arguing against Pelagius's moral optimism, Augustine saw Paul differently. Rather than shy away from Paul's harsh words about the law, Augustine now saw them as the strongest argument against the potential of human nature. And so, against Pelagius, Augustine stressed that Paul was speaking chiefly about the *moral law* in Romans and Galatians. Not only did the ceremonial law fail to justify, but even the moral law had no power to bring life. Instead, Paul states that it was given to "make transgressors" and to "increase the trespass," exposing and magnifying human nature's moral weakness, in order to reveal humanity's need for grace. For Augustine the advent of Christ brought this *lex litterae*—this death-dealing law of the letter—to an end by offering grace and the Spirit in the *lex fidei,* the law of faith. Thus Augustine's well-known dictum: "The law was given that we might seek grace, and grace was given that we might fulfill the law."[16]

Though Augustine introduced a new emphasis into Pauline exegesis, its subsequent influence would not be significant initially. It was domesticated—partly by Augustine himself and partly by the manner in which his interpretation of Paul was transmitted alongside others in *glosses* and *florilegia*. In such a form, medieval theologians were unable to appreciate what was distinctive about Augustine's Paul, or to consider its potential implications. Besides, the medieval context had a different set of concerns. Theologians combined the effort to preserve the inherited exegetical tradition with the need to address new theological questions. So, for example, as the sacraments took center stage in ecclesiastical life, theological reflection turned to the Old Testament and

16. Augustine, *De spiritu et littera* 19.34.

its Levitical "sacraments" as a place to define the church's own distinctive sacramental doctrines.[17] When considering the sacraments of both Testaments, continuity and distinction needed to be held in tension. And for this, the common understanding of Paul's doctrine of the law as the ceremonial law continued to be the dominant interpretation.

To give just one example where this traditional interpretation is operative, consider the dictum found throughout the writings of the twelfth and thirteenth centuries: "*The law was given as a sign for the perfect, a scourge for the proud, and a pedagogue for the simple.*" This dictum appears to have originated from the school of Anselm of Laon,[18] and was variously repeated among the Paris *magistri*.[19] In the commentaries and glosses, this sentence appears especially as an explanation of Romans 5:20 and Galatians 3:19.

The threefold function of the law here expressed focuses only on its role in the Old Testament. The law as "scourge" (*flagellum*, sometimes also *vindictam*) preserves its punitive aspect and corresponds best to the notion found already in the early church that much of the law was given as punishment for Israel's idolatry at Mount Sinai. This "scourge" of the law was another name for the many ceremonial commands—the so-called yoke that Peter spoke of in Acts 15, or the "commands that were not good" from Ezekiel 20:25. The purpose of these countless commandments was nonetheless salutary; they were given so that the people might flee from their burden to seek grace (an adaption of Augustine).

However, those who were already righteous in the Old Testament did not need the law for this reason. Rather, for them it functioned as a "sign" (*signum*), a figure and type of the future redemption of Christ and the new law of the gospel. But these "*perfect*" were few, a spiritual elite of patriarchs and prophets who were proleptically granted insight into the spiritual significance of these ceremonies and ordinances.

17. Cf. Artur Michael Landgraf, "Die Gnadenökonomie des Alten Bundes nach der Lehre der Frühscholastik," "Die Wirkungen der Beschneidung," and "Beiträge der Frühscholastik zur Terminologie der allgemeinen Sakramentenlehre" in *Dogmengeschichte der Frühscholastik*, vol. 3/1 (Regensburg: Friedrich Pustet, 1954), 19–168.

18. Franz Pl. Bliemetzrieder, ed., *Anselms von Laon Systematische Sentenzen*, Beiträge zur Geschichte der Philosophie des Mittelalters, vol. 18/2–3 (Münster: Verlag der Aschendorffschen Verlagsbuchhandlung, 1919), *Sententie Anselmi*, 92–93; *Sententie divine pagine*, 37–38. If the *Expositio in epistolas Pauli* attributed to Bruno of Chartreux (d. 1101) is genuine—something that is no longer held certain—then his comments to Rom. 5:20 may have precedent over Anselm; PL 153:55A-B.

19. The saying was later attributed to Augustine, though such can only be true as reflecting his doctrine of the law overall rather than an actual quotation. See William of Auxerre, *Summa Aurea* IV, tr. 2, c. 1; 19, 121–23; *Summa Aurea* IV, tr. 2, c. 2; 20, 9–10; Thomas, *Sentences* IV, d. 1, q. 1, a. 5, qc. 2, ad 3. Cf. Gabriel Biel, *Sentences* IV, d. 1, q. 1, a. 2, c. 3.

Then there was the vast majority of the people; they had no idea that circumcision, sacrifices, and the like possessed a spiritual meaning that pointed to Christ. These people were the "simple," and were compared to children; they needed constant guidance and supervision. And so for them the law acted as a "pedagogue" (*paedagogum*), teaching them through the sacrifices and ceremonies a rudimentary, "implicit faith" in Christ, a faith "veiled in mystery," until the time of the New Testament when the veil would be taken away.

So, as it was in the early church, for medieval exegetes Paul's argument in Romans and Galatians was largely an argument about the history of salvation. Paul's theology of the law was a theology of the Old Testament. Which means that the problem with Paul's opponents was that they had not paid enough attention to the right calendars. The times had changed, the human race had "come of age," and the school of the old law had finished its task. Yet the law was not against the promise of Christ, even as the Old Testament did not stand against the New. The relationship was one of growth. As the tree is contained in the seed, so the gospel lay hidden in the law. In graduated continuity, salvation history ran its course from law to gospel. And the hermeneutical implications were clearly manifested throughout medieval allegory. It is not without significance that in the Middle Ages Paul is regarded as an allegorical exegete—he is the spiritual commentator of the law par excellence, the one whose chief work is to bring the Testaments together into harmony and establish the "*concordia legis et evangelii*"—the concord of the law and gospel.[20]

When Luther began his first university lectures on the Psalms in 1513, he inherited this tradition of Pauline interpretation, and it is clear that for the next two years he was a faithful heir. Throughout the lectures, Luther interprets Paul's pejorative "under the law" as life under the *ceremonial law* in the Old Testament. It is the time of the *vetus lex*—the old law—the time of types, and shadows, and carnal and temporal promises. On the other hand, to live "under grace" is to be directed by the more spiritual demands and promises of the New Testament, the *nova lex*—the new law—the time of reality, and truth, the time of spiritual and eternal things. At this time, Luther sees the movement from law to gospel simply as the unfolding of salvation history—they are in continuity in the same way that the Old Testament is joined to the New: as prophecy to fulfillment, as type to antitype, as letter to spirit.

20. Atto of Vercelli, PL 134:367C: "... Paulus, loquens de N.T., de V.T. sumens exemplum, confirmat, idipsum ostendit concordinam legis et evangelii; ostendit etiam allegorizandum esse"; cited by Henri de Lubac, *Medieval Exegesis: The Four Senses of Scripture*, trans. E. M. Macierowski, vol. 2 (Grand Rapids: Eerdmans, 2000), 223, 432.

But during this time Luther continued to experience severe religious doubts. He was personally unable to find comfort in the message of the gospel. The fact that he had received an exegetical and theological tradition that defined the gospel as a new law—a new law with deeper, more spiritual demands—exacerbated his spiritual anxiety. What troubled him in particular was the salvation-historical situation of the New Testament Christian. Even though grace had been given through Christ—something the Old Testament saint could only dimly see in hope—the effects of that grace would be measured on the last day against the "gospel"—the righteousness of God that was made known through this new law of Christ. Luther later reflected that the way out of this problem first made itself known when he began to view the law and the gospel distinct from any particular epoch of salvation history: "I lacked nothing before this except that I made no distinction between the law and the gospel. I regarded both as one thing and said that there was no difference between Christ and Moses except *time and perfection*. But when I discovered the proper distinction, that the law is one thing and the gospel is another, I broke through."[21] This happened first in his lectures on Romans in 1515, and then in his lectures on Galatians in 1516. By the time he finished these lectures, Luther no longer understood Paul to be describing the law's distinctively Old Testament function that came to an end at the advent of Christ. Instead, Paul was speaking about how the law functioned at a deeper, more fundamental theological level—applicable to the individual, regardless of the times. Law and gospel were no longer primarily historical categories for Luther but *existential* ones, and as such, their messages are entirely distinct from one another. The "times" of wrath and salvation, of confinement and freedom, of slavery and sonship are Paul's description of two exclusive theological situations, not two successive ages of history. Hence, for Luther, the abrogation of the law is a complete and absolute abrogation—but in the *conscience*. On the one hand, Luther did not deny the clear salvation-historical setting of Paul's argument—the law's pedagogy does have a historical end with the coming of Christ, for as harbinger of the eschaton and the firstfruits of the new creation, Christ in his person brings all things—sin, death, the law, even history itself—to an end.[22] But for the individual who must still struggle against sin and the flesh,

21. WATr 5:210.6f., no. 5518: "Zuuor mangelt mir nichts, denn das ich kein discrimen inter legem et euangelium machet, hielt es alles vor eines et dicebam Christum a Mose non differre nisi tempore et perfectione. Aber do ich das discrimen fande, quod aliud esset lex, aliud euangelium, da riß ich her durch."

22. Cf. *LW* 26:349; WA 40.I:534–35. For Luther's collapse of the eschatological onto the traditional salvation-historical scheme, see Heiko Oberman, "*Iustitia Christi* and *Iustitia Dei*: Lu-

the coming of Christ happens fully in the *daily* coming of faith and the proclamation of the gospel. Thus the person of faith who is *simul iustus et peccator* is also *simul sub lege et sub gratia*, one who stands continually between the times.

The particular shape of Luther's shift on this interpretation of the law and gospel gives several indications of how the distinction would be used in the Lutheran tradition.

First, Luther relates in his lectures that he was beginning to see that in Paul's epistles there was an inseparable relationship between the stated function of the law and the presence of sin—whether it prevented, revealed, or increased sin, "the law impinged upon every sin" (*lex enim omne peccatum tangit*).[23] He thus rejected the idea that Paul was only speaking about the ceremonial law, or for that matter, only about the law's function in the Old Testament. Paul's statements about the Mosaic law were to be applied to the law "in the most general sense" (*generalissime*). Seeing something similar in Augustine's anti-Pelagian interpretation (which he read for the first time in 1515), along with his experience that the struggle against sin continues on even throughout the lives of the baptized, Luther stressed the ongoing—indeed, *daily*—function of the law with respect to sin alongside the ongoing, daily, and complete freedom from the law with respect to faith in the promise of the gospel. This also meant that the gospel in its proper sense did not contain judgment, nor did it contain ethics; it was not a "new law" on a continuum with the old. It was a completely different message. From this one can see the Lutheran emphasis on the negative, that is, accusatory, function of the law in the Christian life. The *lex semper accusat* is not an indictment of the law that remains "holy and just," but of sin, which remains not only in the daily moral failings of Christians but even more so in the proclivity to confuse our devotion to God with devotion to our piety.[24]

The second implication relates to how distinguishing law and gospel is regarded as the key for interpreting the Scriptures rightly. What we have seen is that Luther's shift toward the existential distinction of law and gospel gave

ther and the Scholastic Doctrines of Justification," *Harvard Theological Review* 59, no. 1 (January 1966): 1–26.

23. *LW* 25:62n8; WA 56:68.10–69.21 (Rom. 7:10; *Randglosse* 2).

24. Such is Luther's tacit employment of Augustine's distinction of *uti/frui* in his Heidelberg Disputation (1518): "That wisdom which sees the invisible things of God in works as perceived by man is completely puffed up, blinded, and hardened. The 'law brings the wrath' of God (Rom. 4:15), kills, reviles, accuses, judges, and condemns everything that is not in Christ. Yet that wisdom is not of itself evil, nor is the law to be evaded; but without the theology of the cross man *misuses* the best in the worst manner."

him a new standpoint for addressing the hermeneutical problem of the Old Testament. No longer was the unity of the Old and New Testaments based on the continuity of law and gospel—instead, theological and hermeneutical unity was found by asserting their sharp distinction. For Luther, the existential tension of sin and faith, of law and gospel, is the inescapable experience of the religious human creature. Law and gospel, therefore, are the basic, fundamental categories of one's theological relationship *coram Deo,* before God, and are not unique to any particular people or epoch. It is for this reason then that the Old Testament and the New Testament are united—not because law and gospel are harmoniously linked, but because their radical difference is to be found throughout God's activity in salvation history. Thus, for Luther, the relevance of the Old Testament does not depend upon one's ability to channel it through an allegorical interpretation. The Scriptures' relevance for the Christian depends upon their witness to the common experience of faith. For Luther this faith—in both Testaments—is irreducibly christological, not as some spiritual insight into types and figures, but as the awakened response to God's promise of salvation stirred in the crucible of God's word that kills and makes alive.

This new perspective on Paul first became public when Luther published his commentary on Galatians in 1519. The commentary was eagerly snapped up by humanists and scholars—many of whom would soon become reformers in their own right—and one can quickly see the influence this new reading of Paul and the language of law and gospel had on them. Melanchthon presents it in his *Loci Communes* in 1521, and Johannes Bugenhagen reflects it in his own commentaries in 1524.[25] Lutherans in the subsequent generation would generally follow the main contours of Luther's interpretation of law and gospel in their Pauline commentaries and in their sermons.[26]

But the reception along the Rhine and in Switzerland was somewhat different. Huldrych Zwingli would strike out on the path of Christian humanist reform at roughly the same time that Luther became a public figure. His relation to Luther was ambivalent from the start. He certainly read the Wittenberg professor, but his articulation of the gospel continued to be cast largely in Erasmian terms.[27] With respect to the law, he stressed its permanence as

25. *Annotations 10. Bugenhagij Pomerani In Epistolas Pauli, ad Galatas, Ephesos, Philippensis, Colossenses, Thessalonicenses primam & secundam. Timotheum primam & secundam. Ticum. Philemonem. Hebraeos.* Basel: Adam Petri, 1525.

26. Robert Kolb, "The Influence of Luther's Galatians Commentary of 1535 on Later Sixteenth-Century Lutheran Commentaries on Galatians," *Archive für Reformationsgeschichte* 84 (1993): 156–83.

27. Cf. Martin Brecht, "Zwingli als Schüler Luthers: Zu seiner theologischen Entwicklung, 1518–22," *Zeitschrift für Kirchengeschichte* 96 (1985): 301–19.

an expression of God's eternal, irrevocable will.[28] More significant for him was the idea of *covenant,* developed along with Heinrich Bullinger to combat the Anabaptist position in Zurich.[29] Defending the practice of infant baptism, Zwingli stressed the continuity of the Testaments with the biblical concept of covenant. A child's entry into God's covenant in the Old Testament through circumcision could then be extrapolated to the New Testament for the Christian baptism of children.

It was Bullinger, however, who would develop a thoroughgoing concept of covenant for biblical theology.[30] And it was Bullinger who first brought the Lutheran language of law and gospel into this new context. In the beginning, Bullinger was deeply influenced by Melanchthon's *Loci* of 1521 and some of Luther's early writings. And like them, he began to work out his own theological understanding through commenting on Pauline texts.[31] At Kappel, he lectured on Romans, 1 Corinthians, Galatians, and Hebrews from 1523 to 1526.[32] And while Hebrews became a more central text for his thought, Bullinger would take up Galatians again and publish a commentary in 1535. In both his early Galatians lectures and later commentary it is clear that he had read Luther's commentary.[33] The central theme of the work bears this stamp—justification is not from works but from grace alone. In the commentary, Bullinger explicitly states in the *argumentum* that one must avoid confusing law and gospel. Yet at the same time, he doesn't conceive of the problem in the same way as Luther. The Augustinian emphasis on the law's role to reveal sin is present, but it is also a positive "rule of life" (*regula vitae*). Like the pre-Lutheran tradition, Bullinger wants to maintain the continuity between the Testaments by softening the

28. Cf. *Divine and Human Righteousness* (1523); *True and False Religion* (1525).

29. See Bullinger, *Von dem Touff* (1525); Zwingli, *Antwort über Balthasar Hubmaiers Taufbüchlein* (1525). On Bullinger's relationship with the Anabaptists, see Heinold Fast, *Heinrich Bullinger und die Täufer* (Weierhof, 1959). See also Peter A. Lillback, *The Binding of God* (Grand Rapids: Baker Academic, 2001), 81–109.

30. The definitive text is Bullinger's *De Testamento* (1534). See Charles S. McCoy and J. Wayne Baker, *Fountainhead of Federalism: Heinrich Bullinger and the Covenantal Tradition* (Louisville: Westminster John Knox, 1991), and the discussion of Lillback in *The Binding of God,* 110–11.

31. For Bullinger's interpretation of Paul, see Peter Opitz, "Bullinger and Paul," in *A Companion to Paul and the Reformation,* ed. R. Ward Holder (Leiden: Brill, 2009), 243–66.

32. *Heinrich Bullinger Diarium der Jahre 1504–1574,* ed. Emil Egli (Basel, 1904), 8, 13–15; 10, 8–11; 11, 1–2; *Heinrich Bollinger Theologische Schriften, Band 1: Exegetische Schriften aus den Jahren 1525–1527,* ed. Hans-Georg vom Berg and Susanna Hausammann (Zurich, 1983).

33. See Ernst Koch, "Paulus exegese und Bundes Theologie Bullingers Auslegung von Gal 3,17–26," in *Histoire de l'exégèse au XVIe siècle,* ed. Olivier Fatio and Pierre Fraenkel (Geneva: Libraire Droz S.A., 1978), 342–50.

sharp contrast that Paul seems to be setting forth in chapters 3 and 4. For Bullinger, the law maintains a pedagogical role in both Testaments; though it differs in how it carries out its office, it has the one task (*scopus unicus*), to bear witness to believers that life and salvation come from Christ alone. The law isn't abrogated in the life of the believer; it is perfected (*perfectio legis*), so that one now lives by the law of the Spirit. Though Bullinger doesn't criticize by name, he is undoubtedly displeased with aspects of Luther's approach, calling it blasphemy to speak dishonorably about the law and that "certain theologians" (*theologi quidam*) need to speak with more reverence when talking about the law, its abrogation, and its role in Christian freedom.

Jean Calvin's commentaries come at a time when additional lines have been drawn between Wittenberg and the reformers of upper Germany. Nevertheless, Calvin is still deeply influenced by Melanchthon and Luther and carries on much of the same language on the distinction of law and gospel. But his appropriation also echoes Bullinger's method, which stresses the continuity of covenant over the polarity of law and faith.

In his 1548 commentary on Galatians, Calvin begins with a very clear position in the *argumentum*: "If ceremonies have not the power of bestowing justification, then the observation of them is unnecessary. We must remark, however, that [Paul] does not confine himself entirely to ceremonies, but argues generally about works, otherwise the whole discussion would fall flat. . . . the question could not be stated without assuming the general principle, that we are justified by the free grace of God; and this principle sets aside not only ceremonies, but every other kind of works. . . . in short, Paul here argues negatively from general to particular propositions."[34] Calvin's interpretation of chapter 2 stays with this theme, but by the time he deals with chapter 3, the overarching concept of the covenant begins to change the direction of his interpretation. In 3:19, when Paul asks rhetorically, "Why then the law?" Calvin shifts by noting that Paul is talking not so much about the moral law as about the distinctive features of the Mosaic administration as a whole, namely, the "laying down a rule of life and ceremonies to be observed in worship of God and afterwards adding promises and threats."[35] Furthermore, when dealing with Paul's answer, "on account of transgression," Calvin exhibits some nervousness. He notes, "it is necessary to put readers on their guard on this point; for very many, I find, have fallen into the mistake of acknowledging no other advantage belonging to the law, but what is expressed in this passage. Paul himself elsewhere speaks

34. *OE* 16:8.32–9.1; 9.18–19.
35. *OE* 16:77.2–6.

of the precepts of the law as profitable for doctrine and exhortations. The definition here given of the use of the law is not complete, and those who refuse to make any other acknowledgement in favor of the law do wrong."[36]

Likewise, in the following verses Calvin seems to expend more ink on what Paul is *not* saying than on what he is saying. At each point where Paul seems to be going deeper into the abolition of the law, Calvin pulls the reader back. In 3:25, when Paul says that upon the coming of faith we are no longer under the law, Calvin objects: "Is the law so abolished that we have nothing to do with it? I answer, the law, so far as it is a rule of life, a bridle to keep us in the fear of the Lord, a spur to correct the sluggishness of our flesh . . . it is as much in force as ever, and remains untouched."[37] Finally, Calvin strongly repudiates Luther's existential application of the text: "Some apply the comparison in a different manner to the case of any man whatever, whereas Paul is speaking of two nations. What they say, I acknowledge, is true; but it has nothing to do with the present passage. . . . I deny that Paul here treats of individuals, or draws a distinction between the time of unbelief and the calling [by faith]."[38]

So what is really at issue here? Why is Luther more comfortable with Paul's immoderate language about the law in Galatians 3 and 4 than Calvin or Bullinger is? Why, for Luther, are these passages regarded as paradigmatic for the proper distinction of law and gospel while the early Reformed commentators exhibit unease? It would appear that part of the answer has to do with the point of departure for addressing the problem of conflict and continuity. For the Swiss, continuity was particularly important in the face of the early Anabaptist movement. The Anabaptist rejection of circumcision's relation to infant baptism as corresponding *Pflichtzeichen* (signs of commitment) made them suspect of denigrating the authority of the Old Testament. Thus, for the Swiss, "covenant" became a fundamental concept; in its bilateral structure it encompassed the sacraments, grace, and the obligation of obedience in both Testaments. The distinction of law and gospel, on the other hand, was subsumed under and interpreted by the covenantal dispensations, clarifying the relation of faith to works vis-à-vis the doctrine of justification, but less significant as a controlling hermeneutic for the interpretation of Scripture, preaching, or pastoral care.

Luther, however, had a very different set of concerns. He experienced the conceptual unity of law and gospel as the establishment of a piety of "works righteousness." The exegetical tradition only reinforced this piety as Paul's

36. *OE* 16:77.15–20.
37. *OE* 16:85.34–86.6.
38. *OE* 16:89.12–20.

sharp contrast of law and faith was diminished and subsumed under broader categories. Yet for Luther, Paul seemed quite clear: "the law was not of faith" (Gal. 3:12); righteousness from the law was a wholly other kind than the righteousness of the gospel.[39] The law's inability to justify was thus not limited to its covenantal role in Israel but was grounded in its universal capacity to expose sin and unbelief—a role that Luther argued extended even into the life of the baptized. Consequently, the piety of "works" that Paul condemned could be generalized beyond the original insistence of Jewish ceremonial works to every context in which faith is deemed inadequate or incomplete. "Covenant" (*pactum*), on the other hand, was largely synonymous with the gratuity of promise (*promissio*) set in contrast to the law (cf. Gal. 3:15–16) or as a testament (*testamentum*) and last will (Heb. 9:16–17).[40] As such, "covenant," for Luther, was an expression of the gospel, defined by the scope and nature of Christ's redemption: "For if God is to make a testament, as he promises, then he must die; and if he is to die, then he must be a man. And so, that little word 'testament' is a short summary of all God's wonders and grace, fulfilled in Christ."[41]

The Covenant of Works, the "*Doctrina Legis Abstractive*," and the First Commandment

These divergent approaches to Pauline texts point to emerging differences between the Lutheran and Reformed traditions. On the one hand, both tra-

39. Distinguishing the righteousness of faith and the righteousness of the law as two fundamentally different kinds, that is, two different sources, spheres, and ends, is prominent throughout Luther's writings (e.g. *Sermon on Two Kinds of Righteousness* [1519]; Galatians commentary [1519], ch. 2:16f.; Galatians commentary [1535], preface). For the role that two kinds of righteousness play in Lutheran theology more broadly, see Charles Arand, "Two Kinds of Righteousness as a Framework for Law and Gospel in the Apology," *Lutheran Quarterly* 15 (2001): 417–39; Charles Arand and Robert Kolb, *The Genius of Luther's Theology: A Wittenberg Way of Thinking for the Contemporary Church* (Grand Rapids: Baker Academic, 2008).

40. Space does not permit a discussion of Luther's relation to the late medieval scholastic understanding of *pactum* in connection with the doctrine of merit, that is, *meritum de congruo/condigno*; however, see Oswald Bayer, *Promissio: Geschichte der reformatorischen Wende in Luthers Theologie* (Göttingen: Vandenhoeck & Ruprecht, 1971); and Kenneth Hagen, *A Theology of Testament in the Young Luther: The Lectures on Hebrews* (Leiden: Brill, 1969). Like Luther, Melanchthon defines "covenant" principally in terms of "promise" to which the only correlative is faith: "Ergo in theologia praecipue sunt observanda promissionum vocabula: testamentum, foedus, pactum, promisssio, quibus vocibus divinae promissiones significantur . . . fidei vocabulum est correlativum ad promissiones Christi." *Annotationes in Evangelium Matthaei*, *MW* 4:206–7.

41. *LW* 35:84. Cf. also *LW* 35:358–61.

ditions are part of a larger renaissance of Pauline commentary at the turn of the sixteenth century.[42] But Luther's interest in Paul goes well beyond the humanist admiration of ancient Christian texts and sources, ascribing a preeminence to the apostle as the key to "cracking the nut" of the gospel and as the truest evangelist.[43] Melanchthon goes even further and advances the epistle of Romans as the *scopus* of the entire Scriptures.[44] To be sure, the Reformed tradition would agree with the Wittenbergers on the centrality of the Pauline doctrine of justification. Yet the predilection for the continuity of covenant invited Reformed theologians into different texts, and law and gospel was considered within broader biblical narratives and contexts. After all, looking for the language of covenant in the Scriptures was like trying to find water in the sea. And even where the word was absent, the idea seemed pervasive. While promise and faith were foundational for justification, covenant was regarded as the fundament and essence of the divine/human relationship.[45] Thus, even in Edenic paradise, the concept found a home, as it became increasingly common among the Reformed to speak of the law within a prelapsarian "covenant of works."

Arguably, the first articulation of such a prelapsarian covenant came from Zacharias Ursinus, who cast the Lutheran distinction of law and gospel into this framework: "What is the distinction of law and gospel? The law contains

42. E.g., Lorenzo Valla, *Collatio Novi Testamenti* (1449) (edited and printed by Erasmus in 1505); John Colet, *Ennaratio in Epistolam S. Pauli ad Romanos* (1497); Marsilio Ficino, *In Epistolas Pauli* (unfinished) (1499); Faber Stapulensis, *S. Pauli epistolae XIV ex vulgata adiecta intelligentia ex Graeco cum commentariis* (1512); Wendelin Steinbach, *Commentarius in Epistolam S. Pauli ad Galatas* (1513) and his *Commentarius in Epistolam ad Hebraeos* (1516/1517); Erasmus, *Novum Instrumentum* (1516) (and his *Paraphrases* begun with Romans in 1517).

43. Cf. *LW* 35:362: "The epistles of St. Paul . . . far surpass the other three gospels, Matthew, Mark, and Luke. . . . [They] are the books that show you Christ and teach you all that is necessary and salvatory for you to know. . . . in them you do not find many works and miracles of Christ described, but you do find depicted in masterly fashion how faith in Christ overcomes sin, death and hell, and gives life, righteousness and salvation. This is the real nature of the gospel."

44. "In the Pauline epistles what is written in Romans points the way for the others as a *scopus* or an Attic Mercury" (*MBW* §47, T1:112, 32–33; March 27, 1519); "[Romans is] by far the deepest of all the letters and serving as the *scopus* of the entire Holy Scripture" (*MBW* §68, T1:159, 7–9; December 11, 1519). See Timothy Wengert, "The Biblical Commentaries of Philip Melanchthon," in *Philip Melanchthon (1497–1560) and the Commentary*, ed. M. Patrick Graham and Timothy J. Wengert (Sheffield: Sheffield Academic Press, 1997), 106–48; Wengert, "Philip Melanchthon's 1522 Annotations on Romans and the Lutheran Origins of Rhetorical Criticism," in *Biblical Interpretation in the Era of the Reformation*, ed. Richard A. Muller and John L. Thompson (Grand Rapids: Eerdmans, 1996), 118–40.

45. The previously cited study of Peter Lillback, *The Binding of God*, is an immensely helpful work on the influence of Calvin's biblical theology on Reformed theology in this regard.

the covenant of nature, it is entered into by God with men in creation, that is, it is known by men through nature; and it demands from us perfect obedience toward God, and by performing it, it promises eternal life, by not performing it, it threatens eternal punishment. But indeed, the gospel contains the covenant of grace."[46] However, the Westminster Standards supply the most influential articulation of this "covenant of works." For example, chapter 7 of the Confession of Faith: "The first covenant made with man was a covenant of works, wherein life was promised to Adam; and in him to his posterity, upon condition of perfect and personal obedience." Likewise, chapter 19: "God gave to Adam a law, as a covenant of works, by which he bound him and all his posterity to personal, entire, exact, and perpetual obedience, promised life upon the fulfilling, and threatened death upon the breach of it, and endued him with power and ability to keep it."[47]

One might challenge this concept of an Edenic covenant of works for several reasons, the first being the problem of the biblical texts themselves. Neither the Genesis account nor any other Scripture passage referring to the creation narrative uses the word "covenant." Further, the concept of "works," as the Reformed confessions and divines use it, is derived from the Pauline usage of "works" (ἔργα), which lives in the context of obedience to requirements or commands that may befit rewards and wages. In such a context, works are related to the Mosaic law and are opposed to grace and faith, and cannot give life (Gal. 3:21). The notion of such works in the prelapsarian state is simply not known in Paul's writings. Of course, biblical terminology alone does not make or break such theological concepts (to be fair, terminologically Paul knows no antithesis of law and gospel—polarities tend to be law and faith, law and Christ, law and Spirit, law and grace).

Still, there are theological reasons for which a Lutheran might object to a covenant of works as the original condition and situation of humankind. Such an objection centers on the preeminence of faith and the notion that creation and life could never be a reward for human effort and action. Paul's assessment that the law is incapable of giving life and righteousness (Gal. 3:21)

46. Zacharias Ursinus's Large Catechism, Q. 36. The influence of Melanchthon and Bullinger on Ursinus is well documented. For an overview of the literature, see Lillback, *The Binding of God*, 276–77.

47. WCF 7.2; 19.1. Cf. WSC 12, 16; WLC 20, 22, 30. Other statements and theologians echoed similar themes as those that appear in the Standards. For example, one can find examples already in William Perkins (1558–1602), John Ball (1585–1640), Johannes Wollebius (1586–1629), and Robert Rollock (c. 1555–1599). That Jean Calvin's name is missing from the list is significant, but the debate about whether Calvin also taught something equivalent to a primal covenant of works is dealt with thoroughly in other literature and is beyond the scope of this essay.

is not incidental but is necessarily grounded in its inherent inability to produce or generate in human beings that which it sets forth and describes. To be sure, this impotence is further compounded by the weakness of sinful flesh, but the power to fulfill the law, its holiness and goodness notwithstanding, must come from outside the law itself—God himself must do what the law cannot do (Rom. 8:3–4). The law's strength, goodness, and holiness lie in its descriptive power of the life that God has de facto created for humanity. Thus, even the prelapsarian invitation to obedience is simply a call for the *radix hominis* to be what they already are as creatures made in the image of God. Life is not the result or reward of obedience, but its precondition.

The idea that obedience to the law could be, at least hypothetically, the means by which one gained eternal life was also entertained by Lutherans in the generation after Luther. In 1556, Lutheran theologians gathered in Eisenach to deal with a controversy initiated by Georg Major, who argued that the good works that proceed from faith are "necessary" for salvation. In the course of the debate, Major's opponents suggested that *theoretically* and *abstractly* perfect obedience to the law would result in salvation (*in doctrina legis abstractive*), though after the Fall this was no longer possible.[48] This then became its own controversy, criticized by some as setting up the law as a way of salvation, and confusing the righteousness of faith with the righteousness of the law.[49]

For later Lutherans, part of the confusion lay in the writings of their teacher, Philip Melanchthon. In the Apology of the Augsburg Confession, Melanchthon consistently distinguished between the righteousness of the law and the righteousness of faith as two very different kinds with two distinct *teloi*.[50] The Christian ought to seek both, but not for the same reason. Before God only the righteousness of faith is proper, for only faith can give God the glory that is his due. But before one another, *coram mundo*, the righteousness of the law is not only permissible but required. It was the great confusion and collapsing of these two kinds of righteousness that lay at the heart of the

48. "Bona opera sunt necessaria ad salutem in doctrina legis abstractive et de idea tolerari potest."

49. Most notably, Luther's longtime colleague Nicholas von Amsdorf. For more on the Eisenach Synod, see Matthias Richter, *Gesetz und Heil: Eine Untersuchung zur Vorgeschichte und zum Verlauf des sogenannten Zweiten Antinomistischen Streits* (Göttingen: Vandenhoeck & Ruprecht, 1996), 132–67; Robert Kolb, *Nikolaus von Amsdorf (1483–1565): Popular Polemics in the Preservation of Luther's Legacy* (Nieuwkoop, Netherlands: B. De Graaf, 1978), 145–46.

50. For a very helpful analysis of Melanchthon's Apology along these lines, see Arand, "Two Kinds of Righteousness," 417–39.

scholastic error and that of Melanchthon's opponents.[51] However, in Melanchthon's later writings, he would increasingly establish the doctrine of the law on the basis of a more abstract *lex aeterna*—"an eternal and immovable rule of the divine mind."[52] While Luther spoke of the Pauline doctrine of the law "in the most general sense" (*generalissime*) to stress its universal sin-revealing power in every age, Melanchthon—especially in the later editions of his *Loci Communes*—began to speak of the law as the fundamental basis for humanity *coram Deo*, namely, a relationship defined as one of obedience or disobedience, reward or punishment, rather than Luther's more foundational faith or unbelief.[53]

Luther could occasionally talk about a hypothetical fulfillment of the law, though it is quite rare.[54] But more often one finds statements like the following:

51. Cf. Ap 2.12, 43, and Ap 4.12–16, 43.

52. *CR* 21:685: "Sed Lex Dei est regula eterna et immota mentis divinae"; *CR* 21:686, 688, 711; cf. also *CR* 15:389; 24:385: "Lex, quae est regula iustitiae in Deo, ita est immota, ut oporteat ei satisfacere. Obligat autem lex vel ad obedientiam, vel ad poenam."

53. See Lauri Haikola, "Melanchthons und Luthers Lehre von der Rechtfertigung, ein Vergleich," in *Luther and Melanchthon in the History and Theology of the Reformation*, ed. Vilmas Vajta (Philadelphia: Muhlenberg, 1961), 89–103; Timothy Wengert, *Law and Gospel: Philip Melanchthon's Debate with John Agricola of Eisleben over* Poenitentia (Grand Rapids: Baker, 1997), 177–210.

54. E.g., in the *Disputation on Justification* (1536), the idea is proposed, and Luther agrees, *LW* 34:187. With respect to the prelapsarian prohibition against the eating of the tree in the garden's midst, Luther's later Genesis lectures tend to emphasize more broadly that this prohibition is the giving of "the Word," which establishes the church, the preaching office, and true worship. Since, for Luther, the church is born of the gospel, the notion that this Edenic word is strictly one of law is problematic. "For Adam this Word was Gospel and Law; it was his worship; it was his service" (*LW* 1:146). This illustrates how inapplicable the prelapsarian commands ("have dominion" and "be fruitful and multiply" should be included here too) are for saying much about the theology of the law in the postlapsarian situation. Eden is too distant and incomprehensible to extrapolate such things. Luther does reject a particular antinomian argument that tried to use the absence of the law in the garden as precedent for the law's removal from Christian preaching. But even here he argues that one must distinguish sharply between the law given to Adam before sin and that given after. The theology of law and gospel that is derived from Pauline texts is not applicable to what one reads in Gen. 2, and vice versa (*LW* 1:109): "Is it not a monstrous crime to jumble passages this way when so much is at issue? After sin Adam is not the person he was before sin in the state of innocence; and yet those people make no distinction between the Law given before sin and that given after sin. What Paul says about the Law which came in after sin they deceitfully and blasphemously apply to the Law which was given in Paradise. If sin had not been in existence, then that Law which forbids sin would also not have been in existence, just as I stated above that in the perfect creation there was no need of civil government or of laws, which are like branding irons, or of what Paul calls a school-master (Gal. 3:24)."

> Therefore even if you were to do the work of the law according to the commandment, "You shall love etc.," you still would not be justified by this.[55]

> Therefore even if it were possible that you could do a work that would fulfill the commandment "you shall love the Lord your God with all your heart, etc.," still you would not be righteous before God for this reason . . . for the law does not make one righteous even if it is completely carried out and fulfilled.[56]

> If a man were completely and absolutely to fulfill the law through the power of the Holy Spirit, he would still have to appeal for God's mercy; for God has determined that he will save men through Christ and not through the law.[57]

> [God] has never at any time given nor wanted to give eternal life because of any works—no matter how glorious and great and how much they may correspond to the divine law—but only on account of his ineffable mercy.[58]

> Even if anyone were to fulfill the law, he would nevertheless not thereby be righteous because the purpose of the law is something else than justification.[59]

The difference here appears to be two different accents on what it means to fulfill the law. In the "covenant of works," the Westminster Standards stress the obedient actions of the human creature, that is, as the title of the covenant implies, life given as a reward for works. Luther, on the other hand, repeatedly points to faith as the definition of righteousness before God, and not merely as a subsequent surrogate for a failed righteousness of works, but as the true meaning and fulfillment of the law. Such was Luther's view of the law when interpreted by the first commandment. For Luther, the first commandment is the chief commandment. It is not only the most important—all other commandments are an elaboration and instantiation of the first. "The First Commandment is the chief source and fountainhead that permeates all others;

55. WA 40.I:218; *LW* 26:122.

56. WATr 6:6720.

57. WATr 1:85.

58. WA 39.I:238.

59. WA 39.I:213.

again, to it they all return and upon it they depend, so that end and beginning are completely linked and bound together."[60] "Because this commandment is the very first of all commandments and the highest and the best, from which all others proceed, in which they exist and by which they are judged and assessed, so its work . . . is the very first, highest, and best from which all others must proceed, in which they must exist and abide, and by which they must be judged and assessed."[61] Thus, if one fulfills the first commandment, all the others are fulfilled. "For the one who has the first commandment, has everything."[62] No commandment can be kept without the first. On the other hand, if obedience to another commandment comes in conflict with the first, then the former must be abandoned for the sake of the latter: "If a situation should arise where you would have to give up either your father or God, you must say, 'Farewell, father, with the fourth commandment and with the whole second table. I know nothing of you, but have completely forgotten you.' Now it is not a matter of the fourth commandment or the second table, but of the first, whether God is true, whether glory is owed Him, whether the Son of God is to be heard."[63] The first commandment requires nothing less than faith itself: "Faith is the true worship and the main work of the first commandment."[64] "The righteous one is made so through faith, which believes that God is gracious. He commanded the believer to believe this saying 'I am the Lord your God. You shall have no other gods beside me.'"[65]

Here we meet the mystery of the first commandment as the nexus of law and gospel. For Luther can also see the word of this commandment as a *promise*: "It is the promise of all promises, the fountain and head of all religion and wisdom, embracing the promise of the gospel of Christ. This is the proper sense of the first commandment because it prescribes nothing when it says, 'I am the Lord your God.'"[66] It is, as Heinrich Bornkamm observes, "an affirmation which demands, and a command which promises."[67] As two

60. Large Catechism, in *BC*, 430.

61. *LW* 44:30; WA 6:209.

62. WA 28:725.13.

63. WA 40.II:578:3–4; *LW* 12:276.

64. WA 5:394.33–34; cf. WA 39.I:90.8: "Fides est opus primi praecepti."

65. WA 5:399.2.

66. From Luther's glosses on Exod. 20, very possibly written during his time in Coburg. WA 30.II:358.1: "Promissio omnium promissionum fons & omnis religionis & sapiencię caput, Euangelium Christum promissum complectens. Hoc est proprie primum praeceptum, quia nihil praecipitur, dicens: Ego sum dominus deus tuus."

67. Heinrich Bornkamm, *Luther and the Old Testament*, trans. Eric Gritsch and Ruth Gritsch (Philadelphia: Fortress, 1969), 165.

sides of the same profundity, the promise "I am yours" aims at faith and the command "have none but me" aims at unbelief. If the law in its deepest sense calls for faith, then this same law, in fact, prohibits using it as a means toward salvation. To "have a God" means that he alone will give us all good things, including life and salvation. So Luther says, "when those who are self-righteous keep the law, they deny the righteousness of faith and sin against the first, second, and third commandments, and against the entire law, because God commands that he be worshiped by believing and fearing him. Therefore by their very *keeping* of the law they act in a manner that is most *contrary* to the law. . . . In keeping the law, therefore, they not only do not keep it, but they also deny the first commandment, the promises of God and the blessings promised to Abraham."[68]

The different accent between Lutheran and Reformed is not insignificant, but neither is it entirely irreconcilable. In the Reformed writings, the prelapsarian covenant of works is not driven by divine necessity, as if no eternal relationship between God and humanity is possible without such an agreement. The Westminster Confession speaks of this covenant as a divine, "voluntary condescension": "The distance between God and the creature is so great, that although reasonable creatures do owe obedience unto him as their Creator, yet they could never have any fruition of him as their blessedness and reward, but by some voluntary condescension on God's part, which he hath been pleased to express by way of covenant."[69] Likewise, in the writings of Francis Turretin (1623–1687), the requirement of obedience and promise of reward are an invitation to greater intimacy, "so that man now excited by the promise of God can certainly expect happiness, not from his mere philanthropy alone, but also from a covenant (on account of his truthfulness and fidelity)."[70] Lutherans stress the response to this invitation as a response of faith and trust, while the Reformed stress the perpetual obedience that arises from such faith, but conceptually the two are rooted in the divine creative act and the gift of God's word to his human creatures.

Nevertheless, theologically and pastorally, accents matter. If they do not indicate a fundamental doctrinal disagreement, they do betray certain presuppositions about theological method, its task, and its goal.

68. *LW* 26:253–54, 257.

69. WCF 7.1.

70. Francis Turretin, *Institutio Theologiae Elencticae* (1679), 8.3.1–2.

Existential and Sapiential Theology

Over thirty years ago, Otto Herman Pesch produced a monumental study on Thomas Aquinas and Martin Luther, in which he attempted to bring their disparate theologies of justification into systematic relation with one another.[71] After meticulously looking at the disparate contexts, and clarifying the terminological, conceptual, and methodological differences of the two theologians, Pesch found much that could be coordinated into fruitful dialogue and even compatibility. But Pesch also discovered that this exposed a deeper, more fundamental incongruity between Aquinas and Luther that reflected conflicting paths of theological discourse. This conflict does not begin at the level of doctrinal content (*Denkformen*) but at the underlying level of distinct theological modes of thought and intention with respect to the theological task (*Denkvollzugsformen*). Pesch characterized this difference as "sapiential" versus "existential" theology.

Sapiential theology represents Aquinas's approach. It is a second-order discourse that assumes the subjective response of faith within first-order discourse, but strives to treat theological questions from a neutral, more objective standpoint. Because the theologian is a rational creature, the theological task calls one upward beyond the contingent and transient to seek an understanding of reality in terms of ultimate causes and "by means of that cause . . . form a most certain judgment about other causes, and according thereto set all things in order."[72] Such is the call of wisdom (*sapientia*) for Aquinas, to trace the paths of God's own ineffable intellect, and thus from such a vantage consider and correlate all other derivative truth—theological, philosophical, moral.

Luther, on the other hand, exhibits an approach that Pesch characterizes as "existential." This approach to theology not only assumes the first-order context of revelation and faith, but cultivates its understanding *within* the ongoing act of faith itself. Theology's "affirmations are so formulated that the actual faith and confession of the speaker are not merely necessary presuppositions but are reflexly thematized."[73] To rise above the situation in order to contemplate ultimate causes is not only impossible for Luther, it is indicative

71. Otto Herman Pesch, *Theologie der Rechtfertigung bei Martin Luther und Thomas von Aquin: Versuch eines systematisch-theologischen Dialogs* (Ostfildern, Germany: Grünewald, 1985). See also his "Existential and Sapiential Theology—the Theological Confrontation between Luther and Thomas Aquinas," in *Catholic Scholars Dialogue with Luther*, ed. Jared Wicks, SJ (Chicago: Loyola University Press, 1970), 61–81.

72. *ST* II-II, q. 45, a. 1.

73. Pesch, "Existential and Sapiential Theology," 76.

of the sinful condition to do so. The wisdom of the cross calls us to forgo the lofty vistas that seem to offer a better perspective on the beauty and goodness of God's glory in creation.[74] Rather, at the foot of the cross we are given only to deal with the *this-ness* of God in Christ and the *this-ness* of our sinful condition. We cannot transcend this situation and through some thought experiment slip out from underneath the hand of our Creator or the condition of our fallen self to consider theological questions in a neutral space. Rather, we remain in and must speak within the context of divine address that continually impinges upon our identity, our will, and our future: "The proper subject of theology is man guilty of sin and condemned, and God the Justifier and Savior of man the sinner. Whatever is discussed in theology outside this subject, is error and poison."[75]

Such an existential approach seems evident in Luther's distinction of law and gospel. Not only does Luther consider law and gospel beyond the traditional salvation-historical schema as two mutually exclusive relations to God, but he finds efforts to transcend this conflicted state of affairs theologically precarious at best. A "distinction" is not a logical category for the sake of doctrinal clarity; for Luther it is a verbal noun—*an act* that faith must do, lest it give itself over to unbelief. Thus, Luther would say that properly distinguishing between law and gospel is, in actual fact, only accomplished by the Holy Spirit. On the other hand, to develop theological distinctions and doctrines on the basis of concepts considered in the abstract (e.g., "law" or "righteousness") leads one away from how one de facto encounters and experiences these in the concrete.[76] Thus the "righteousness of God" revealed in the gospel is not a universal standard or divine attribute of "righteousness" but rather the historical and christological exhibition and benefaction of God's faithfulness and love—"the essence of the gospel is its address to individual lives, not the eternal disposition of God toward the world."[77] So also the "law" must always

74. The basic tenet of Luther's Heidelberg Disputation (1518), *LW* 31:35–70.

75. *LW* 12:311.

76. Thus Luther's description of his breakthrough, *LW* 54:442; WATr 5:210: "There [Rom. 1:17] I saw what righteousness Paul was talking about. Earlier in the text I read 'righteousness.' I related the *abstractum* and *concretum* together and became sure of my cause. I learned to distinguish between the righteousness of the law and the righteousness of the gospel. I lacked nothing before this." See also Johann Altenstaig, *Vocabularius theologiae* (Haguenau, 1517): "Abstractum et concretum differunt, ut clarum est secundum logicos. Quia abstractum dicit solam formam in se, sicut castitas, veritas, albedo etc., sed concretum dicit duo, sc. formam cum substrato vel cum subiecto simul, sicut castum, verum album."

77. John M. G. Barclay, *Paul and the Gift* (Grand Rapids: Eerdmans, 2015), 111.

confront fallen humanity in its existing sinfulness, and thus as an accusation. The Christian's unfettered delight in the law lives only in faith, *in spe*, not *in re*.[78]

This seems to be why Luther does not consider Eden a legitimate point of departure for developing a doctrine of law and gospel. The prelapsarian knowledge of God and self is inaccessible to us. The unity of God's love and wrath is hidden from our experience. We can only deal with God clothed in his word, who—clothed in our flesh—exhibits in his own person the very antithesis of law and gospel, judgment and forgiveness, death and resurrection. And as such, he is the exemplar for our existence *coram Deo*.

When the analogy of existential and sapiential theology is carried further, it would appear that the Reformed tradition, though finding much in common with Lutheran doctrine, is prone toward the theological method of *sapientia*. The critic might claim otherwise, but such a method does not denote hubris, as if the theologian believes she can peer into the hidden things of God, or clamber up to the ineffable heights, boosted by Scripture and hoisted by speculation. No, *sapientia* is rather seen as an invitation to contemplate the vision of God's glory and thus "enjoy him forever"—the spilling over of the manifold benisons of heaven that "like streams conduct us to the fountain."[79] Whereas Luther was fixed on the Scriptures as divine address and the word of God as *viva vox*, Calvin could with equal force portray the Scriptures as "spectacles" through which one can rightly trace the paths of the knowledge of God imprinted upon his many manifest works and unfolded by his divine providence, even as the beginning and end of all things are held together in Christ.[80] Though our present existence is conflicted and our experience of God in this life is filled with contradiction, the sapiential theologian is called to affirm the underlying unity as a testimony to God's own oneness and sovereignty.

Likewise, the experienced conflict between law and gospel prompts the sapiential theologian to seek a resolution, a unity above and beyond divine wrath and grace, judgment and forgiveness. Perhaps such a unity stands at the perimeter of our fallen state—in Eden and the new Jerusalem. Yet, for

78. The contrast between what is known and possessed by faith and hope and the empirical now is a central theme in Luther's theological method. See the discussion of this topic in Bernhard Lohse, *Martin Luther's Theology in Its Historical and Systematic Development* (Minneapolis: Fortress, 1999), 74–75.

79. Calvin, *Institutes of the Christian Religion* 1.1.1.

80. Cf. Calvin, *Institutes of the Christian Religion* 1.6.1. See also the helpful comparison of Luther and Calvin on this subject by H. Paul Santmire and John B. Cobb, "The World of Nature according to the Protestant Tradition," in *The Oxford Handbook of Religion and Ecology* (Oxford: Oxford University Press, 2006), 116–24.

the Christian, in whom the presence of the Spirit already anticipates a new creation, there is the possibility of meditation and reflection on the coherence of the word that flows from the unity of the Godhead and the goodness of his providence.

So where does that leave us? If the contrast between the Reformed and Lutheran distinction of law and gospel is rooted in such a deep methodological and teleological difference, can there even be the possibility of rapprochement? Perhaps such a goal is not fitting after all. As Pesch indicates at the end of his work, on the far side of the attempt to understand one another, there still remains the possibility of complement. In fact, a consequence of such an effort to understand is the enlargement of how one perceives the theological task and scope of the Christian message. Perhaps the relationship between the Reformed and Lutheran approaches to law and gospel will not sound a singular, unified voice but will offer the wider church a pair of central themes upon the gospel of our Lord Jesus to insert into the polyphony (and cacophony) that is contemporary theology.

Likewise, each tradition presents the other with a challenge from which it may benefit. To the Lutheran one may ask whether every context requires such existential dualism. Is there a time and occasion when the horizon of one's vision ought to be broadened, animated by the promise that the Christ who reveals God in the crucified one will one day be "all in all" (Col. 3:11)? In a context when overarching metanarratives have been exposed or stripped away and lives are increasingly compartmentalized and fragmented, there is a longing for a comprehensive account, a new story to replace the shattered stories of self and society. There is a transformative power to the Reformed vision that looks beyond the present condition to what once was and what will be.

On the other hand, the Lutheran approach is an invitation to take seriously Paul's antithesis—the sharp rupture of the present by the advent of the eschaton, which leaves the church and its members in a paradoxical state. That state is not some Manichaean dualism in which part of us exists in the flesh and part in the spirit. Rather, it is the struggle of the holistic claims of two ages, two worlds, two mountains, two cities. When the conscience experiences this contradiction of experience and promise, one cannot transcend to a neutral space, free of conflict. Thus, when the law confronts us with our shortcomings, our sin, and even our piety and progress, the conscience will not be consoled by the notion that the law is eternal, holy, and good. The grand sweep of covenantal obligations and reciprocities cannot and does not say the one and only thing that faith, at that moment, must hear: "as far as the east is from the west, so far does God remove our transgressions from us."

Perhaps there is a need for both voices in Christendom. Perhaps the church must attend to both paths of theology, to concede that a theology that comforts, directs, convinces, and convicts cannot be a monolithic system or a single approach. Perhaps, as Pesch says at the end of his work, "there must always be a sapiential theology . . . and an existential theology for the blessing of Christianity."[81]

81. Pesch, *Rechtfertigung*, 955: "Daruber hinaus aber könnte das Werk beider Theologen Bedeutsames lehren hinsichtlich Struktur und Ansatz des theologischen Vollzuges. Es wird zum Segen der Christenheit immer eine sapientiale, heilsgeschichtliche, schöpfungsbezogene Theologie unde ebenso immer eine soteriologische, christolozentrische, existentielleTheologie geben müssen."

Chapter 8

A Reformed Response to the Lutheran Tradition

Katherine Sonderegger

"The true knowledge of the distinction between the Law and the Gospel is not only a glorious light, affording the correct understanding of the entire Holy Scriptures, but without this knowledge Scripture is and remains a sealed book."[1] So begins the militant proclamation of our theme—law and gospel—by that nineteenth-century worthy of Concordia Seminary, C. F. W. Walther. It seems fitting to me to begin my reflections on this most Lutheran theme with an American voice—or perhaps better, with that of a Swabian Lutheran well planted in the New World, at the émigré community in Saint Louis, Missouri. I want to spend most of my time here on Walther's sharp division between law and gospel in the Holy Scriptures, but not before I mention a more contemporary Lutheran voice—one equally incisive as Walther, but more wedded to the German experience before and after World War II—that of Werner Elert. Famous for his debate with Karl Barth, Elert gives voice to the distinction Walther defends, but in the idiom of mid-twentieth-century personalism and existential phenomenology. Here's Elert from *Law and Gospel*:

> "*Lex semper accusat*" says Melanchthon in the Apology to the Augsburg Confession: the law always accuses. With these words he expresses in the most concise formula not only Luther's view, but also Paul's. . . . [Karl Barth] states that law and gospel stand in a dialectical relationship. Absolutely correct. But the question remains what one means by dialectic. If one means thereby a dialectic of the substance, this would imply what we said at the outset, that when the one speaks the other is reduced to

1. C. F. W. Walther, thesis 4, in *God's No and God's Yes: The Proper Distinction between Law and Gospel* (Saint Louis: Concordia, 1973), 24.

> silence and vice versa. "The Law," Barth says, "is nothing else than the necessary form of the Gospel, whose content is grace." The explanation for this reduction of the substantive dialectic of law and gospel to the verbal dialectic of form and content lies in Barth's statement: "The very fact that God speaks to us, that, under all circumstances, is in itself, grace."[2]

The idea that God speaks only grace to man, Elert concludes firmly, "is a fundamental error."[3] After a robust rebuke of Calvin, Elert concludes the essay with a tight summary of the whole: "Either the law or the gospel is the end of God's ways with men, but not both. They are as opposed to one another as death and life. It is the gospel in which we place our faith."[4]

Now I would like to take these two bold voices as heralds and guides for a deeper reflection on law and gospel as scriptural or, perhaps better, as structural, biblical themes. I hasten to assure you that I do not do this in utter blindness to the fullness, diversity, and complexity of Lutheran theology on the great causes of justification, grace, and law. (I hear Robert Jenson and Paul Hinlicky pleading in my ear for a broader, richer, more ecumenical vision; I hope to show later what I have learned from them.) I ask Walther and Elert to stand surety for the whole here, not because a rich and historical tradition can be properly reduced in this way—a kind of Weberian ideal type—but rather because these two raise in a vivid and courageous way the deepest question that faces us as dogmatic theologians: Shall we read the Holy Scriptures in this way, or not? If law and gospel are not the pair that cut all the way down into the very heart of Scripture, what might take their place? Can we read the Bible in any other way; or will it, stripped bare of this dualism, remain "a sealed Book," without grace, without light, without power to heal, to instruct, to convict and cure? How should Christians read the Holy Word of God? These are the questions Walther and Elert embolden me to ask.

Is the Bible a "Sealed Book"?

Let me begin with a rather brash question of my own: Can the Bible be a "sealed book"? Walther and Elert propose that Holy Scripture is the kind of

2. W. Elert, *Zwischen Gnade und Ungnade* (Munich: Evangelischer Presseverband für Bayern, 1948); ET, *Law and Gospel*, trans. E. H. Schroeder (Philadelphia: Fortress, 1967), 11.

3. Elert, *Law and Gospel*, 5.

4. Elert, *Law and Gospel*, 48.

work that can be fundamentally misread and misunderstood. It can stand impervious to our attempts to take up and read; the seals can remain unbroken. The solvent to be applied to the Scriptures is the "substantial dialectic" of law and gospel. This pair penetrates the obdurate covers over the whole, reduces the "contradictions" that lace the interior, and "opens the gates to Paradise," to echo Luther's famous phrase. Now there is much to be said about this dialectical pair, but I want to linger here a moment on the prior conviction—that such a pair is demanded by the book of Scripture itself.

Is the aim of Christian doctrine to provide a "framework," a structure or analytic tool by which a closed text becomes open? Is the Bible a work that can be "read under a description"; "read as" a member of a class, a kind? Is the proper task of dogmatics to provide such a description? Is this, in the end, what we mean by "second-order" statements in theology, a deep "grammar," as late Wittgensteinians would have it, that orders and renders coherent the "first-order" utterances of Scripture? If so, we might well wonder, What is the source of such upper-level analysis? Whence this *regula fidei?*

I think these are deep questions, and not ones given to simple replies. One way to read the rise of the modern in Christian theology is as a studied, self-conscious attempt to recognize a class or identifying genre to which the Bible belongs. Is the Bible, for example, an instance of "ancient literature"? Famously, Schleiermacher, in his lectures on hermeneutics, advocated for reading the Bible like any other text, drawing upon historical setting, genre studies, and the knowledge of authorship and authorial intent. The Bible belongs to the ancient Near East, and to the scattered Mediterranean cities of the late Roman imperium. Samuel Coleridge cut his critical teeth on the genre of prophecy as a form of poetic diction; D. F. Strauss, more menacingly, on the genre of *mythos,* or plastic thought. What we now group in a rather shopworn carryall as "historical criticism" is an extension and expression of the modern conviction that the Bible is a collection of historical books, anchored deep in the cultures of the ancient world, and laid bare by the insight, critical tools, and recognition of the remote that constitute historical knowing. Indeed, the "new perspective on Paul"—the far-flung family presided over by the Lutheran bishop and scholar Krister Stendahl—brings the higher criticism of modernism to the epistles, worldview, and convictions of the apostle Paul. All these modernist descriptions of the biblical books seem so often at odds with dogmatic and spiritual convictions about Holy Scripture; and indeed, to come of age in their presence has been, to lean on Schweitzer's memorable words, a "painful school of honesty." But I think we should not allow these conflicts to mask some startling commonalities. "Law and gospel," as I read this pair in Walther and

Elert, seem also to offer a genre, a description, and an analysis into which the Holy Bible is to fit; and through this structural and second-order pair, the *lux ex Orient* is to shine.

The aim, I believe, is this: we are to read the whole of the Bible, from Genesis to Revelation, as the outworking of either divine law or divine pardon; each part and the books therein composed belong to one camp or the other camp; *tertium non datur*. In his evening addresses, Walther ranges over pastoral examples, where first law, then gospel, must be applied. He parses specific biblical verses, half-verses, parables, and large-scale events as divided into well-patrolled areas, law or gospel, and the wise pastor discerns which area has opened up before the faithful, and how the pastor is to lead, first through anguish, despair, and sorrow, then to green pastures and the joy of the sinner redeemed. These categories are "mutually exclusive," Elert warns; when "one speaks the other is silent," for just this is the discrimen of a real or substantial dialectic. I cannot shake the visual impression here of a *template* that rests over the whole, something like the decoders beloved by so many of us in childhood, through which the proper and true meaning of the text emerges, to chasten, to subdue, but then also to console and free. The Bible, that is, belongs to a mixed genre, the law-gospel, and it reveals its sweetness and marrow to the devout soul only when the perplexing and hard exterior is punctured, and the inward sections divided firmly and clearly into their true divisions, law or gospel. "In this sign, conquer" seems to be the motto of this dialectic.

Well, why not? you might well ask. Does the Bible not need interpreters? The Ethiopian official does not know how to read the prophet Isaiah until Philip draws near in the Spirit and opens the book before him. Such a biblical exemplar, further, shows that structured, guided reading does not seem particularly modern, but rather belongs to the very first movements of Christian reading of the Holy Scriptures. And perhaps we might want to cast the net wider: Do not rabbinic Jews, from at least the early days in Javneh, aim to break up the Bible into camps, genres, descriptions: Law, Prophets, Writings; Torah, Nebiim, Ketuvim? Think of the templates Augustine famously throws over the New Testament: Trinitarian statements or verses that are to be read "relationally," and others "substantially"; or christological statements that belong to the Son's days of humility and lowliness, and those that belong to his deity, and eternal glory. The Tome of Leo practices divisions of just this sort; even Cyril finds Gospel verses that express our Lord's humanity and meekness, and others his exaltation and full deity. Only so did the early doctors of the church believe that the Scriptures were properly read and properly defended against the errors of their opponents. Nicene orthodoxy appears built—we might even go this far—on the firm foundation of an analytic reading of Holy Scripture.

Closer to home, we might press on in this vein to Luther and Melanchthon, to the whole college of magisterial reformers. No one could fail to spot the prominence accorded law and gospel in the Smalcald Articles; in the earliest editions of Melanchthon's *Loci*; in the settlement thrashed out in the Formula of Concord; in Luther's prefaces to the Bible and his pathbreaking commentary on Galatians. We might also consider the insight some Lutherans call the "canon within the canon": Do we not read and rank our Holy Scriptures by Luther's axiom, *was Christum treibt?* Do we not bend over the pages of the Bible in search of the "manger in which Christ lies," to borrow Luther's lovely, evocative image? Every schoolchild knows that Luther cast a cold eye on certain books of the Bible; the letter of James, that "right strawy epistle," hardly earns its keep in the New Testament, and the book of Revelation fares little better. Calvin famously did not include it in his majestic commentary series on the whole Bible. Such bold use of division and analysis in the reading of the Bible suggests that Christians of every age classify and group whole sections of Holy Scripture, and learn to read it only as a work "under a description": a book that preaches Christ, for example, or that "shows the way of the cross" or instructs the faithful in the "path of radical renunciation." Perhaps the seals of the Bible have always needed breaking, awaiting the rupture of class, of dialectic, of genre and aim. Perhaps modernism in biblical interpretation simply continues, sharpens, and clarifies an ancient practice, a *rule* for holy reading of holy things. And, as Walther shrewdly remarks in another evening talk, the history of the church and the faithful cannot stand outside the *providentia Dei*; in the midst of every rebellion and waywardness, God remains sovereign, working his purpose out. Just so, the dialectical reading of Holy Scripture develops under the watchful eye of a gracious and almighty Lord.

Scripture Needs No Analytic Grid to Be Understood

So what might we say, in the end, to this Lutheran pattern and analytic, law and gospel, as key to Holy Scripture? My aim here is not to extend the very sad polemics between Reformed and Lutheran houses of God, nor uncover a yet more subtle way of differentiating the two prominent wings of the sixteenth-century Reformation of the Latin Church. Much as I admire Francis Turretin, I do not believe an elenctic theology serves the church well, nor does it seem to me the surest path to upbuilding the faithful. I consider Luther one of my fathers in the faith and a doctor of the church; so my aim here is to reflect from within this broad Reformation of the church to its proper confession and study of Holy Writ. Is this the proper way to read Scripture? Does it open a sealed book? Perhaps more pointedly, do the seals in truth need to be broken?

For my part, I do not believe the Bible is a book that is sealed. I say that the Bible does not require a dialectic or analytic grid to pry open its interior, or to set forth its gracious light in all its radiant glory. I don't believe the Bible is that sort of book—indeed, I don't believe it belongs in a "sort" or "kind" at all, but is instead unique—and we should receive it as a form of divine presence, a mystery, a fullness, a sacrament, and light. The Reformed tradition is fond of speaking of Holy Scripture as "perspicuous" and "self-interpreting," and I would want to affirm these insights, though I suspect by sounding a rather different key. I do not think the Bible is best understood as *revelation*, though to be sure it contains revealed truths. We do not recognize the surpassing uniqueness of Holy Scripture, I say, by focusing upon *referent*: the Bible is not first and principally *about* something; though again, it, to be sure, contains descriptions and indications and referents of all kinds. The Bible is first and principally, I say, a *nearness*, a divine drawing-near, a *mysterion*; it is the radiance of the holy fire who is God. When we read and meditate and feed upon Holy Scripture, we, like Gabriel, stand in the presence. God is veiled, most certainly! I do not mean that we gaze upon almighty God in Scripture somewhat as a child gazes at photos of her summer camp in a long-forgotten scrapbook. The Bible is not referential in that way, either. No! God is hidden, invisible, beyond form; exalted, glorious, infinite, and infinitely free. Were the much-lamented John Webster still here among us, he would want me to underscore just now the full *creatureliness* of Holy Scripture; and indeed I do. I do not aim to undermine, ignore, or deracinate the Bible as a material, creaturely, and historical work: it cannot be divine presence as is the Holy Spirit himself, in the world and in the human heart. Nor can it be a full correlate to Jesus Christ, the living Word. The fullness of God is pleased to dwell in the Son in a manner wholly divine, unique, infinitely rich. I do not mean that Holy Scripture is presence in this sense! No, rather, I aim to set forth the Bible as a *means* of presence, a creaturely manifestation of the one God, who lives and speaks and rules from the thornbush, radiant and not consumed. And yes, perhaps in a more concentrated solution that Luther drew up, I would say that the Bible is the "manger in which the Lord God dwells." Now, of course, I have not even touched the hem of the garment by saying all this. A full doctrine of Holy Scripture will have to say much, much more about inspiration and historicity and covenant unity and authorship—and that is the work of another day. But I mean here to advance the notion—the confession, really—that the Bible *radiates* divine presence, and the Lord's whole goodness passes over us as we shelter in this mighty rock.

What Is the Bible About?

So we return by another route to the dialectic of law and gospel, and ask, from this new vantage, how we might regard the task of division and analysis through this Lutheran pair. Let me begin by asking the simple question that I think—not surprisingly—does not yield a simple answer: Just what is the Bible about, for our Lutheran teachers? What is its purpose and aim and great work? I think we might begin here with the conviction that for Walther and Elert the Bible is a book about salvation. That need not mean that it is exclusively about our salvation—the Holy Writings can contain much that is of passing note, of historical interest, or everyday, flat factuality. But principally the Bible tells the work of our redemption; but not for that day only but for us, we who hear these words, today. Now, I think this is a characterization of the Bible that is so deeply familiar to us, so dear to us, that we may not consider how radical this claim truly is. Note that the Bible remains *referential* here, but not necessarily *propositional.* The Bible contains teachings about God, about the people Israel, its history and covenant and cult; it tells of exodus and exile, of prophetic and royal reform, of divine instruction to penitents and to victors; of a humble birth in a little darkened city, of great deeds of power and acclaim, of teachings and commands and blessings, of the works of the night, and of the great light that pours out of a tomb, early on the first day; and of the first witnesses who carry the word about all these teachings, these events ringed about with the Spirit's power. The Bible contains and refers to all these things. But according to Luther and the Lutheran tradition, Holy Scripture is not most properly characterized by propositions or statements *about* these things. The Bible is not revelation *in this sense.* It is not *esoteric,* disclosing truths about divine reality that could not be had in the stolid world of the everyday. Nor does it principally set forth doctrines that must be affirmed in order to know God truly. Yes, they are there. But the Bible is not an instruction book, at its heart. Rather, the Bible is a work of our salvation, a mighty bursting forth from the sinner's tomb. What must I do to be saved? *This* question is taken up, answered, and shattered in the pages of this book.

Now if the Bible is this sort of book—deliverance to the captive—then law and gospel serve a slightly different end than do those categories of genre and type, so familiar to modern and some precritical readers of Scripture.

We say something distinctive when we identify the Holy Scriptures as composed of law and gospel than when we affirm poetry or prophecy, narrative or *phrónēsis*, parable or saying source. The law-gospel distinction springs from the *relational* or, in modern dress, the *existential* character of Scripture as saving word. The Bible is not simply divided up into genres that suitably capture the text within its covers. Instead, we are urged to break the seals of Scripture by taking to heart the truth that these words are *pro me; pro nos*: they concern us. We might borrow a page from modern discussions of faith to say that law and gospel are "self-involving"; they are the words, terrible or consoling, of God's mighty work *toward us*. We are included, entailed, by the very categories we use to clarify and rank the holy text. This is the justification for narrowing our focus on the rich expanse of Holy Scripture to these two, and these alone. Law and gospel are the terms of our eschatological destiny: before eternal God, we are accused; or we are pardoned, consoled, reckoned righteous. For all the complex legacy of modern Lutheran doctrines of faith, we can still say in a simple fashion that Christian faith just is the deep, personal recognition that law and gospel concern me; more, they *determine* me.

Now, it seems to me that we might pause here to seek the grounds for such a strong personalist and binary reading of Holy Scripture. Is this the proper—indeed, only—way of construing God's ways with us? Is the entirety of Holy Scripture an outworking of divine judgment, such that the offer of grace and the rebuke of the sinner is the purpose and sum, the content and *scopus*, of the whole of the Bible? Why would we say that? Let me suggest one possible reply to this question, drawing on a wonderfully suggestive comment of Robert Jenson's. In his characteristic terse and compressed style, he remarkably suggests both the answer *and* the problem that such a scriptural dialectic poses. In the brisk, little book entitled *Lutheran Slogans: Use and Abuse*, Jenson writes:

> Why is "narrative" so important [to the proper reading of Scripture]? . . . Israel's Scripture was authoritative for the first believers before they were believers and remained so thereafter. But this could have gone several ways. Why should the wisdom tradition in Scripture not have shaped the community of Jesus' disciples into a sect of "philosophers" in the ancient sense, "lovers of wisdom"? The Scripture's Wisdom literature is not notably narrative. Or why should not the church have been molded by Scripture into a movement to bring the blessings of Mosaic law to the world? In themselves, also the legal codes narrate very little.[5]

5. R. Jenson, *Lutheran Slogans: Use and Abuse* (Delhi, NY: ALPB Books, 2011), 79.

There, in brief compass, the problem! But also, in equally brisk and brief compass, the solution:

> It was and is the gift of a small second volume, attached to the first Scripture, that determined how Scripture would shape the Christian movement. For that volume comprises the Gospels' story of what happened with Jesus, and in various forms the claim that this story is the climax of Israel's Scripture. Thus the church was constrained to read Israel's Scripture as the sort of discourse that can have a climax, that is, as narrative, and then to read the two testaments together as one great meganarrative of God's work with his people.[6]

In a wonderful footnote, Jenson shows just how this providential reading is supposed to work. "The rabbinic movement," he writes, "that became the Judaism we know was also blessed with a second volume, the Mishnah. This is a collection of legal commentary, applying sacral law to daily life." This is good, of course, as it stands; but then comes the tour de force! "As the New Testament constrains the church to read the Old Testament as narrative, with theological and moral comment, so the Mishnah—with equal legitimacy—constrains Judaism to read the Old Testament as Torah, with narrative context."[7]

First, the explication; now, the application. Jenson proposes that a central category in his work, narrative, is justified as the dominant character of the whole of Scripture because the New Testament and, supreme in it, the Gospels are narratives. That "second volume" casts its light over the whole, and controls how we read the entire Bible. Just so, the brilliant light of the Mishnah distills the multiple genres of the Hebrew Bible into law, or Torah. Something that follows or fulfills or completes *determines* how we read and characterize the whole: that is Jenson's lesson. It seems to me that something of this pattern can be seen in the Lutheran effort to *define, determine,* and *categorize* Holy Scripture as a book about salvation, about law and gospel. If Jenson is right, we do not discover the proper analytic categories for the Bible by adding up the genres within it, or scouring the texts for leading types and themes. The Bible is not "narrative" as a whole *in virtue of* the predominance of story in its pages. In fact, we might even find ourselves persuaded, on other grounds, that the text could *equally* well be read in another way, to belong to another whole kind. Just this is what Jenson believes we find in Jewish reading

6. Jenson, *Lutheran Slogans*, 79.
7. Jenson, *Lutheran Slogans*, 79n106.

of the Bible, controlled as it is by the mishnaic commentaries. Notice here that the subject matter of the Bible, its aim or type, is not assimilated to its *content*. When we use the term "narrative" for Jenson, or "law and gospel" for Walther, we do not pick out specific, cardinal passages, nor do we add up the instances of the genres within the pages of Holy Writ. No! We can be so bold as to acknowledge that large tracts of Scripture are not narratives; we could freely admit that large portions do not concern the law or the saving gospel; we could even bow before a competing claim, ceding coherence and plausibility to the whole canon as Torah or perhaps as liberation, say, or mystical union. We are making a decision about the whole, that is, on grounds distinct and perhaps prior to the material content of the Bible, book by book, genre by genre.

What the Bible is *about*, I might say in summary, is not determined by what is in it. To be sure, these second-order categories cannot range entirely free of the text! I am not proposing that a plausible megacategory for Holy Scripture could be "auto repair" or "ancient Roman drama." There must be something like "fit" or "coherence" between category and text, a plausibility and constraint; yet the category, all the same, need not *emerge* from the text, nor be simply a summary of it. We have instead something like a "metacategory" that controls the whole, the lens through which we see each part, recognize, order, and interpret it. What the *part* is about can be discovered and stated by knowing the megacategory, the genre of the *whole*. This is what unseals the book.

Now, whence these megacategories? Jenson, remember, suggests they emerge from sacred writing appended to the Scriptures of Israel, the New Testament and Mishnah. But we might ask, need these supercategories belong to the sacred writings themselves? Might they emerge also from the life of prayer, from Christian witness, martyrdom, discipleship; from the *consensus gentium* or *consensus fidelium*? Might they come from the church and its traditions? These defining categories serve as *regula fidei*, I suggested earlier; might these be anchored in Christian practice and community, in the *totus Christus*? I don't think we need to settle these neuralgic questions about Scripture and tradition here—if only we could!—but I do think that the entire pattern of law and gospel as a scriptural supercategory can be seen as the deliverance of a faithful monastic and pioneer, an Augustinian whose torments with Christian righteousness broke through old patterns of reading the Bible and brought revolutionary pardon and liberty to the whole. Luther and Melanchthon learned to read the Bible through the medieval pattern of preaching, sacrament, and holy works; they learned to read it anew through a fresh encounter with Paul's mighty letter to the Romans in the midst of an inner struggle over the sinner in the presence of a holy God. This large complex of ecclesial practice, personal piety, and scholarly study yielded a new master narrative, the account of salvation through Christ's own grace and merit, received by faith alone. The Bible is the record of this great divine work of redemption. It is a book of salvation.

Now, if this very compressed account of Holy Scripture as law and gospel can suffice, it will go some way to meeting some standard objections raised about this dialectical pair. Consider Melanchthon's famous axiom "the law always accuses," a phrase central to the dogmatic exegesis of Walther and Elert. We might object: Is that so? Does the law *always* accuse? Is it such a harsh, judgmental, unrelenting prosecutor? Is this the proper way to read the Pentateuch? Do we not find words of consolation, offers of grace and pardon there too? How can we read Psalm 119 if we consider law to be nothing but trial and faultfinding and curse? What possible defense could we mount against the "new perspective" or E. P. Sanders's "covenantal nomism" were we to see the Torah as little more than a heartless judge, a demanding taskmaster? Why would David dance before the ark of the covenant with all his might if those tablets of the law were nothing but accusation and guilt and terror? Is this in truth the way of Israel, the way of the covenant? Such questions have dogged the Lutheran account of the accusing law, from the Reformed scholastics and the modern students of rabbinic Judaism and its Scriptures. Parallel objections have been raised about Walther and Melanchthon as interpreters of Luther. Is the "distinction between law and gospel" in truth a "glorious light"? Does it yield the proper way to read Luther himself? Certainly we find Luther excoriating "Moses" in light of the sweet and gracious Lord Christ—but does he always paint Moses in such garish hues? Is Luther not a more delicate, a more deft reader of Holy Scripture than all that? Does he not seem to hold open a door, from time to time, to the "third use of the law"; does he not give some ground to Melanchthon's later acceptance of the law as guide to a disciplined Christian life? Do not the specific texts of Luther, the fine-grained reading of his work, prompt the same objections that many Bible scholars have raised about the law as accuser? The texts under study, in Luther and in the Bible, seem to resist the categories laid upon them; they do not fit, it seems, or cohere, but rather inhibit, deform, constrain. Such, we might say in brief, is the objection to law and gospel as controlling key to Holy Scripture.

But this broad strand of Lutheran Scripture reading is not left defenseless against these objections; not at all! These Lutheran exegetes knew too that the apostle Paul taught that the law is good, righteous, and holy; they too knew that "those who did these things would live by them." They were not blind to the promises, the grace, the sweetness of the Mosaic code, nor did they consider the teachings of Christ a counterstroke against the whole Pentateuch. Something much more sure-handed, in the reading of Scripture and of Luther, is going on here than these objections suggest. The Lutheran claim, instead, is that Luther gave to the faithful a form of reading that allowed grace and judgment to pervade the whole, to lie embedded in the entire witness of Scripture, distinct, divided, yet not separated or confused.

The law, they say, is a form of *conditional* address to creatures: if you follow this commandment and do it, you shall live. In just this way, the law can offer holy promises: do this and it will go well for you in the land. The law in this sense can teach, instruct, guide; indeed, it is a good shepherd. The law, in this Lutheran reading, is far from flat, homogenized, uniform; rather, the law, from earliest days, was understood to have moral, ceremonial, and juridical elements, and each had their own persistent conditions. The Reformed scholastic interest in temporal covenants finds its parallel here: the law, in its Lutheran interpretation, had historical elements, its flourishing for a season and a day, and then its quiet passing away, its fulfillment or end. The very notion that law could *end*, that it could have provisions, statutes, and ordinances that would not abide but rather pass away: this was an insight and crisis that both Christianity, in all its forms, and rabbinic Judaism had to encounter, understand, and accommodate. There was an era for the sacrificial cultus of the temple; and it is no more. There was a time for a high priest or a Sanhedrin or royal house; and it is over. There was for the people Israel a binding covenant of dietary laws and circumcision; and for Christians, that time has passed away. But the Ten Words abide; their time is always and forever. Moreover, the law abides in Christ's own teaching and example. He gives law in the Sermon on the Mount; he chides and instructs; he judges and casts out; he bows in the end to a judgment against himself and to a death the law he follows curses and declares unclean.

The gospel, on the other hand, was understood, from Luther forward, as a form of address wholly positive, unconditioned, and everlasting. It belonged, and was supremely exemplified in Jesus Christ, the Living Gospel, but it belonged too to the Old Testament and the covenant life of the people Israel. Though Walther and Elert both speak at times as though gospel *supersedes* the law, neither in fact succumb to such a wooden and tone-deaf reading of Israel's Scriptures. Instead, gospel can be found within the joy of the Lord's presence in his temple, embedded in the promise of return, in the offer of pardon, in the declaration of divine favor and election. It is the very presence of gospel within the Old Testament that emboldened Calvin to declare Israel's cultus *sacramental,* and not merely "material" or "carnal" rites. It is the very presence of gospel within the Old Testament that makes a single Bible out of two Testaments, and underwrites the christological reading of the whole. Law and gospel in truth are entwined, joined together, as a complex but single strand, running throughout the entire Bible: that is the claim for this pair as master concept, as saving truth of the Holy Scriptures.

So what, in the end, should we say as Christians, and I as a Reformed theologian, about this complex master category, law and gospel? As we have seen, it is a far more powerful, far more sophisticated and fine-grained concept than most critics allow. It is not defeated or superseded by objections anchored in historical reading of covenant law or of the apostle Paul. Its engine is not anchored in specific texts or the summation of genres and types. It is, I believe, a particularly elegant, devout, and challenging form of *Christology*: it is a thoroughgoing christological interpretation of the Bible, an unembarrassed proclamation of Scripture, whole and entire, as Word of God, incarnate for our salvation. Baptism and the Lord's Supper are means of grace, certainly; but even more is the entire Bible a means of saving grace. In its law it breaks down and breaks through smug security; it holds before sinners' eyes their own guilt and penalty; in the sobering words of John Agricola, it "crushes the sinner." But the Bible is not just law, nor is it predominantly law. No, grace abounds even more! The whole Bible, Old and New Testament, sets forth Christ, who is, above all else, gospel. The free pardon, the righteousness and consolation, the liberty and gracious exchange: all these are the marks of Christ, stamped deep into Scripture's very core. It is its final structure and end. This rich dialectic of law and gospel, law entwined with gospel, law leading to gospel, is the glorious legacy of Lutheran exegesis for the whole church.

Yet it is not, as you know, the way I read the Holy Bible. I do not have a master concept or pair for the whole of Scripture, nor do I believe the Bible requires such an analysis to break open its seals. The whole of the Bible is not "for us and for our salvation" in this strong sense. Nor is it christological in this thoroughgoing, structural, architectural way. The Bible, I say, is the sacramental nearness of the whole glory of God. If it has a referent as a whole, it is about God, not about us and our salvation. Divine sovereignty, divine aseity and glory and life: these are the perfections of God exemplified in the pages of Holy Writ. I suppose the psalmist says it best: Not to us, O Lord, not to us, but to thy name be the glory. Perhaps this is the legacy of Reformed Christendom I might offer as commentary and companion to law and gospel; not *against* them, certainly, but beside and beyond them too. There is much more to be said, of course, about the proper reading of Holy Scripture and about the Reformed account of justification and sanctification, about gospel and law. But not everything should be said in one place or all at once. Rather, perhaps another axiom or confession might say the one thing I wish to add as a final word. As the Lutheran J. S. Bach concluded all his compositions, so I perhaps should end this chapter: Soli Deo Gloria!

Chapter 9

Continuing the Conversation: A Lutheran Reflection

Mark C. Mattes

When visiting the Berliner Dom, the iconic church in the heart of Berlin, one cannot help but be awestruck not only by the spaciousness of the sanctuary but also by the four gigantic statues of the magisterial reformers guarding each of the sanctuary's four corners: Luther, Melanchthon, Calvin, and Zwingli. For those whose family roots belong to traditions that challenged the Prussian Union (such as my own), the presence of both Lutheran and Reformed *magistri* in the same worship space draws attention. In real life, could all four have worshiped together without substantive disputes arising? One is apt to think that Luther and Zwingli would quickly get into a row over the presence of Christ in the Supper, while Melanchthon and Calvin would just as quickly team up, given that they shared similar views on the Supper and a systematic approach to theology. The united presence of these four witnesses testifies both to the ideals of the Prussian Union and to the current Evangelische Kirche in Deutschland. Likewise, for the *Uniert* tradition, these four figures not only trigger reformational ideals by which to live but also symbolize the possibility of a unified approach to doctrine. Centuries of Pietism, rationalism, and Protestant liberalism smoothed over the doctrinal sore spots erupting between these four. For that congregation's builders, these spiritual movements that tended to relativize doctrine were more important than the confessional differences dividing the reformers.

The differences between Lutherans and Reformed come even more to the fore when the Reformed voice is represented by the Westminster Confession's "bicovenantal" approach to theology, which subsumes the distinction between law and gospel under the overarching framework of "covenant," and the Lutheran, by those influenced to one degree or another by C. F. W. Walther's

Proper Distinction between Law and Gospel,[1] which highlights the opposition between law and gospel. This paper will describe some of these differences, propose a connection between Lutherans and the Reformed on law and gospel, and offer suggestions for future discussion.

Lutheran and Reformed Differences *Noch Einmal*

The heart of the disagreement between Lutherans and the Reformed on law and gospel is this: The Reformed find the concept of "covenant" to be an overarching paradigm that encompasses and situates law and gospel. For Lutherans, there is no such overarching, encompassing, neutral paradigm. Instead, there is a real rupture or difference between law and gospel for which there is no supervening, reconciling category, or third party. For Lutherans, law is command while gospel is promise. Law directs human behavior; gospel repeats and delivers God's loyalty, especially to sinners with troubled consciences. But, for the Reformed, there is one word of God, not two. Law and gospel constitute a "twofold administration of the covenant of grace,"[2] or, as Karl Barth later put it, the "Law is nothing else than the necessary form of the Gospel, whose content is grace. Precisely this content demands this form, the form which calls for its like, the Law's form."[3] Clearly, for the Reformed, salvation is by grace. However, even though the law is not the basis for salvation, it is the fundamental framework for divine-human interaction.

In contrast, for Lutherans, God's mercy and faith in God's mercy are the fundamental framework. In response to Barth, few articulate the core difference on law and gospel between Lutherans and the Reformed as well as Hermann Sasse:

> Both communions wish to distinguish the Gospel from the Law and yet indicate the relation which subsists between them. Both acknowledge that the chief article of the Christian faith is the forgiveness of sins: the Lutherans consider it the *whole* content of the Gospel, while the Reformed consider it the *principal* content of the Gospel. Both know that Christ

1. Translated by W. H. T. Dau (Saint Louis: Concordia, 1986). A fine pastoral restatement of Walther's work is John T. Pless, *Handling the Word of Truth: Law and Gospel in the Church Today* (Saint Louis: Concordia, 2015); see especially 17–24.

2. See Scott Swain's essay, thesis 2, above.

3. Karl Barth, "Gospel and Law," chapter in *Community, State, and Church: Three Essays* (Gloucester, MA: Peter Smith, 1968), 80.

preached the Law as well as the Gospel, even as the Old Testament contains the Gospel as well as the Law. Both know that the church must proclaim the whole Word of God, both the Law and the Gospel. The difference lies in the fact that the Reformed believe that both Law and Gospel are parts of Christ's real work, and consequently are essential functions of the church; the Lutheran Church, on the other hand, teaches that the preaching of the Law is the "strange," and the preaching of the Gospel is the "real," work of Christ, and that accordingly, although the church must also preach the Law—how else could it proclaim the Gospel?—the only thing which is essential to its nature as the church of Christ is that it is the place, the only place in all the world, in which the blessed tidings of the forgiveness of sins for Christ's sake are heard.[4]

For Lutherans, that God has two distinct words bears even on the doctrine of God. Luther admonishes sinners "to flee from and find refuge in God against God" (*ad deum contra deum confungere*).[5] Luther's language of flight "from God, to God," specifying a clash within God's own life between the expectations of divine holiness and a compassion that "grows warm and tender" (Hos. 11:8–9), could perhaps be affirmed by the Reformed as a rhetorical embellishment to highlight divine mercy, but never be confessed as a real conflict within the divine life as such, given that God is eternal law. For the Reformed, Luther's description of "God against God" (*Gott gegen Gott*), Christ as the conscience's defense against God's own accusing law, does not sound insightful but instead Marcionite at best, schizophrenic at worst. For Luther, in contrast, God's law may be eternal, but God is not equivalent to eternal law.

Example of the Woman Caught in Adultery

For Lutherans, "grace" is not merely the favor of God's condescension to deal with mortals. It is surely that, but its nature is clearer when seen more specifically as mercy. For Lutherans, sinners are saved not only from sin, death, and the devil, but also from the law, indeed, God's very own law. *Lex semper accusat*. Such a view is not *imposed upon* Scripture but *grows out* of Scripture. We can

4. Hermann Sasse, *Here We Stand: Nature and Character of the Lutheran Faith*, trans. Theodore G. Tappert (Adelaide, South Australia: Lutheran Publishing House, 1979), 129.

5. WA 5:204.26–27. See Vítor Westhelle, "Luther's *Theologia Crucis*," in *The Oxford Handbook of Martin Luther's Theology*, ed. Robert Kolb, Irene Dingel, and L'ubomír Batka (Oxford: Oxford University Press, 2014), 163.

see this strife within God's own life in Jesus's dealing with the adulteress (John 8). God's law is clear: "If a man commits adultery with the wife of his neighbor, both the adulterer and the adulteress shall surely be put to death" (Lev. 20:10). Leviticus offers no loopholes or provisions in the fine print: adulterers are to be executed. In this circumstance, if mercy should apply, it would be "Aim for the head!" Put the sinner out of her misery! But when Jesus was put to the test with this specific situation by his opponents, those obsessed with personal, religious, and social purity, Jesus threw the accusation back at them: "Let the one who is without sin among you be the first to throw a stone at her." Jesus preached the accusing law to the woman's accusers. He thoroughly disempowered them. They wanted to use the law to feed their self-righteousness, and to entrap Jesus as an "antinomian" in the process. But their machinations only empowered Jesus's case against them: before God we have no righteousness of our own to bring. *Coram Deo,* it is not only our sin, but also our goodness that is problematic.

Now, we need to be very clear: Jesus was not just opposing his enemies, the scribes and Pharisees. He was opposing God's own law in Leviticus. How could Jesus do such a thing? Isn't he God in the flesh? As the Redeemer, isn't he to be righteous and so uphold the law? No doubt, he himself "fulfilled" the commandment not to commit adultery. But with this sinful woman he fails to uphold the law because he refused to allow anyone to strike her dead. One can picture his willingness to take the sentence for her if the stones were to fly.

Of course, the story of the woman caught in adultery is one of entrapment, specifically of Jesus. When all is said and done, the scribes and Pharisees were less interested in upholding the law than in accusing Jesus. But given Jesus's opposition to executing the consequences of the law, they had a legitimate, that is, biblical and legal, charge against Jesus. Not only is the law vulnerable to being used violently in the hands of evil people, but it also fails to deliver the core of God's economy with sinners: mercy to the repentant.

In Jesus's defense of this sinful woman we encounter God contra God. God as mercy extended in Jesus's intervention for a sinner in opposition to God who expresses himself in communal order and ritual purity. In receiving such mercy, the woman must flee from the God who wants her dead to the God who will do nothing other than claim her as his own—for Jesus's sake.

This incident is no mere outlier. It is the story of Israel itself. Israel's story is that of exile and return, death and resurrection, since the nation was chronically unfaithful to its Lord and so suffered God's judgment. God's people were ever humbled by Canaanites, Egyptians, Babylonians, Greeks, and Romans, instruments through whom God chastened the people. The scribes and Pharisees play out the script of pride and rebellion as well as their predecessors did. By seeking to uphold the letter of the law, the scribes and Pharisees fall short of Israel's vocation to protect the powerless, such as the widow and the orphan, the stranger and the foreigner, "to do justice, and to love kindness, and to walk humbly with . . . God" (Mic. 6:8), caring for the least, and seeking out "the lost sheep of the house of Israel" (Matt. 15:24). The inner logic of such merciful behavior is grounded in the primary narrative of Israel, the exodus. God's people had been redeemed from slavery in Egypt. Knowing the plight of being abused as slaves, redeemed hearts should be open and generous to those entrapped, even if it is due to their own sin. God's command to Hosea to marry the prostitute Gomer illustrates God's own covenant love to his wayward people (Hos. 3:1).

Sin is not merely about moral culpability. It is also about victimization. Sinners fool themselves into thinking that they are free, that they can walk out of or away from their sin. They have no more power to do this than addicts have the ability to walk out of addictions solely by willpower. Sin, like addiction, has captured the sinner. The law can show people the right way but is impotent to rescue them from bondage and situate them on a life-giving and wholesome path. The woman certainly does not deny her culpability. She was caught in the act. But her sin is not the only fact of her life. She too is a daughter of Abraham. Her only hope for rescue is Jesus. Jesus Christ is her defense. He stands against her adversaries. Even more importantly, he stands against God's own *Torah*. He brings this defense home to the adulteress in the words of absolution, words that reconcile her to God in the present: "Neither do I condemn you . . ."

That word of absolution, given from the one who himself "knew no sin" but was made sin for us (2 Cor. 5:21), is liberating. The woman is liberated from her accusers, but even stronger, from God's own accusation, God's own law. Her defender is none other than Jesus, before whom the law is silenced. Her life is now defined through Jesus, by his affirmation of her, by his validation of her, not as a sinner, but as a daughter of Israel. She must have been astonished! In such a redefinition of her life, the directive "go and sin no more" is plausible. Defined now by God's love, rescued from death, hers is a natural, spontaneous heart of gratitude. A new path or way is opened for her because her identity is no longer that of "sinner" but is instead that of "redeemed." Captivated by God's mercy, she herself can be merciful. Having appropriate boundaries established by Jesus in his discernment of righteousness for one oppressed by the law, she can maintain the appropriateness of sexual boundaries channeled in the marriage union.

The view of God gathered from this story testifies neither to a Marcionite nor a schizophrenic God. Instead, it is a God who insists on mercy and who will have our relationship to him be based on nothing other than mercy; God is in fact most glorified when we live from his mercy alone. God's "alien work" of accusation exists solely for the "proper work" of mercy. The rupture between law and gospel ("Let him who is without sin among you . . .") is established for the sake of the gospel ("Neither do I condemn you; go, and from now on sin no more").

Freedom from the Law as Tyrant

Describing this strife even within the divine life, Luther in the *Lectures on Galatians* (1535) sees Paul as advocating that Christ and the law are engaged in a "remarkable duel":

> This also serves to support the idea that we are justified by faith alone. For when this duel between the Law and Christ was going on, no works or merits of ours intervened. Christ alone remains there; having put on our person, He serves the Law and in supreme innocence suffers all its tyranny. Therefore the Law is guilty of stealing, of sacrilege, and of the murder of the Son of God. It loses its rights and deserves to be damned. Wherever Christ is present or is at least named, it is forced to yield and to flee this name as the devil flees the cross. Therefore we believers are free of the Law through Christ, who "triumphed over it in Him" (Col. 2:15). This glorious triumph, accomplished for us through Christ, is grasped not by works but by faith alone. Therefore faith alone justifies.[6]

The Reformed tradition is less likely to see the law as a tyrant that bullies and from which sinners need freedom. Now, as noted, the Reformed tradition, sounding similar to the Lutheran, sees the moral law presented in the Mosaic covenant as "a letter that kills and a ministry of death." But for Westminster, this is qualified. Such a ministry of death is not "because the Mosaic covenant *qua* covenant is a republication of the covenant of works," but rather is "due to the weakness of fallen human nature and to the fact that the Mosaic covenant publishes the moral law only 'on tablets of stone' and not 'on tablets of human hearts.'"[7] If we could get the law off the tablets and into hearts, sinners would be less prone to sin, more prone to righteousness. The transition from law to

6. *Lectures on Galatians* (1535), *LW* 26:371–72.

7. Scott R. Swain, "The Gospel in the Reformed Tradition," essay in this volume.

gospel, for the Westminster tradition, comes across as decidedly smoother than for Lutherans. For Lutherans, the ministry of death is no mere mask of kindness, perhaps like putting a lame animal down. It is wrath. It is the wages of sin.[8] And it cannot be harmonized with gospel through a more encompassing, neutral category. It can only be absorbed by Jesus's own mercy and brought to its own end, a death of death. Only then is new birth, new life, possible through trusting in the gospel.

In part, the difference between the Lutherans and the Reformed is due to the fact that the Reformed theory of atonement, at least as presented in bicovenantal theology, is thoroughly Anselmic: the law defines the work of Christ, not vice versa. The Reformed stress Christ's "active obedience" and accord it a significance higher than what most Lutherans would. While not oblivious to Christ's active obedience, his fidelity to his mission, Lutherans are especially apt to highlight Christ's passive obedience, especially in light of the truth that Christ's death leads to his resurrection. That is, the goal in Christ's atoning work is precisely to lead to new life and not merely restitution within the moral order. For Anselm, Christ's atoning work exists within law and reinforces law as structuring the relationship between God and humans. Luther sees things quite differently. Christ simultaneously fulfills and abrogates the law. The law is fulfilled not just in that Christ himself was sinless in his fidelity to his mission but also in that, becoming the greatest, indeed only sinner, Christ dies the death penalty imposed by that law.[9] But in demanding Christ's death, the law is abrogated since it has executed its own Lord. Believers' troubled consciences are thus free from the law. It is not the law but Christ who reigns supreme in them. No longer available for self-justification, the law abides only in that we still live in a creation that requires order, the flesh or self-centeredness needs to die daily, and people need guidance.

Covenant

For Lutherans, the story of the Scriptures is primarily one of God who justifies sinners and sinners who live as justified. The concept of covenant is best understood in terms of law and gospel and not vice versa. For Lutherans, when

8. "The voice of the Law terrifies because it dins into the ears of smug sinners the theme: 'In the midst of earthly life, snares of death surround us.' But the voice of the Gospel cheers the terrified sinner with its song: 'In the midst of certain death, life in Christ is ours.'" See "Psalm 90," in *LW* 13:83.

9. *Lectures on Galatians* (1535), *LW* 26:281.

"covenant" is used as a neutral, comprehensive category in which law and gospel are placed, human behavior is seen as a visible manifestation of the effectiveness of God's grace. Thereby, the hiddenness of new life in Christ (Col. 3:3) is muddled, if not in fact violated. The Reformed are convinced that if visible indicators or markers of God's grace do not become manifest in personal or social life, then perhaps we are dealing with something other than God's grace. Lutherans are quite convinced that there are no rubrics, let alone metrics, by which spiritual growth or progress can be measured. That is not to say that no such spiritual growth exists. But more than likely it is growth in the awareness that if a sinner needed Jesus yesterday, how much more does that sinner need him today! Lutherans are far quicker than the Reformed to maintain that the Christian life is "hidden with Christ in God." If hidden, it is not accessible to measurement. For Lutherans, the spirituality of such self-monitoring returns us to the fleshpots of medieval Roman Catholic asceticism, curves sinners back in upon themselves, and fails to honor the liberation for which Christ died and rose.

For Lutherans, unlike the Reformed, the concept of "covenant" does not impinge on law and gospel but just the opposite. Hence, "covenant" in the Scriptures is often an iteration of promise, though, admittedly, not always. So, God's covenant with Noah grants the promise that "When the bow is in the clouds, I [God] will see it and remember the everlasting covenant between God and every living creature" (Gen. 9:16), and God will never again destroy the earth through a deluge. After the sorry history of Genesis 1–11, in which Adam and Eve rebelled, Cain killed Abel, violence led to the flood, drunken Noah lay naked, and Babel was destroyed, God chose Abraham, Sarah, and their descendants to establish a new beginning. The covenant with Abraham is iterated several times in Genesis, but at its core is the promise that God will grant Abraham progeny, land, and blessing (Gen. 12:2–3). The covenant with Moses begins with the *promise* "I am the LORD your God, who brought you out of the land of Egypt, out of the house of slavery" (Exod. 20:2; Deut. 5:6), and then specifies commands, the "ten words," which ultimately led not to life but death, not to blessing but curse (Deut. 30:15–20), and exile in Babylon. God's covenant love (*hesed*) was reiterated to David, promising God's commitment to David and his family (2 Sam. 7). The history of promise associated with the concept of covenant reaches its climax in the prophetic promise of a new covenant (Jer. 32:36–43; 33:6–9; 33:14–16), which Christians see as enacted and administered in Jesus's blood, and which Lutherans specifically see as distributed in the Lord's Supper. Prior covenants find their fulfillment and purpose in this new covenant established in Jesus's blood.

The Nature of Reform

At stake in the differences between Lutherans and the Reformed is the nature of reform itself. Lutherans advocate a continuous need to rehear the justifying word that liberates from both sin and the law's accusations. The Christian life grows out of this constant need to rehear the gospel, which secures sinners in God's grace and shapes their identities as God's beloved children. In contrast, the Reformed see justification as a onetime event, marked by regeneration, and from there leading to one's growth in personal holiness. The vocation of the believer is to live a holy life, and the law is a salutary guide in determining holiness. Ideally, all of society would be claimed by the gospel.[10] The goodness of the church ought to permeate society. Such sentiment has had an important historical and contemporary impact on the United States, leading to the conviction that the USA is a "Christian nation."[11]

Credit should be given where it is due. The United States has received much good on account of this heritage. I suspect the roots for establishing the United States as a republic grew out of this Puritan legacy. After all, Calvin's Geneva was a republic. But this legacy is mixed. Its Puritan dream continues to inspire the Christian Right in America today. Every society must debate the balance of order and freedom it needs. The Puritan legacy certainly contributes to our sense of social order today. But here we need wisdom. In contrast to the convictions of the libertines in the sixties, morality can be legislated. Indeed, all law is nothing other than the legislation of morality. But *faith* cannot be legislated. So, from a Lutheran perspective, Christians should not seek to legislate Christian values per se but human values instead as informed by natural law. Additionally, insofar as this Puritan heritage is somewhat utopian, and the fact that many "progressive" denominations, such as the United Church of Christ and the Presbyterian Church USA, are rooted in the Reformed tradi-

10. In contrast, Lutherans are more apt to associate "sanctification," similar to its roots in Hebrew thinking, with utensils set aside for ritual use. Earthly things are quite "holy," because they are instruments through which God creates and sustains the world. Hence, in *Lectures on Galatians* (1535) Luther writes, "Thus this Wittenberg of ours is a holy village, and we are truly holy, because we have been baptized, communed, taught, and called by God; we have the works of God among us, that is, the Word and the sacraments, and these make us holy." See *LW* 26:25. My sense is that the righteousness "by association" advocated here would not cut it for the Reformed.

11. See, for example, John Winthrop's sermon preached shipboard before the establishment of the Massachusetts Bay Colony, "A Model of Christian Charity," in William C. Placher, *Readings in the History of Christian Theology*, vol. 2, *From the Reformation to the Present* (Philadelphia: Westminster, 1988), 109.

tion, it may also impact the Religious Left. Both Religious Right and Left see the Christian faith, if it were genuinely practiced, as able to transform society and perfect it. Thereby, God's kingdom comes on their timetable and by their chosen means.

It would seem that this vision more directly derives from the vision for reform so important in the late Middle Ages, but at a "more ambitious" level: "The drive to piety, to bring all real Christians (which were, of course, a minority, the saved, and didn't include the foreknown to damnation, even if they were nominally members of the Church) up to the fully Godly life, inflects the agenda of social reform, and gives it a universalist-philanthropic thrust. And the demands of civility, which entailed some reordering of society, in turn give a new social dimension to the pious, ordered life."[12] In the Reformed mind, our behavior, both personally and socially, ought to reflect God's glory. God has designed us precisely for this correspondence in thought, word, and deed. Such correspondence accords with our nature, and to fall short of it is to fall short of our nature. It is to be visible, manifest, and public because that indicates its authenticity and reality.[13]

For the Reformed, the law can help perfect not only the individual, but society as a whole, if only society would follow it. No wonder Reformed church buildings tend to be modeled after school auditoriums and Reformed clergy tend to wear academic gowns, like professors, and not traditional vestments. The church is primarily to train believers in the discipleship by which they can grow in holiness and to transform society so that it grows in holiness. In contrast, Lutheran church buildings look all too Catholic, as if the Reformation never happened. Of course, a closer look at Lutheran church buildings will show that in most of them the pulpit, altar, and baptismal font are paramount. Those furnishings highlight the centrality of grace coming for sinners in Word and sacrament. For Lutherans, the worship service as such is less about school and more about receiving God's mercy.

Ironically, Luther, revered as "the Reformer," simply falls short of this Reformed version of reform. For Luther, reform is primarily about the establishment of the gospel as grace, and that in preaching and catechesis. He noted that life was just as bad among evangelical Lutherans as among Roman Catholics, but doctrine was sound.[14] And, it was the soundness of doctrine

12. Charles Taylor, *A Secular Age* (Cambridge, MA: Belknap Press of Harvard University Press, 2007), 105.

13. H. Richard Niebuhr, *Christ and Culture* (New York: Harper and Row, 1951), 217–18.

14. Table Talk, no. 624, Fall 1533, *LW* 54:110.

that counted. Now, of course, that dispute with Rome led to major changes and ruptures in late medieval life, especially challenging the assumption of the difference between the "religious," those who follow the evangelical counsels of poverty, chastity, and obedience as a higher calling, and "secular people" who live out ordinary lives in the world. For Luther, good works were good not because they established merit as the medieval system taught, but because they helped the neighbor in need. Diapering the infant is every bit as sacred as spending hours in prayer. Luther's argument that laity became priests and priests laity altered the fabric of marriage, monasticism, charity (the common chest), parenting, and education in marked ways. But Luther's vision of society is never utopian. He sees no perfection prior to the last judgment; at best there are glimpses of justice seen in this world, with the promise of fulfillment and wholeness in the life to come.

Again, Lutherans are far more apt to see the Christian life as hidden, not open to measurement. It is not that faith does not bear on public life or that one concedes to the regnant secularistic worldview. Lutherans seek neither "exile" from public life (like Mennonites) nor "conquest" of public life (like the Reformed). Instead, "The Lutheran stress on active righteousness widens our vision regarding the left-hand realm and seeks to identify the common ground for moral reflection between Christians and non-Christians"[15] insofar as such common ground can be established. Lutherans are apt to be whistle-blowers but never utopians.[16] The gospel restores us to creation, not social engineering of either the Right or the Left. Lutherans advocating traditional stances on abortion and marriage in the public realm do so because these stances accord with natural law, not the quest for an America as a "city shining on a hill." In a sense, if we use Charles Taylor's criteria of reform, Lutheranism fails as a "reform movement"—and confessional Lutherans are good with that.

What, then, is truly pleasing to God? What glorifies God? For the Reformed, human behavior is a means of reflecting God's glory. For Lutherans, in contrast, faith alone not only saves, but also is sufficient to express God's glory in human life. Indeed, before God, it is faith alone that only ever could accord with God.[17] Given divine apophaticism (that God always transcends

15. Charles P. Arand and Joel Biermann, "Why the Two Kinds of Righteousness?" *Concordia Journal*, April 2007, 131.

16. See, for example, the case of resistance with the Magdeburg Confession of 1550: David Mark Whitford, *Tyranny and Resistance: The Magdeburg Confession and the Lutheran Tradition* (Saint Louis: Concordia, 2001).

17. Reformed theologian Brian Gerrish notes that of Luther "the believer does not earn this divine imputation with his faith, neither is there any legal fiction: God counts the confidence of the

any descriptors applied to him), at least for the Lutheran perspective, there is no *proportio* (comparative relation) by which to measure the proximity of human behavior in relation to the divine. The difference between God and humanity can be bridged only christologically.[18] For Lutherans, faith is at the heart or core of all people, whether they acknowledge God's divinity or not. Human behavior, like human feeling, is an outgrowth of faith. Indeed, for Luther, faith is everything in the human spiritual walk. It "consummates" the divinity in believers:

> Faith consummates the Deity; and if I may put it this way, it is the creator of the Deity, not in the substance of God but in us. For without faith God loses His glory, wisdom, righteousness, truthfulness, mercy, etc., in us; in short, God has none of His majesty or divinity where faith is absent. Nor does God require anything greater of man than that he attribute to Him His glory and His divinity sound and unblemished; that is, He has whatever a believing heart is able to attribute to Him. To be able to attribute such glory to God is wisdom beyond wisdom, righteousness beyond righteousness, religion beyond religion, and sacrifice beyond sacrifice. From this it can be understood what great righteousness faith is and, by antithesis, what a great sin unbelief is.[19]

We take Paul at his word: "We see through a glass darkly . . ." (1 Cor. 13:12). For Lutherans, it would be presumptuous to think that metrics exist to determine whether or to what degree human behavior glorifies God. Instead, what gives God his due is the faith that accords with the reality of the divinity of God. Counter to medieval Catholicism, justification by faith is no "legal fiction," because faith alone in Christ accords with the reality that not even our good deeds could ever engender righteousness before God (*coram Deo*). Just the opposite: it is fiction to believe that human behavior ever could, even in principle, justify. Luther operates with an apophatic view of God. But he could never affirm God's goodness on the basis of Dionysian mysticism. In the Dionysian itinerary of ever

---

heart as 'right' because that is what it is. Its rightness lives in the fact that faith, for its part, does not make God an idol but takes him for exactly what *he* is: the author and giver of every good, the precise counterpart of the believer's confidence. In a sense faith, by believing, is the 'creator of divinity' in us: it lets God be God." See "By Faith Alone," in *The Old Protestantism and the New: Essays on the Reformation Heritage* (Edinburgh: T. & T. Clark, 1982), 86.

18. See Knut Alfsvåg, *What No Mind Has Conceived: On the Significance of Christological Apophaticism* (Leuven: Peeters, 2010), 176–259.

19. *Lectures on Galatians* (1535), *LW* 26:227.

onward transcendence, there is nowhere on which to lay one's head. Instead, for Luther, Dionysian apophaticism is bridged christologically. Through the lens of Jesus Christ as God's mercy, all of creation can be affirmed as gift, God is secured for believers as goodness itself (indisputably testified in the witness and ongoing ministry of Jesus), and God's ways can be affirmed as wise (as is exuberantly described in the Psalter), but not outside of or apart from the gospel.

Christ Shapes Christian Life

What is the shape of the Christian life? Quickly, the Reformed respond that God's law guides us; otherwise how could we possibly tell what is God's way and what is not? As noted, the Reformed see the Christian as able to make steady advance in holiness. For Lutherans, the shape of the Christian life is Jesus Christ himself.[20] Such shaping is not done apart from trials, but precisely through them. God uses crosses and trials so that when his work of refashioning believers is complete, they will be "in the image of the crucified."[21] While Luther does not use the terminology of "narrative identity," in which people tell the story of their lives through integrating their own understanding of their past along with their hoped-for future in order to provide coherence for their lives, it can be a helpful tool for understanding how, for Lutherans, it is not believers primarily who interpret Scripture but Scripture that interprets believers. In a narrative identity Christians interpret their past, present, and future through the stories, histories, and genres of Scripture. When we hear or read Scripture, we identify with one or more of the characters or some voice in the literary genre. So, for example, when we hear the parable of the prodigal son (Luke 15), we put ourselves in the shoes of the prodigal or the elder brother, or perhaps even the waiting father (if we did that, we perhaps would be similar to the "Christs" that Luther urged us to be!). The prodigal who has already heard the law's accusation in the pigsty now hears the gospel as he is embraced by the father.

But the elder brother ought to hear a word of law, at least indirectly or implicitly, because he should in fact have a bigger, more generous, more welcoming heart like his father's, to embrace his own brother, even though legally

20. For a pastorally sensitive presentation of Christian life as Christ in action in believers, see Harold L. Senkbeil, *Sanctification: Christ in Action* (Milwaukee: Northwestern, 1989), and *Dying to Live: The Power of Forgiveness* (Saint Louis: Concordia, 1994).

21. FC SD 11.48–49.

he owes his brother nothing (nor does the father). No doubt Christ was indirectly challenging the Pharisees in his characterization of the elder brother and defending the "lost sheep of the house of Israel." If we could be as generous and forgiving as the father, it would be because we have received generosity from God, and so accordingly can spread generosity. We lose nothing when we forgive, and are generous when we already have everything in Christ. Both libertinism and legalism are rejected in the parable.

So, is God hard or benevolent? The answer lies in whether the word is heard by the proud, self-secure elder brother or the broken, penitent prodigal. Law and gospel are not superimposed on Scripture because the entire message of the Scriptures at every juncture is summarized in the *Magnificat*. As the Mother of God teaches us: God has "brought down the mighty from their thrones / and exalted those of humble estate" (Luke 1:52).[22] God has both an alien and a proper work. And the alien work exists for the proper. This is why any attempt at one "word," "covenant," or program that sidesteps, marginalizes, or mixes God's alien work of humbling the proud and God's proper work of exalting the lowly (such as Mary herself) fails to adequately express the Scriptures. The pattern in Scripture is that of exile and restoration or death and resurrection, leading to a new Eden, a new heavens and earth, a new Jerusalem.

So, there is nothing about an "indefinite God." God is always quite definitive—even when hidden. God hides elsewhere precisely so that we will be led to look for him on the cross. God puts down the mighty from their thrones because they refuse to live out of fearing, loving, and trusting in God, the true source of goodness, above everything else, and trust instead in their own pride, ambition, and self-definition. But God rescues the lowly, whether brought low through accusation, or difficult circumstances (but there we would encounter more the hidden God [*Deus absconditus*] and not God as lawgiver).

More than anything, Christ shapes Christians through the worship service. Christian life grows out of prayer (*oratio*), meditation (*meditatio*), and spiritual trial (*tentatio*). Thereby, we live our lives through the lens of the Scriptures, receiving our identity, like the prodigal or the adulteress, from Christ, who validates us as God's creatures. Hence, Christ effectuates Christian life through preaching and the sacraments: through baptism, which drowns the old person and raises up the new; through the Lord's Supper, which forgives sinners and unites them with Christ; and through the preaching of the word, which slays sinners, regenerates believers, and empowers believers to live out their lives in their vocations in service in the world.

22. See Luther's *The Magnificat*, *LW* 21:295–358.

Third Use as the Meeting Point between Lutherans and Reformed

Given the fact that for the Reformed the third use of the law is the primary use of the law, there can be little agreement on this topic between the Reformed and Lutherans who deny the third use of the law outright. For those Lutherans, since Christ has abrogated the law, and thus liberated believers from the law, to sneak law into Christian life through the backdoor does violence to the work of Christ or feeds the illusion that the believer has a "continuous self," one not dying and rising daily in return to baptism. Additionally, if the matter of a third use is really the need for guidance, what could a third use add that is not already there with a first use, that is, the *usus politicus*? It would seem that on purely logical grounds the case against a third use of the law, so strongly advocated by mid-twentieth-century existentialist readings of Luther, would have the upper hand over the authors of the Formula of Concord, who advocated the third use in article 6 of that document.

Luther employs a number of ways to describe the role of Christ and law in the new life in Christ. Repeatedly, he embraces the concept of spontaneity, that good fruit derives from good trees. Grace genuinely renews nature so that reborn humans do the good without compulsion that God intended humans to do from the very beginning. Luther is confident that the new identity granted in the word of promise takes hold in believers' hearts and shapes their behavior to become more and more in accordance with Christ's. This stance is linked to his imagery derived from bridal mysticism that the soul is married to Christ, and thereby shares in the properties of Christ.

For example, in the *Lectures on Galatians* (1535), Luther portrays a stance on human behavior that fits with his notion of spontaneity. He looks at human "doing" in a threefold way and shows how a "theological" approach to doing is different from a "natural" or a "moral" approach. "Natural" doing is like eating or walking. "Moral" doing is establishing virtue or avoiding vice. Naturally, it is appropriate for the righteousness *coram mundo,* active righteousness, but not the righteousness *coram Deo,* passive righteousness, that has been advanced as a path for Lutheran engagement in public life or the development of a character ethics.[23] But thirdly, Luther speaks of a "theological" doing, behavior as an outgrowth of faith. No doubt this is good works established no longer on the basis of accruing merit for one's eternal welfare but instead is an outgrowth of

23. Joel D. Biermann, *A Case for Character: Towards a Lutheran Virtue Ethics* (Minneapolis: Fortress, 2014).

faith, which is the do-all in the Christian life.[24] Faith, of course, for Luther is no mere *notitia*, though it includes that. It is primarily *fiducia*, complete trust in Christ, especially in the face of the accusations of the law and the punches of the devil, and from which all thinking and doing arise. As Luther defines it in the "Preface to Romans" (1546 [1522]), faith is active.[25] Because it is located in the heart and so centers the core of life, it defines one's thoughts and actions. It is precisely the flesh that would war against this theological doing, which calls for exhortation against that flesh, in essence the third use of the law. For Luther, good works exist both for the neighbor and for the new being to control the old one.

However, the language of exhortation is likewise present in Luther. The fact that the law *always* accuses does not mean that the law *only* accuses. Luther claimed:

> The New Testament, properly speaking, consists of promises and exhortations, just as the Old, properly speaking, consists of laws and threats. In the New Testament, the gospel is preached and this is just the word that offers the Spirit and grace for the remission of sins which was procured for us by Christ crucified. It is all entirely free, given by the mercy of God the Father alone as He shows His favour towards us, who are unworthy, and who deserve condemnation rather than anything else. Exhortations follow after this; and they are intended to stir up those who have obtained mercy and have been justified already, to be energetic in bringing forth the fruits of the Spirit and of the righteousness given them, to exercise themselves in love and good works, and boldly to bear the cross and all the other tribulations of this world. This is the whole sum of the New Testament.[26]

24. "Therefore faith is the 'do-all' in works, if I may use this expression. Thus Abraham is called faithful because faith is diffused throughout all of Abraham. When I look at Abraham doing works, therefore, I see nothing of the physical Abraham or of the Abraham who does works, but only Abraham the believer." See *Lectures on Galatians* (1535), *LW* 26:266.

25. "Faith, however, is a divine work in us which changes us and makes us to be born anew of God, John 1[:12–13]. It kills the old Adam and makes us altogether different men, in heart and spirit and mind and powers; and it brings with it the Holy Spirit. O it is a living, busy, active, mighty thing, this faith. It is impossible for it not to be doing good works incessantly. It does not ask whether good works are to be done, but before the question is asked, it has already done them, and is constantly doing them." See "Prefaces to New Testament," *LW* 35:370.

26. *The Bondage of the Will*, trans. J. I. Packer and O. R. Johnston (New York: Revell, 1957), 180. Lucas V. Woodford notes, "But let's be clear. It is not wrong to teach morality. It's not wrong to aspire to goodness, practice specific virtues, or to teach character. It's not wrong to be disciplined. Society and culture need these things. Our children need these things. We need these things, just as we need

Given that this claim is specifically addressed to a distinctly Christian audience and not merely the wider public in which the first use of the law governs to provide order, it sounds suspiciously similar to what the authors of the Formula of Concord identified as a third use of the law. It summarizes an important practice that Luther did as a preacher: admonish his congregation to good works! Luther's sermons tended to be expository and catechetical, a fitting model for contemporary preaching to those so often unaware of the ABCs of Christian faith and life.

Linked with this language of exhortation is that of "keeping the law." Hence, Luther writes, "Therefore Moses, together with Paul, necessarily drives us to Christ, through whom we become doers of the Law and are accounted guilty of no transgression. How? First, on account of faith in Christ; secondly through the gift and the Holy Spirit, who creates a new life and new impulses in us, so that we may keep the Law also in a formal sense. Whatever is not kept is forgiven for the sake of Christ."[27] Likewise, "Now, against this evil God found a remedy and determined to send Christ, his Son, into this world, that he should shed his blood and die, in order to make satisfaction for sin and take it away, and that the Holy Spirit then should enter the hearts of such people, who go about with the works of the Law, being unwilling and forced to it, and make them willing, in order that without force and with joyous heart they keep God's commandments."[28] The medieval *viatores* were seeking primarily to accrue merit when they offered good works. By the very nature of the case, they were turned in on themselves and fed the illusion that they could do something that could count *coram Deo*, if even only congruently. Evangelicals (in the Lutheran sense) do good not for the sake of accruing merit but instead because outside of themselves they see their neighbor in need, and seek to assist, thereby conforming to the Golden Rule, loving their neighbor as themselves. It is a response to God's goodness in creation and redemption: "For all of this I owe it to God to thank and praise, serve and *obey* him."[29]

God's Law. In fact His Law must be taught as a guide for the Christian life. However, the law will never reform the Old Adam. It is not the motivation for the virtuous life of holiness." See "Vice, Virtue, and Baptismal Therapy," *Seelsorger: A Journal for the Contemporary Cure of Souls* 2, no. 1 (July 9, 2016): 50. See http://www.wolfmueller.co/a-journal-for-the-contemporary-cure-of-souls-seelsorger-2-1-released/.

27. *Lectures on Galatians* (1535), *LW* 26:260.

28. "Sermon for the Fourth Sunday after Easter," in *The Complete Sermons of Martin Luther*, ed. John Nicholas Lenker (Grand Rapids: Baker, 2000), 2:114.

29. Small Catechism, in *BC*, 355 (emphasis added). And as the *Haustafel*, itemizing the ethical obligations within community, ends, "Let all their lessons learn with care, / So that the household well may fare." *BC*, 367.

In addition to the language of spontaneity (Christ in action) and exhortation (awareness of the flesh's inclination to self-centeredness), there is also the language of "delight" in the law. Like exhortation, this language is not subsidiary in Luther. The language is important because it indicates a stance of new persons in Christ: the regenerate rejoice in God's ways. Throughout his career, Luther was concerned for how the word makes sinners to be reborn. New birth is never for Luther the Arminian, revivalistic "decision for Jesus" that is so pervasive in North American "spirituality." For Luther, the new birth is always tied to the external word (*verbum externum*), granted in preaching, absolution, and the sacraments. However, to remember Luther's paradigm of interpreting Christian life through baptismal death and resurrection, resurrection precisely leads to new birth. To underappreciate the transformative power of new life in Christ in no way serves the gospel as Luther understood it. Hence, in his central teaching document, the Large Catechism, he writes:

> From this you see that the Creed is a very different teaching than the Ten Commandments. For the latter teach us what we ought to do, but the Creed tells us what God does for us and gives to us. The Ten Commandments, moreover, are written in the hearts of all people, but no human wisdom is able to comprehend the Creed; it must be taught by the Holy Spirit alone. Therefore the Ten Commandments do not succeed in making us Christians, for God's wrath and displeasure still remain upon us because we cannot fulfill what God demands of us. But the Creed brings pure grace and makes us righteous and acceptable to God. Through this knowledge we come to love and delight in all the commandments of God because we see here in the Creed how God gives himself completely to us, with all his gifts and power, to help us keep the Ten Commandments: the Father gives us all creation, Christ all his works, the Holy Spirit all his gifts.[30]

Why a third use? Is not the first use sufficient if law is understood as guidance and not only as accusation? As noted, the fact that the law *always* accuses does not mean that the law *only* accuses; it also instructs, both believers and nonbelievers. "The law of God is used (1) to maintain external discipline and respectability against dissolute, disobedient people and (2) to bring such people to a recognition of their sins." The Formula of Concord goes on to say, "It is also used when those who have been born anew through God's Spirit, converted to the Lord, and had the veil of Moses removed for them live and walk

30. Large Catechism, in *BC*, 440.

in the law."[31] Given Luther's emphasis on exhortation and his insistence that those reborn can delight in the law, we can acknowledge that exhortation has a different feel to the Christian than does the first use of the law, which is, or ought to be, fitted into the structures of social order. How so? It is the feel of a parent admonishing a child in contrast to a public school teacher providing directives to a class. Such a child need not fear the threat of abandonment or total rejection from the parent. The child is secure in the parent's arms, knowing that the parent has only good in mind for the child. The child can sense that the admonition is for his or her welfare.[32] Luther preaches, "This [the gospel] will cause the heart to rejoice and find delight in God, and will enable the believer to keep the Law cheerfully, without expecting reward, without fear of punishment, without seeking compensation, as the heart is perfectly satisfied with God's grace, by which the Law has been fulfilled."[33] Indeed, "For when the heart hears that Christ fulfils the Law for us and takes our sin upon himself, it no longer cares that impossible things are demanded by the Law, that we must despair of rendering them, and must give up our good works. . . . This is because the heart now has in Christ all that the Law demands, and it would be sorry indeed if it demanded less. Behold, thus the Law is delightful now and easy which before was disagreeable, difficult and impossible; for it lives in the heart by the Spirit."[34] God uses the gospel to shape Christians to become each day more like Christ. But God also uses the law to provide Christians guidance, to struggle against the flesh, and to stand in awe of the wisdom with which God has ordered the world. The law in no way exists to provide continuity to the self. The continuity of the self for the Christian is found in Christ alone, who finally is the agent working in and through all Christian actions (Gal. 2:20).

The authors of the Formula of Concord were neither stupid nor unfaithful to Luther. They concede:

> If the faithful and elect children of God were perfectly renewed through the indwelling Spirit in this life, so that in their nature and all their powers they were completely free from sin, they would need no law and therefore no prodding. Instead, they would do in and of themselves, completely voluntarily, without any teaching, admonition, exhortation, or prodding of the law, what they are obligated to do according to God's will, just as in

31. FC SD 6.1, in *BC*, 587.

32. This point is based on conversations with Chaplain Russell Lackey, Grand View University.

33. "Sermon for the Third Sunday in Advent," in *The Complete Sermons of Martin Luther*, 1:99.

34. "Sermon for the Second Sunday after Epiphany," in *The Complete Sermons of Martin Luther*, 1.2:68.

> and of themselves the sun, the moon, and all the stars follow unimpeded the regular course God gave them once and for all, apart from any admonition, exhortation, impulse, coercion, or compulsion. . . . Therefore, in this life, because of these desires of the flesh, the faithful, elect, reborn children of God need not only the law's daily instruction and admonition, its warning and threatening. Often they also need its punishments, so that they may be incited by them and follow God's Spirit.[35]

In many respects, the third use of the law is a commentary on article 6 of the Augsburg Confession, "Concerning the New Obedience."[36] Interestingly, article 5, "Concerning the Office of Preaching," specifies how the mercy proffered in justification by grace alone through faith alone, delineated in article 4, is administered to sinners. Article 6, then, specifies the shape of the justified life that issues in a *new* obedience. It is new because works are no longer about acquiring merit but instead are about accomplishing good in the world. Pegging Lutherans as "quietists" is certainly untrue to the Augsburg Confession! It is also new because it is an outworking of Christ in believers. Christ is the *novum* in believers' lives. Precisely because the adulteress was granted mercy and not lapidated, she was empowered herself to grant mercy to others. Precisely because the prodigal was embraced and not scorned, he too was empowered to be generous and forgiving to others. The gospel regenerates, and in that newness of life one receives different motives, ones that lend toward Christlikeness in daily vocations. Thus, our prayer that God's will be done is answered in our transformed will. The shape of Christian living is thus Christlike as well. For Luther, Christ is both sacrament (gift) and example.

How could the affirmation of the law in the life of the Christian ever be harmonized with the stance of Luther in *Lectures on Galatians* (1535), the law until Christ? For Luther, the law continues to have relevance in Christian life because the Christian is a divided self, flesh and spirit. Only in the afterlife will believers be completely free of the old being.[37] The law has come to its

35. FC SD 6.6 and 9, in *BC*, 588.

36. AC 6, Latin text, in *BC*, 41: "Likewise, they teach that this faith is bound to yield good fruits and that it ought to do good works commanded by God on account of God's will and not so that we may trust in these works to merit justification before God. For forgiveness of sins and justification are taken hold of by faith, as the saying of Christ also testifies [Luke 17:10]: 'When you have done all [things] . . . say, "We are worthless slaves."' The authors of the ancient church teach the same. For Ambrose says: 'It is established by God that whoever believes in Christ shall be saved without work, by faith alone, receiving the forgiveness of sins as a gift.'"

37. "Therefore the Christian is divided this way into two times. To the extent that he is flesh, he is

end (*telos*) in bringing sinners to Christ, and Christ is its end (*finis*) in that it no longer reigns in the conscience, where only Christ now reigns supreme.[38] That acknowledged, the law continues to challenge the sinful flesh remaining in believers and guides them in God's ways. Given that such ways are increasingly unknown in the current culture, a robust catechesis will give the law its due, for believers as well as nonbelievers.

While Lutheranism affirms a "third use of the law," it can never, unlike the Reformed faith, accord it the chief role for the law. For Lutherans, the chief use is the theological use, to lead us to Christ. Primarily it is Christ who shapes the life of Christians. The Reformed advocate progressive growth and improvement in the Christian life, in some cases even seeking to gauge or monitor it.[39] Visibility, not invisibility ("your life is hidden with Christ in God"), marks its distinctive approach. For Lutherans, such monitoring—using some kind of metrics or rubric to discern growth—comes across as a return to a spirituality marked by incurvation on oneself. For Luther, there is a growth in holiness: through the agency of the Holy Spirit, "holiness has begun and is growing daily" as we "await the time when our flesh will be put to death, will be buried with all its uncleanness, and will come forth gloriously and arise to complete and perfect holiness in a new, eternal life." But, "now, however, we remain only halfway pure and holy. The Holy Spirit must always work in us through the Word, granting us daily forgiveness until we attain to that life where there will be no more forgiveness. In that life there will be only perfectly pure and holy people, full of integrity and righteousness, completely freed from sin, death, and all misfortune, living in new, immortal, and glorified bodies."[40]

For some, that may seem a mediocre standard. But given the variegated contours of human nature, its drives, passions, foibles, mixed intentions, and the like, precisely as we encounter it historically, socially, and deep within our

under the Law; to the extent that he is spirit, he is under the Gospel. To his flesh there always cling lust, greed, ambition, pride, etc. So do ignorance and contempt of God, impatience, grumbling, and wrath against God because He obstructs our plans and efforts and because he does not immediately punish the wicked who despise Him. These sins cling to the flesh of the saints. Therefore if you do not look at anything beyond the flesh, you will remain permanently under the time of the Law. But those days have to be shortened, for otherwise no human being would be saved (Mat. 24:22). An end has to be set for the Law, where it will come to a stop. Therefore the time of Law is not forever; but it has an end, which is Christ. But the time of grace is forever; for Christ, having died once for all, will never die again (Rom. 6:9–10). He is eternal; therefore the time of grace is eternal also." See *Lectures on Galatians* (1535), *LW* 26:342.

38. *Lectures on Galatians* (1535), *LW* 26:11.

39. As one example, see Jonathan Edwards, *A Treatise concerning Religious Affections*, http://www.jonathan-edwards.org/ReligiousAffections.pdf.

40. Large Catechism, in *BC*, 438.

own souls, it is realistic and humane. The language of progress in the Christian life is by no means absent from Luther. But Luther's tendency is to see progress as a daily return to baptism, to conversion, to forgiveness, and to the need for Christ. We do not progress to something other than or outside of faith in this life, but ever from faith to faith, ultimately until we are wholly defined by Christ:

> He [Christ] is the sun and is set for our example, which we must imitate. For this reason there will always be found among us some that are weak, others that are strong, and again some that are stronger; these are able to suffer less, those more; and so they must all continue in the imitation of Christ. For this life is a constant progress from faith to faith, from love to love, from patience to patience, and from affliction to affliction. It is not righteousness, but justification; not purity, but purification; we have not yet arrived at our destination, but we are all on the road, and some are farther advanced than others. God is satisfied to find us busy at work and full of determination. When he is ready he will come quickly, strengthen faith and love, and in an instant take us from this life to heaven. But while we live on earth we must bear with one another, as Christ also bore with us, seeing that none of us is perfect.[41]

Future Directions

The Reformed worry that Lutherans misrepresent the gospel as libertine: if Christ is the end of the law, then do as you please. Lutherans worry that the Reformed misrepresent the gospel as pharisaical. A helpful step forward would be to actually evaluate Lutheran and Reformed sermons, on a specific assigned text, especially from preachers who seek to conform to the confessional writings of their specific tradition, to test and see if such worries are founded. My deepest hunch is that Reformed preachers will be found who instinctively and artfully do law and gospel, while Lutheran preachers will be found who are gifted in admonition (all the while honoring the gospel as free). But representative sermons highlighting differences between Lutherans and Reformed should also be examined and discussed.

Both traditions would be wise to acknowledge where the other has an edge in the contemporary world. Given that many young Americans and Euro-

41. "The Fifth Sunday in Lent," in *The Complete Sermons of Martin Luther*, 1.2:212.

peans suffer from anomie, a sense of purposelessness, would not the Reformed quest that all of life be lived for the glory of God provide a welcome and effective basis to help youth (and older folks)? Contemporary anomie is a result of the North American and European creation of the "unencumbered self," which affords maximal personal liberties (provided no harm to others is done) for the self in its task to create itself on the basis of its own authenticity and uniqueness. Such "selves" are far better at parallel play than genuine teamwork, and so suffer loneliness and chronic low-grade depression. Given Augustine's dictum that human hearts are restless until they rest in God, it is inevitable that *autopoietic* (self-defining) selves would be morose. Lutherans would do well to acknowledge the purposelessness that haunts so many Americans and Europeans and address it through their doctrine of vocation.

On the other hand, given that so many young people feel broken, like the prodigal or the adulteress, is not a healthy Lutheran dosage of mercy likewise requisite for genuine care of souls? For example, when I ask my students, many of whom come from nonchurched or underchurched backgrounds, "What is at the core of religion?" they unhesitatingly respond, "Rules!" Never once in over two decades of college teaching have I had a student say that the core of Christian faith is God's mercy or kindness. That gives me pause for some concern: How is it that Christians do such a poor job conveying the gospel? Are dominant Christian traditions in North America, evangelical or Roman Catholic, so concerned about rules that any message of God's mercy is undermined or circumvented?

Future consultation may wish to explore to what degree, if any, Luther's affirmation of Christian synergy or cooperation with God, not for salvation but as part of the ongoing creation, corresponds to the Reformed notion of covenant? Hence, Luther writes, "It has pleased God not to give the Spirit without the Word, but through the Word; that he might have us as workers together with Him, we sounding forth without what He alone breathes within wheresoever he will."[42] The Reformed notion of covenant seems to convey a kind of partnership between God and humanity that apart from Luther's "cooperation" is not as accented in the Lutheran tradition.

42. *The Bondage of the Will*, 184; see also 267–68.

Chapter 10

Continuing the Conversation: A Reformed Reflection

Kevin J. Vanhoozer

As an American who lived for twelve years in the UK, I could have used Christopher Davies's *Divided by a Common Language: A Guide to British and American English,* had it been available at the time.[1] A similar guidebook might have helped me understand the two-day discussion between Lutheran and Reformed theologians on law and gospel. These venerable Protestant traditions indeed have much in common, most notably the language of *sola Scriptura* and *solus Christus,* shorthand for what Philip Schaff refers to as the formal and material principles of the Reformation, respectively. It would be tragic, then, to think of these two church traditions as "two holy nations divided by a common language."[2]

In addition, I have a vested interest in becoming bilingual and achieving fluency in Lutheran theology, for I have recently tried to play Protestant peacemaker. My recent book (*Biblical Authority after Babel: Retrieving the* Solas *in the Spirit of Mere Protestant Christianity*)[3] is an attempt at damage control as concerns the common (mis)perception that Protestants, despite their common affirmation of *sola Scriptura,* are hopelessly divided about what Scripture means. If I was all ears during these discussions, then, it was not because I wanted my side to "win," but because I want to understand the Reformed/Lutheran differences over law/gospel in order to rebut arguments that they constitute more evidential grist for the mill of pervasive interpretive pluralism.[4]

1. Mayflower Press, 1997.

2. I allude to the saying, often attributed to Bernard Shaw, that "England and America are two countries divided by a common language."

3. Grand Rapids: Brazos, 2016.

4. See Christopher Smith, *The Bible Made Impossible: Why Biblicism Is Not a Truly Evangelical Reading of Scripture* (Grand Rapids; Brazos, 2011), and Alister McGrath's *Christianity's Dangerous*

If we are honest, however, we have to admit that while the law/gospel language is the same, the same cannot be said for what the two traditions do with it. Ludwig Wittgenstein's advice when it comes to understanding language is timely. Roughly, it amounts to the adage: "Look not for the meaning; look at the use."[5] The best way to understand what people mean in using words like "law" and "gospel" is to observe as closely as possible what they *do* with such words: when they are used, how they are used, what they are used for, and in what context they are used.[6] Our Reformed/Lutheran colloquium did not afford us the opportunity to enter into each other's cultures or forms of life, but we did try to learn each other's language games as best we could by attending to the particular ways things were said, and under what conditions.

Everyone who tries to master a foreign tongue knows how important it is to learn language and culture together. The Lutheran/Reformed divergence on law/gospel stems not simply from different uses of words (language games) but also from different beliefs, values, and practices (forms of life). To get at the deep theological differences, then, it will be necessary to infer what distinctive insights and values inform these two cultural-linguistic communities.

Law and Gospel

What follows is my attempt to summarize what we said about our respective ultimate concerns and our respective ways of viewing theology. It is not a comprehensive record but an attempt to systematize, under three headings, the areas of our chief disagreements.

Idea: The Protestant Revolution—a History from the Sixteenth Century to the Twenty-First (New York: HarperOne, 2007), both books that associate the Reformation with interpretive pluralism.

5. What Wittgenstein actually said was "the meaning of a word is its use in the language" (*Philosophical Investigations*, trans. G. E. M. Anscombe, 3rd ed. [New York: Macmillan, 1968], section 43).

6. The Formula of Concord recognized this point, long before Wittgenstein, when it explained the dissent among the theologians of the Augsburg Confession over whether preaching the gospel is a preaching of repentance as well as grace: "the little word 'gospel' is not used and understood in the same, single sense at all times" (FC SD 5.3, in *BC*, 582).

Law and Gospel: Dialectical Distinction or Covenantal Relation?

For Luther there is one word of God, and "one and the same word strikes sinful man both as law and as gospel."[7] Accordingly, the most central Lutheran concern is to distinguish law and gospel—and to keep them distinct. This is a familiar note to anyone who has worked through C. F. W. Walther's *Proper Distinction between Law and Gospel.*[8] Originally delivered as thirty-nine lectures, the published version sets forth twenty-five theses on the importance of rightly distinguishing the law and gospel from each other. Here, for example, is thesis 4: "The true knowledge of the distinction between the Law and the Gospel is not only a glorious light, affording the correct understanding of the entire Holy Scriptures, but without this knowledge Scripture is and remains a sealed book." Significantly, the next twenty-one theses are all negative statements that specify the ways in which "the Word of God is not rightly divided" by the failure to distinguish law and gospel.

In brief, the distinction seems to be that the law demands, then kills, whereas the gospel promises, and gives life. Paul's gospel concerns the power of God for salvation, a revelation of God's righteousness for faith (Rom. 1:16–17). Although no one can be justified by doing the works of the law, the good news is that God has made known a righteousness "apart from the law" (Rom. 3:21). Interestingly, "Luther . . . sharpens the expression to read 'against the law.'"[9]

The law/gospel dialectic is Luther's legacy to the whole church. According to Mark Mattes, keeping the dialectic alive is "the most important ecumenical challenge and gift that Lutherans offer other Christians."[10] The dialectic sums up God's dual work, both alien (condemning) and proper (confirming; comforting). With apologies to Wordsworth: for Luther, it is not the dissecting but the synthesizing of the dialectic that murders it. Any one word or concept (like "covenant") that sidesteps God's alien work fails to preserve the dual nature of what God is doing everywhere and at all times in Scripture to everyone.

Ludwig Feuerbach's name was not explicitly mentioned or brought to center stage, but I detected among the Lutherans a (justified!) concern about the ease with which we project our best thoughts onto God—in particular, God as eternal law (God is law = law is God)—in our attempt to tame the lion of Judah. I think I heard the Lutherans lament the ease with which their

7. Paul Althaus, *The Theology of Martin Luther* (Philadelphia: Fortress, 1966), 264.

8. Saint Louis: Concordia, 1986.

9. Althaus, *Theology of Martin Luther*, 257.

10. See Mark C. Mattes, "Properly Distinguishing Law and Gospel as the Pastor's Calling," *Logia* 24, no. 1 (2015): 37.

own tradition so quickly lost Luther's sure touch as concerns the law/gospel distinction. By the seventeenth century, Lutheran orthodoxy had come to view God's theoretical essence as law. This eternal divine law, a nonaccusatory guiding law that mirrors God's will, is, in Steven Paulson's words, "a lie . . . a South Dakotan jack-alope." Hence the third use inexorably became "the primary use, and the primary use was equated with the mind and will of God himself." This was the besetting temptation of Protestants, including Lutherans who, according to Paulson, happily returned to their jail cells in Babylon (i.e., schemes for attaining a righteousness from the law). Preserving the law-gospel dialectic is thus a necessary guard against projecting our own ideas of divine perfection onto God.

For the Reformed, the law is not there primarily to kill Christians, but to direct their lives. The law is an expression of God's eternal character and will. To lay out in speech God's will for creation is first and foremost to acknowledge as gift this instruction in the ways of God, and hence a guide to wisdom and flourishing (Ps. 1). That the law has become a threat—a letter that kills—is not the essential truth about the law but a historical accident, contingent on human fallenness.

The most central Reformed concern is therefore not to preserve the dialectic but to relate law and gospel—and keep them related. For the Reformed, rightly to understand law and gospel, both in their distinction and relation, is to situate them within the broader rubric of the covenant.[11] Reformed theology cares about giving an "orderly account" of both law and gospel, and this ultimately involves giving an account of redemptive history.

The Canonical Location of Persons "Under the Law"

There was widespread agreement that the term "law" is susceptible of many uses, some of them positive.[12] The sticking point seems to be the relation of law to specific persons. In particular, the Reformed tend to focus on salvation history that begins with humans as creatures (i.e., Genesis), and hence under a law that expresses God's will as a "perfect rule for righteousness." Conversely, Lutherans tend to focus on salvation history that begins with humans as sin-

11. See, for example, Ryan M. McGraw, "The Threats of the Gospel: John Owen on What the Law/Gospel Distinction Is Not," *Calvin Theological Journal* 51 (2016): 79–111, esp. 80.

12. Michael Allen's essay notes that the Leiden Synopsis identifies six uses of the term "law" in Scripture.

ners (i.e., Galatians), and hence under the law that kills and condemns. This difference in anthropological starting point gave rise to one of the most intense exchanges concerning the Reformed "covenant of works." Call it the first *feud* of the law (and yes, there will be three feuds).

A covenant, according to Cocceius, is "a law, to which has been annexed a promise exciting one to expect good in the form of communion."[13] To Lutheran ears, the positive connotation the Reformed give to the idea of a covenant of works in prelapsarian Eden, signaled by the pairing of "law" and "promise," generates grammatical, conceptual, and theological dissonance. It also makes it sound as though law is more fundamental than gospel, and that humans may not be wrong to think that there is at least a theoretical possibility that they can earn salvation by satisfying the requirements of the law: "Do this and live."

Reformed theologians are known for taking Augustine's description of Adam's relation with God as a covenant and running with it.[14] What is often insufficiently acknowledged, however, is that Reformed theologians insist that God's establishing this covenant is itself the result of a prior gracious initiative, so that there is no question of "law" preceding "grace." Moreover, the eternal life promised Adam as a result of his obedience is not something that Adam "earns," but is simply the condition of his receiving this blessing as a gift. As Bavinck says: "There is no such thing as merit in the existence of a creature before God, nor can there be since the relation between the Creator and a creature radically and once-and-for-all eliminates any notion of merit."[15]

When Lutherans speak of persons "under law," they tend to have humans not as creatures but specifically as sinners in mind. The works of the law appear in this context not as the basis for reaping covenant blessings but as the opposite of justification by faith (Gal. 2:16). One Lutheran commented that the language of "covenant" is not the problem, but "works" is. From a Lutheran perspective, the point of the Adamic prohibition was not to tell Adam what to *do* but rather what to *be*: a person who wholeheartedly trusted the word of God, that is, a person of faith. Interestingly, N. T. Wright has recently argued for a "covenant of vocation" with Adam in contrast to a "works-contract."[16] Perhaps this might provide a way to negotiate our way beyond the first feud of the law.

13. Cited in Heinrich Heppe, *Reformed Dogmatics* (Grand Rapids: Baker, 1978), 281.

14. Augustine, *City of God* 16.27.

15. Herman Bavinck, *Reformed Dogmatics*, vol. 2, *God and Creation*, trans. John Vriend (Grand Rapids: Baker, 2004), 570.

16. N. T. Wright, *The Day the Revolution Began: Reconsidering the Meaning of Jesus' Crucifixion* (New York: HarperOne, 2016), ch. 4.

The second feud of the law concerns the status of its second use as a means of condemning sinners as unrighteous. The intent of this use of the law is to lead people to despair of themselves and to hope in Christ. Lutherans associate this second use of the law, its "true and genuine meaning,"[17] with the "alien" or "improper" work of God insofar as it is here an instrument of God's wrath, a severe pedagogy: "The Spirit speaking though the law terrifies, kills, and is a consuming fire for the conscience."[18] Faith involves *dying* to the law (Gal. 2:19), which means turning a deaf ear to its accusations: "The law is to be interpreted through the gospel."[19]

The third feud of the law follows from the above and concerns the status of the Mosaic law. Is it a republication of the original covenant of works? Or is it, as the Reformed prefer to say, enfolded in the one continuous covenant of grace? To the extent that Lutherans read the law/gospel distinction through Galatians, they associate the law of Moses with the Judaizers' insistence to live by the letter of the law (Gal. 2:11–16; cf. Acts 15:5). In light of the Reformed emphasis on covenant, Lutherans wonder whether, and to what extent, the Reformed interpret the gospel through the law.

For the Reformed, the Mosaic covenant includes God's gracious provisions for sin's covering. Israel's sin offerings were a graphic object lesson of the truth that "without the shedding of blood there is no forgiveness of sins" (Heb. 9:22). There is a difference of Reformed opinion concerning the presence of a "works principle" in the Mosaic covenant, and thus whether it is a conditional "law covenant" rather than an unconditional "promise covenant."[20] The notion of a works principle in a covenant of grace no doubt grates against Lutheran sensibilities. It is therefore important to see the Sinaitic works principle as typological. For example, in his commentary on Hebrews 8:6, John Owen interpreted the works principle in the Mosaic covenant typologically to refer to Israel's failure to remain in the promised land.[21] The purpose of the works

17. So Althaus, *Theology of Martin Luther*, 254.

18. Althaus, *Theology of Martin Luther*, 256.

19. Althaus, *Theology of Martin Luther*, 259.

20. Compare John Murray, *The Covenant of Grace: A Biblical-Theological Study* (Phillipsburg, NJ: Presbyterian and Reformed, 1988), and Meredith Kline, *By Oath Consigned: A Reinterpretation of the Covenant Signs of Circumcision and Baptism* (Grand Rapids: Eerdmans, 1968). There is a further question as to whether covenant theology proceeds from a prior law-gospel distinction rather than vice versa. See Michael Horton, *God of Promise: Introducing Covenant Theology* (Grand Rapids: Baker, 2006), 85.

21. John Owen, *An Exposition of the Epistle to the Hebrews* (Edinburgh: Banner of Truth, 1991), 6:80–92.

principle, so interpreted, was not to encourage Israel to achieve salvation by keeping the law, but to remind them of their inability and point them to God's gracious provision for their sins, proximately in the blood of bulls and goats but ultimately in the Suffering Servant, the promised Messiah.

There is no covenant partner that is righteous, no not one—*except* the Messiah, God's faithful servant and obedient Son. The Mosaic covenant typologically indicates that salvation is indeed through works: *Christ's* work as covenant mediator. According to Bavinck, "the covenant of grace, insofar as it was made with Christ, was essentially a covenant of works."[22] This is why Calvin insists that Christ, because of his perfect obedience, *merits* our salvation.[23] God himself undertakes the "work" of covenant obedience, even to the point of dying on the cross (Phil. 2:8). In Turretin's words: "Thus what was demanded of us in the covenant of works is fulfilled by Christ in the covenant of grace."[24] Grace restores and perfects nature inasmuch as Christ recapitulates the histories of Adam and Israel, though with active (and passive) obedience. Christ fulfills the law because he perfectly obeys its commands and representatively suffers its curse. Those who through faith are members of the new covenant enjoy union with Christ and are no longer under the curse of the law (Rom. 8:1). Still, they give thanks to the positive commands for the law for directing their Spirit-given freedom.

Gospel and Law in Preaching and Theology

Under this heading I have just a few remarks—really, just a hunch to hazard—about the place and purpose of the law/gospel distinction in Lutheran and Reformed theology and ministry. It struck me that Lutherans view preaching as the privileged form of doctrine, while the Reformed formulate doctrine in order to serve preaching.

Preaching addresses specific audiences at specific times and places. I heard a loud and clear cautionary note from our Lutheran colleagues about the ease with which "theological alchemy" turns gospel into law, not least by formulating doctrinal truths about God's essence. Systems of theology take the sown Word and plow straight furrows, yet, as Paulson says, the Word, not the soil,

22. Herman Bavinck, *Reformed Dogmatics*, vol. 3, *Sin and Salvation in Christ*, trans. John Vriend (Grand Rapids: Baker Academic, 2006), 227.

23. Calvin, *Institutes of the Christian Religion* 2.17.1.

24. Francis Turretin, *Institutes of Elenctic Theology*, ed. James T. Dennison Jr. (Phillipsburg, NJ: Presbyterian and Reformed, 1997), 268.

is the active ingredient, and the Holy Spirit gives "ears where and when it pleases him."

According to Paulson, preaching "is not explanation or meaning." What the preacher says is not doctrine but a deed: "a doing rather than an explanation, a thing, not a sign." The doing is, I think, dialectical: the preacher's primary task is to keep the tension of the Word alive, neither turning gospel into law (that way legalism lies) nor separating gospel and law (that way lies antinomianism). It is one thing to explain substitutionary atonement, quite another to insist on the necessity of death for sinners. Luther's students "experienced something dramatic—the living distinction of law and gospel."

Lutherans seem to prioritize preaching above formulating doctrine, or perhaps preaching as the primary form doctrine should take. The very attempt to describe God's essence apart from the proclamation of forgiveness produces a "holy essence" of God, a naked majesty without any gospel. The radical nature of Luther's gospel—that God has done all in Christ—is difficult to formulate in terms of essences and laws.

Whereas for Lutherans preaching the law/gospel dialectic provokes an existential crisis, the Reformed see the law/gospel distinction as something that can be taught (learned) and walked (lived). The Reformed both care about and enjoy parsing the conceptual grammar of the law/gospel distinction, says Kapic, "because they believe one's understanding of this relationship has massive pastoral consequences."

The Reformed view the law as a gift from God, an element in the economy of redemption that can lead to greater godliness, but not because the law itself has transformative power. On the contrary, the law is more like a map than a motor: it guides, but it does not generate energy. On the contrary, it is grace that establishes both faith (in the gospel) and obedience (to the law). To make disciples, one must not only wrestle with the devil (satanic accusations in particular) and die to self; one must also practice resurrection and participate in local assemblies of believers who, by living out the life of Christ under the instruction of his revealed will, enact living parables of the kingdom of God. The Spirit uses the law to form communities that live in communion with Christ and with one another.

"Here We Stand"

There is nothing more basic in theology than making judgments: identifying things, distinguishing things, and relating things. Whence come the contrasting characteristic theological judgments, namely, the Lutheran tendency to *distinguish* law and gospel and the Reformed tendency to *relate* them? What are the historical-genetic factors that contribute to Lutherans and Reformed leaning toward antinomianism and legalism, respectively?

Bavinck chalks up the fundamental difference to the Reformed thinking theologically and the Lutherans anthropologically: "From this difference in principle, the dogmatic controversies between them . . . can be easily explained."[25] This explains the Reformed tendency to subordinate everything to God's eternal election and the Lutheran tendency to focus on the Christian's historical-existential justification. If we think this generalization too hasty, how then should we understand the differences that divide our two interpretive communities?

Pastoral Theology: Hermeneutics and Homiletics

Lutherans and Reformed share a common Protestant language. However, language involves both the *said* and the *saying*. I was intrigued by Mattes's comment that the tendency in Reformed hermeneutics is to look to Scripture for information, whereas Lutherans look to Scripture for (relational) address. I want to explore this point from a slightly different perspective.

Lutherans vigilantly guard the peculiar illocutionary force of law discourse, namely, its accusatory function. The law does not merely state imperatives: it condemns. Indeed, "It kills sinners."[26] We can therefore distinguish law as locution (statement of God's will) and law as illocution (accusatory force). Not only can sinners not fulfill the law because they transgress this or that commandment; more radically, they cannot fulfill the law because their hearts are inclined in God- and gospel-denying directions. The law accuses because it exposes the corruption of the sinful heart.

At the same time, there is one word of God. One and the same locution can have either condemnatory or promissory (illocutionary) force, and which force it has depends not on the preaching but on the hearing: "Faith . . . moves from the law to the gospel."[27] It is the Spirit who enables sinners to hear preaching about Jesus Christ as gospel rather than law. The question this

25. Herman Bavinck, *Reformed Dogmatics*, vol. 1, *Prolegomena*, ed. John Bolt, trans. John Vriend (Grand Rapids: Baker Academic, 2003), 177.

26. Mattes, "Properly Distinguishing Law and Gospel," 41.

27. Althaus, *Theology of Martin Luther*, 265.

poses is whether, for Lutherans, the perlocutionary effect (faith) determines the illocutionary force (promise) rather than vice versa (as is usually the case in speech acts).

Scripture, as the Word of God, is divine discourse, and Reformed theologians are keen to acknowledge the whole counsel of God (Acts 20:27), including the full range of divine speech acts. However, instead of letting the hearer's stance determine whether a given biblical passage is law or gospel, the Reformed tend to interpret all of Scripture as covenantal discourse, and to understand covenant as entailing both privileges and responsibilities.

Erik Herrmann may have put his finger on our respective pastoral emphases: Luther's preeminent concern was occasional, local, and immediate. We might also add "individual-centric" inasmuch as individual persons are the primary recipients of the divine address.[28] In contrast, Calvin wanted to set up the household of God in Geneva:[29] "For the reformers in general and for Calvin in particular, Soli Deo Gloria (to God alone be glory) was the design of life and good works were caring for one's neighbor, working for justice and right dealings, building churches, pubs, hospitals and universities for the honor of the Great King."[30] These contrasting pastoral postures lead to a second strategic difference.

Moral Theology: Law and Ethics

According to Herrmann, Luther views the law's function positively in his earlier lectures on the Psalms. It was only when he began to comment on Romans and Galatians that Luther came to understand that Paul was speaking of the law not simply in terms of one stage of redemptive history (i.e., before or after Christ) but as something of perennial concern. Luther came to see the law/gospel distinction not merely as salvation-historical but as *existential*: individuals struggle against sin in the flesh in the here and now, and either law or gospel may impinge at any moment.[31] While both Lutherans and Reformed affirm

28. It is misleading to associate Lutheran theological method with individualism, however, given the importance Luther attached not only to catechisms and confessions, but also to the priesthood of believers.

29. Some have called this a "theocracy," but this should not be confused with "theonomy."

30. Michael Horton, "Was Geneva a Theocracy?" *Modern Reformation* 1, no. 2 (March/April 1992), http://www.the-highway.com/theocracy_Horton.html.

31. "For Martin Luther the law and the gospel expressed his own existential experience [though] . . . he never resolved it existentially. For as long as he lived he understood himself as standing con-

"continuity and discontinuity," they do so in different grammatical registers: redemptive-existential and redemptive-historical, respectively.

Bernd Wannenwetsch suggests that Luther's mature understanding of the law takes a "narrative dramatic perspective from which it cannot be abstracted without losing substance."[32] From this narrative-dramatic perspective, what is ethically first and foremost is the first commandment: "Thou shalt have no other gods before me." All other commandments are simply an outworking of this fundamental requirement to have faith in God and his promise. "I am the Lord your God" is a promise that frees individuals from the burden of making themselves righteous, yet it is a threat to me if I insist on being my own god or on serving some other god than Yahweh.

Luther saw the first commandment as containing within itself all the other commandments: "Let God be God!" If we could only remember not to have any other gods before the one true God, everything else would be fine. How then does one fulfill the law? If I have rightly understood the Lutheran position, it is not by obeying particular commands but rather by transcending morality altogether. To put it in Kierkegaardian terms: to try to fulfill the law by obeying it is to remain on the ethical stage of existence, whereas Luther thinks we need to move to a higher existential stage, namely, faith.

Christians are *simul iustus et peccator*. Insofar as saints are in Christ, they conform to the law spontaneously, which is why the fruit of the Spirit are no longer "works of the law." The law nevertheless continues to have significance for those who are simultaneously saints and sinners. It serves as a standing reminder—a wake-up call—that the battle between the old and new man is not over, and thus reminds disciples not to fall asleep to the urgency of holding on in faith to Christ. Theology—which for Luther is primarily gospel proclamation—exists to help disciples to stay awake, ever vigilant to the danger of thinking that it is *I* who live, not Christ in me (cf. Gal. 2:20).

The Reformed look to the law not merely to accuse but to direct: "The law of God in its most basic form refers to the divine rule in the government of all things external to God."[33] Believers are no longer under the law of Moses in its *condemning function*, but it continues to have a helpful orientation function as guide to wise and flourishing living along the grain of the created order laid

---

demned and forgiven before God at the same time" (David P. Scaer, "Law and Gospel in Lutheran Theology," *Logia* 3 no. 1 [1994]: 27–28).

32. Bernd Wannenwetsch, "Luther's Moral Theology," in *Cambridge Companion to Martin Luther*, ed. Donald McKim (Cambridge: Cambridge University Press, 2003), 124.

33. Paul Nimmo, "The Law of God and Christian Ethics," in *Christian Dogmatics: Reformed Theology for the Church Catholic*, ed. Michael Allen and Scott Swain (Grand Rapids: Zondervan, 2016), 292.

down (*lex*) by God's creative speech acts. The law is not a violent imposition on humanity; on the contrary, it represents the instruction manual, as it were, for what it means to do humanity in ways that lead to human flourishing and the glory of God. The faithful are to live out the life of Christ in them, which is why Paul speaks of the "law of Christ" (1 Cor. 9:21) and the "law of the Spirit of life" (Rom. 8:2) to refer to the Spirit's enabling believers, as it were, to flesh out Jesus's commandment (John 15:12–13).

For the Reformed, the law of Moses and the law of Christ refer to two different stages of redemptive history, before and after the gift of the Spirit (John 14:15–17; 16:7, 13; cf. Acts 2:32–33). Those works produced by this third use of the law are spontaneous signs of gratitude for the grace poured out in Jesus Christ. Christian ethics is the joyful project of acting out the freedom we have in Christ, which is why the burden of the "law of Christ" is light.

Lutherans may still worry that talk of the third use of the law compromises justification by faith. Perhaps the way forward is to find a new term that captures both the Lutheran concern for faith and the Reformed concern for faithful obedience. Matthew Bates has recently suggested just such a term: "allegiance." Allegiance combines belief with lived loyalty. According to Bates, we are saved neither by works nor even by faith alone, but by allegiance to Jesus as Lord.[34]

Doctrinal Theology: Cruciform versus Covenant

Herrmann wonders whether Otto Pesch's contrast between "existential" and "sapiential" theology, originally deployed to explain the difference between Luther's and Aquinas's ways of doing theology, may also help explain the difference between Lutheran and Reformed.[35] It is an intriguing suggestion. By "sapiential," however, Pesch means "speculative," in the sense of adopting a theoretical posture. It is, of course, impossible to remain theoretical when God addresses us, and for Luther this is always the context of faith's response. Lutherans reject ways of doing theology from any "objective" standpoint, some alleged theoretical perspective above and apart from the always particular divine address.

34. See Matthew W. Bates, *Salvation by Allegiance Alone: Faith, Works, and the Gospel of Jesus the King* (Grand Rapids: Baker Academic, 2017).

35. O. H. Pesch, "Existential and Sapiential Theology—the Theological Confrontation between Luther and Thomas Aquinas," in *Catholic Scholars Dialogue with Luther*, ed. J. Wicks (Chicago: Loyola University Press, 1970), 59–81.

To this, Reformed theologians can only say "Amen"! And perhaps, "not so fast." Reformed theologians like William Ames view theology as the project of "living to God," and the emphasis on lived knowledge—or in my terms, on demonstrating our understanding by fitting participation in the drama of redemption—is precisely what Reformed theologians mean by "sapiential." Furthermore, whereas Lutherans focus on the grace revealed by the cross, the climax of the drama of redemption, the Reformed want to think about the other acts in the drama of redemption—creation and consummation—on the grounds that disciples need to know where they are in the story and where they are going in order to participate rightly.[36]

For Luther, the sapiential is the staurological (from Gk. *stauros*, "cross"). I refer to Luther's idea of *theologia crucis* ("theology of the cross"), set out in the Heidelberg Disputation (1518) in contrast to a theology of glory. The key biblical text is 1 Corinthians 1:21, which contrasts the wisdom of the world with the cruciform wisdom of God. Reformed theologians are not squeamish in speaking about God's glory (e.g., "The chief end of man is to enjoy God and glorify him forever"). Does it therefore follow that Reformed theology is a subset of what Luther referred to as the "theology of glory"?

Luther's "system" of theology is not that of "an organized set of doctrines" but that of "a consistent principled procedure." Luther said, "*Crux probat omnia*" ("the Cross tests all"), and this is also his challenge to sapiential systematics. For Luther, the wisdom of the cross is dialectical and serves as the index of a system's incompleteness: "He deserves to be called a theologian . . . who comprehends the visible and manifest things of God seen through suffering and the cross."[37] Doing theology for Luther involves *oratio* (prayer), *meditatio* (meditation), and *tentatio* (struggle), which he correlates with the Holy Spirit, Scripture, and the devil, respectively.[38] The particular *tentatio* Luther has in mind is the individual's struggle to respond to the divine address wholeheartedly, and not simply with intellectual assent. To respond to the message of the cross ultimately requires dying to self. In this drama, the devil encourages unbelief, and speaks a single line on which he works myriad variations: "Did God really say?" (cf. Gen. 3:1).

For Lutherans, law and gospel belong together in a soteriological dialectic: we grasp the gospel only by passing through the law, and we grasp the law

36. See my *Faith Speaking Understanding: Performing the Drama of Redemption* (Louisville: Westminster John Knox, 2014).

37. Thesis 20 of the Heidelberg Disputation, in Timothy Lull, ed., *Martin Luther's Basic Theological Writings* (Minneapolis: Fortress, 1989), 43.

38. See John W. Kleinig, "*Oratio, Meditatio, Tentatio*: What Makes a Theologian?" *Concordia Theological Quarterly* 66, no. 3 (2002): 255–67.

only by passing through the gospel.[39] Mattes mentioned in this connection Luther's tendency to read the Bible from a "narrative-dramatic" perspective that summons readers to identify with a particular character or voice in the Bible, thence to wrestle with the existential issue at stake.

May we speak of a Reformed theology of the cross? May it ever be![40] Reformed theologians tend to interpret the cross as the climax of a series of covenants that together help to explain the realization of God's gospel promise and coming of God's kingdom. Indeed, we could say that the whole drama of redemption that spans Old and New Testaments is the story of how the one covenant of grace unfolds: "For the law was given through Moses; grace and truth came through Jesus Christ" (John 1:17). Far from being a simple law/gospel dialectic, the contrast is a gloss on John's preceding statement: "And from his fullness we have all received, grace upon grace" (John 1:16 ESV) or "one blessing after another" (NIV). The gracious provision of the cross was the climactic substance of a whole series of its shadowy anticipations. Reformed theologians deploy covenant as a way of preserving law and gospel in a well-ordered rather than dialectical relation. The works principle helps to explain the saving significance of Christ's work, and the sense in which Christ's active and passive obedience together represent the "end" of the law.

Reformed theologians operate not only with the premise of Christ's cross and the aim of inculcating faith, but also with the premise of Christ's comprehensive Lordship and the aim of making disciples. Calvin's *Institutes* is not simply a summary of theology but a *summa pietatis* (summary of piety).[41] Christian doctrine orients the heart and provides directions for faithful discipleship. The *Institutes* thus provides training in Christian piety or *paideia*. The way of Reformed wisdom thus involves knowing how to respond to Christ's Lordship, not only when one is standing at the foot of the cross, but in all times, places, and circumstances.

Indeed, perhaps one way to summarize our respective concerns is to see them as emphasizing different aspects of Christ's work as the lens through which to look at the whole of theology: for Lutherans, the cross (*crux probat omnia*) or, perhaps more generally, Christ's state of humiliation; for the Reformed, the accent is placed on the new humanity of the crucified Christ associated with his resurrection and ascension (the comprehensive Lordship

39. Althaus, *Theology of Martin Luther*, 260.

40. See Michael Allen, "John Calvin's Reading of the Corinthian Epistles," in *Reformation Readings of Paul: Explorations in History and Exegesis*, ed. Michael Allen and Jonathan A. Linebaugh (Downers Grove: IVP Academic, 2015), esp. 175–86.

41. See further Matthew Myer Boulton's excellent study, *Life in God: John Calvin, Practical Formation, and the Future of Protestant Theology* (Grand Rapids: Eerdmans, 2011), 45–58.

of Christ), that is, on the *duplex gratia* of justification and sanctification. The resurrection and ascension also highlight the importance of the Christian's *eschatological* and not simply existential situation: Christian pilgrims are already/not-yet there, in the heavenlies, with Christ (Eph. 2:6).

In sum: Lutheran theologians tend to use Scripture for pastoral purposes—to preserve the existential tension of the law-gospel dialectic—in order to keep the believer's focus on Christ and guard against slipping into self-justificatory, self-congratulatory, and self-righteous habits of thinking that we can save ourselves by doing something. The overriding concern is to contain and confront the sinner's "inner control-freak" (*homo incurvatus in se*) by bringing to mind the ever-so-easy-to-forget truth that we can do nothing to save ourselves and that Christ has done everything. In contrast, Reformed theologians read the Scripture as diverse acts in a unified drama of redemption whose climax is the death and resurrection of Jesus Christ, the turning point of the ages, and the event that institutes the new covenant, the glorious substance of which the earlier covenants were but shadows, but which, like those earlier covenants, entails both privileges and responsibilities, grace and gratitude, everything the new covenant community needs to order its corporate life as corporate praise.

Where We Go from "Here"

Are there ways to preserve our respective concerns but keep the conversation moving forward? Let me count the ways (three).

Discernment

The most important requirement for gaining mutual understanding is listening discernment. For example, is it right to describe the difference between the Lutheran and Reformed approaches to the law/gospel distinction in terms of an existential versus a covenantal orientation and framework, or to characterize Lutherans as attentive to the *saying* of the Word of God, in particular the contrasting illocutionary forces of law and gospel, and Reformed as attentive to the *said*? Is it fair to describe Lutheran theology as especially attuned to the way in which the cross tests every other doctrine, in contrast to the Reformed, who are alert to the broader covenantal history and context of the cross? Genuine differences need to be acknowledged, but we also need to guard against reducing these differences to simplistic slogans.

I hope that my contrast between the dramatic/existential (Lutheran) and dramatic/redemptive-historical (Reformed) serves more as a heuristic device that yields understanding than as a caricature that distorts understanding. I found some comfort in Mark Mattes's suggestion that to be addressed by the word of God is simultaneously to be exegeted by God inasmuch as our response to the divine address reveals us as people who relate to God either in faith or by works. This seems to corroborate my suggestion that Luther views individuals as having their being and identity dramatically determined by their encounter with God's word.

Dogmatic Rank

Elsewhere I have argued that acknowledging differences in dogmatic rank is the key to the unity-in-diversity that is mere Protestant Christianity.[42] Not every doctrinal difference is a matter of preserving the integrity of the gospel, though some (e.g., the Trinity; bodily resurrection of Jesus) are. I am happy to report that during the course of our discussions neither side dropped the H-bomb (heresy) on the other. On the contrary, we had no trouble acknowledging one another as branches from the same trunk, fellow members of the body of Christ, able to sup together at the communion table.

Still, it is incontrovertible that the differences that cause Lutherans and Reformed to go their own ecclesial ways are still operative. Dan Treier and I have likened the second-order dogmatic differences behind the denominational divisions that separate Lutheran and Reformed churches to the situation in the early church that led to Paul and Barnabas going their separate ways.[43] According to the narrative in Acts 15:36–41, Paul and Barnabas "sharply disagreed" about whether or not to take John Mark with them. At this level of disagreement, it is not the integrity of the gospel that is at stake but the shape of its ministry. Significantly, Christian fellowship remains even when leaders, and their churches, pursue different ministries.

To be sure, the way one relates law and gospel is of greater significance for theology than the presence or absence of John Mark was. There is, nevertheless, a formal parallel inasmuch as each involves a decision about how best to

42. Kevin J. Vanhoozer, *Biblical Authority after Babel: Retrieving the* Solas *in the Spirit of Mere Protestant Christianity* (Grand Rapids: Brazos, 2016), 204–6.

43. Kevin J. Vanhoozer and Daniel J. Treier, *Theology and the Mirror of Scripture: A Mere Evangelical Account* (Downers Grove: InterVarsity, 2015), 202–4.

conduct the ministry. In this respect, the episode of Paul and Barnabas foreshadowed the Protestant parting of the ways some fifteen hundred years later. The point is that different construals of Christian mission and ministry, and the second-order doctrinal disagreements that may occasion them, are not matters on which the gospel itself stands or falls. There is room in mere Protestant Christianity to acknowledge the legitimacy of various pastoral emphases and theological themes.[44] As Dan Treier and I say in our book: "Fellowship need not be broken even though collaboration may prove impossible."[45]

Dialogue

Can we go further, and see Lutheran/Reformed distinctives not only as a burden to endure but as a gift to celebrate? I believe we can, with the help of a Russian Orthodox mediator, the literary critic Mikhail Bakhtin.

Bakhtin argues that dialogue is less an arena for debate than a crucible in which to discover greater textual understanding. In a genuine dialogue, neither party's perspective is absorbed into the other (Bakhtin resists Gadamer's notion of a "fusion of horizons"). Rather, in a genuine dialogue each interlocutor remains "outside" the other. Consequently, Lutherans may be able to see what is behind their Reformed interlocutors' backs (and vice versa). Bakhtin's fundamental contribution amounts to this: it is through dialogue that interpreters gradually realize the meaning potential of a text. It is not that dialogue adds material content to the text (Scripture is materially sufficient); rather, because each party in the dialogue occupies a different position/perspective, each is able to contribute something to the discussion that the other had not seen. To read only within one's own interpretive community risks imprisoning the biblical text within one's own cultural moment, historical horizon, or theological orientation.

On Bakhtin's view, cultural distance—in this case, the linguistic-cultural distance between the Lutherans and the Reformed—is not an obstacle to but a condition of a deeper understanding of the biblical text. Again, we need outsideness (otherness) fully to appreciate the treasures buried in Scripture.

44. See, for example, Michael Allen's description of how the Lutherans and Reformed explain the relationship between grace and human freedom in terms of two kinds of righteousness (alien/proper) and federal theology (covenant of works/grace), respectively (R. Michael Allen, *Justification and the Gospel: Understanding the Contexts and Controversies* [Grand Rapids: Baker Academic, 2015], 111–22).

45. Vanhoozer and Treier, *Theology and the Mirror of Scripture*, 203.

Could it be, for example, that Luther's unique background afforded him a new insight into the meaning of justification? And could it be that Reformed theologians' insight into the centrality of the covenant represents another vein of gold ore? And is it possible (I now wax even bolder) that Lutheran and Reformed traditions, in all their distinctiveness, are themselves instruments the Spirit uses to give gifts to the church, namely, more testimonies to the riches of the wisdom summed up in Jesus Christ? It may take two or more theological frameworks fully to do justice to the truth of Scripture's testimony, just as it took four Gospels to tell the one story of Jesus Christ. Such Pentecostal plurality is not to be despised.

Bakhtin's notion that dialogue between diverse interpreters (and interpretive traditions) generates "creative understanding" bears more than a passing resemblance to the reformers' own predilection for church councils and colloquies. Though it is sometimes painful to endure the lack of consensus over such doctrines as the Lord's Supper, the dialogue itself can be salutary if it leads not only to greater understanding but also to greater interpretive virtue and epistemic conscientiousness. The basic point is that the Lutheran-Reformed dialogue on law and grace provides for a certain outsideness inside catholic orthodoxy. One can only hope that future dialogue will result in what Andrews Walls says happens whenever one tries to translate the gospel into a new culture: "It is a delightful paradox that the more Christ is translated into the various thought forms and life systems which form our various national [and denominational] identities, the richer all of us will be in our common Christian identity."[46]

On the Way from Emmaus

Travel and living in different cultures are often educational. And often that's what it takes to learn a foreign language: immersing oneself in the culture and tradition of its use. Dialogue takes time, and we had only forty-eight hours. This was just about enough time to understand how each tradition was using language, and thus to overcome our initial culture shock. As it took time for the disciples to realize who Jesus was, so it will take us time to discern the nature of our differences, though I hope we already know these differences are of second-order dogmatic rank.

46. Andrew F. Walls, *The Missionary Movement in Christian History: Studies in the Transmission of Faith* (Maryknoll, NY: Orbis, 1996), 54.

For some ten years now, I have been involved in conversations with Evangelicals and Catholics Together (ECT). In the epilogue I coauthored with Rusty Reno, in a book marking the twentieth anniversary of ECT, we similarly reflected about our dialogue. Our working title was "Conversations on the Way to Emmaus."[47] We were talking, yes, but we were unable to fellowship at the Lord's table. By way of contrast, our Lutheran-Reformed dialogue has a distinctly different feel: we may be divided on certain issues, but we agree on the gospel and we discern the body in one another's churches. We are having conversations on the road *from* Emmaus, and our hearts continue to burn within us as, together, we continue to open the Scriptures for one another.

47. R. R. Reno and Kevin J. Vanhoozer, "Epilogue," in *Evangelicals and Catholics Together at Twenty*, ed. Timothy George and Thomas G. Guarino (Grand Rapids: Brazos, 2015), 165–70.

Contributors

Michael Allen is John Dyer Trimble Professor of Systematic Theology at Reformed Theological Seminary (Orlando, FL). His books include *Sanctification* (Zondervan Academic) and, edited with Scott Swain, *The Oxford Handbook of Reformed Theology* (OUP).

Charles P. Arand is Professor of Systematic Theology at Concordia Seminary (Saint Louis). His books include *Testing the Boundaries* (Concordia) and, with Robert Kolb, *The Genius of Luther's Theology* (Baker Academic).

Erik H. Herrmann is Associate Professor of Historical Theology at Concordia Seminary (Saint Louis). His writings include "The Babylonian Captivity of the Church," in *The Annotated Luther* (Fortress), and "Luther's Absorption of Medieval Biblical Interpretation and His Use of the Church Fathers," in *The Oxford Handbook to the Theology of Martin Luther* (OUP).

Kelly M. Kapic is Professor of Theological Studies at Covenant College. His books include *Embodied Hope* (IVP Academic) and *God So Loved He Gave* (Zondervan).

Jonathan A. Linebaugh is Lecturer in New Testament at Cambridge University and Fellow of Jesus College. His books include *God, Grace, and Righteousness in Wisdom of Solomon and Paul's Letter to the Romans* (Brill) and, edited with Michael Allen, *Reformation Readings of Paul* (IVP Academic).

Piotr J. Małysz is Associate Professor of Divinity at Beeson Divinity School. His books include *Trinity, Freedom, and Love* (T. & T. Clark) and, edited with Derek Nelson, *Luther Refracted* (Fortress).

Mark C. Mattes is Department Chair, Philosophy and Theology, Grand View University. His books include *The Role of Justification in Contemporary Theology* (Eerdmans) and *Martin Luther's Theology of Beauty* (Baker Academic).

Steven Paulson is Professor of Systematic Theology at Luther Seminary. His books include *Lutheran Theology* (T. & T. Clark) and *A Brief Introduction to Martin Luther* (Westminster John Knox).

Katherine Sonderegger is the William Meade Chair in Systematic Theology at Virginia Theological Seminary. Her books include *That Jesus Was Born a Jew* (Pennsylvania State University Press) and the first volume of an ongoing *Systematic Theology* (Fortress).

Scott R. Swain is President and James Woodrow Hassell Professor of Systematic Theology at Reformed Theological Seminary (Orlando, FL). His books include *The God of the Gospel* (IVP Academic) and, edited with Fred Sanders, *Retrieving Eternal Generation* (Zondervan Academic).

Kevin J. Vanhoozer is Research Professor of Systematic Theology at Trinity Evangelical Divinity School. His books include *Biblical Authority after Babel* (Brazos) and *Faith Speaking Understanding* (Westminster John Knox).

Index